Whillans's Tax Tables

Budget Edition 2012

Edited by
Claire Hayes CTA
Kevin Walton MA

Consultant Editor
Rebecca Benneyworth BSC, FCA

 LexisNexis®

Members of the LexisNexis Group worldwide

United Kingdom	LexisNexis, a Division of Reed Elsevier (UK) Ltd, Halsbury House, 35 Chancery Lane, London, WC2A 1EL, and London House, 20-22 East London Street, Edinburgh EH7 4BQ
Australia	LexisNexis Butterworths, Chatswood, New South Wales
Austria	LexisNexis Verlag ARD Orac GmbH & Co KG, Vienna
Benelux	LexisNexis Benelux, Amsterdam
Canada	LexisNexis Canada, Markham, Ontario
China	LexisNexis China, Beijing and Shanghai
France	LexisNexis SA, Paris
Germany	LexisNexis Deutschland GmbH, Munster
Hong Kong	LexisNexis Hong Kong, Hong Kong
India	LexisNexis India, New Delhi
Italy	Giuffrè Editore, Milan
Japan	LexisNexis Japan, Tokyo
Malaysia	Malayan Law Journal Sdn Bhd, Kuala Lumpur
New Zealand	LexisNexis NZ Ltd, Wellington
Poland	Wydawnictwo Prawnicze LexisNexis Sp, Warsaw
Singapore	LexisNexis Singapore, Singapore
South Africa	LexisNexis Butterworths, Durban
USA	LexisNexis, Dayton, Ohio

First published in 1948

© Reed Elsevier (UK) Ltd 2012

Published by LexisNexis
This is a Tolley title

Printed and bound by CPI Group (UK) Ltd, Croydon, CR0 4YY

Visit LexisNexis at www.lexisnexis.co.uk

Preface

Welcome to the new Edition of Whillans's Tax Tables. All of the usual material that you need to refer to is here again; to make the book as user friendly as possible, we have organised it so that each topic is covered on a separate page. In particular, I would like to draw your attention to the section on penalties. With the new penalty regime for late filing and late payment being rolled out gradually, it is important to keep on top of the latest position. In our penalties section you can see at a glance which penalty regime is in force for which periods, across the taxes.

Rebecca Benneyworth

Administration

Bank base rates

Period	Rate
from 5 March 2009	**0.50%**
5 February 2009–4 March 2009	1.00%
8 January 2009–4 February 2009	1.50%
4 December 2008–7 January 2009	2.00%
6 November 2008–3 December 2008	3.00%
8 October 2008–5 November 2008	4.50%
10 April 2008–7 October 2008	5.00%
7 February 2008–9 April 2008	5.25%
6 December 2007–6 February 2008	5.50%
5 July 2007–5 December 2007	5.75%
10 May 2007–4 July 2007	5.50%
11 January 2007–9 May 2007	5.25%
9 November 2006–10 January 2007	5.00%
3 August 2006–8 November 2006	4.75%
4 August 2005–2 August 2006	4.50%
5 August 2004–3 August 2005	4.75%
10 June 2004–4 August 2004	4.50%
6 May 2004–9 June 2004	4.25%
5 February 2004–5 May 2004	4.00%
6 November 2003–4 February 2004	3.75%
10 July 2003–5 November 2003	3.50%
6 February 2003–9 July 2003	3.75%
8 November 2001–5 February 2003	4.00%
4 October 2001–7 November 2001	4.50%
18 September 2001–3 October 2001	4.75%
2 August 2001–17 September 2001	5.00%
10 May 2001–1 August 2001	5.25%
5 April 2001–9 May 2001	5.50%
8 February 2001–4 April 2001	5.75%
10 February 2000–7 February 2001	6.00%
13 January 2000–9 February 2000	5.75%
4 November 1999–12 January 2000	5.50%
8 September 1999–3 November 1999	5.25%
10 June 1999–7 September 1999	5.00%
8 April 1999–9 June 1999	5.25%
4 February 1999–7 April 1999	5.50%
7 January 1999–3 February 1999	6.00%
10 December 1998–6 January 1999	6.25%
5 November 1998–9 December 1998	6.75%
8 October 1998–4 November 1998	7.25%
4 June 1998–7 October 1998	7.50%
6 November 1997–3 June 1998	7.25%
7 August 1997–5 November 1997	7.00%
10 July 1997–6 August 1997	6.75%

Due dates for tax

Capital gains tax

Normally 31 January following end of year of assessment. (TMA 1970 s 59B)

(See also *Extended due dates* under **Income tax**, below.)

Corporation tax

Must be paid electronically for tax due on or after 1 April 2011.

Generally (TMA 1970 s 59D)

9 months and 1 day after end of accounting period.

Instalments for larger companies (TMA 1970 s 59E, SI 1998/3175)

A 'large company' is any company responsible for paying the bank levy, and one whose augmented profits (see p 63) exceed £1.5m a year, divided by 1 plus the number of any active associated companies. A company is not a large company in respect of an accounting period if its total liability for that period is not more than £10,000, or if its profits for an accounting period are £10m or less and it was not a large company in the 12 months preceding that accounting period. For most large companies (those with no ring fence profits) the amount of each instalment for a 12 month accounting period will be one quarter of its total liability. The amount of each instalment for any accounting period longer than 3 months but shorter than 12 months is calculated using the formula $3 \times CTI/n$ where CTI is the amount of a company's total liability for that accounting period, and n is the number of months in the accounting period. The due dates of instalments are as follows:

    1st instalment: 6 months and 13 days from start of accounting period (or date of final instalment if earlier);

    2nd instalment: 3 months after 1st instalment, if length of accounting period allows;

    3rd instalment: 3 months after 2nd instalment, if length of accounting period allows;

    Final instalment: 3 months and 14 days from end of accounting period.

Close companies: tax on loans to participators

9 months and 1 day after the end of the accounting period. To be included in instalment payments for large companies (see above) (TMA 1970 s 59E(11)).

Income tax

Payments on account (TMA 1970 s 59A, SI 1996/1654)

A payment on account is required where a taxpayer was assessed to income tax in the immediately preceding year to an amount exceeding the amount of tax deducted at source in respect of that year (subject to a de minimis limit, see below).

The payment on account (which includes Class 4 NIC) is made in 2 equal instalments due on:

    (a)   31 January during the year of assessment, and

    (b)   31 July in the following year of assessment.

No payments on account are required where either:

    (a)   the aggregate of the liability (including Class 4 NIC) for the preceding year (net of tax deducted at source) is less than £1,000 (£500 for 2008/09 and previous years (SI 2008/838)); or

    (b)   more than 80% of the taxpayer's income tax and Class 4 NIC liability for the preceding year was met by tax deducted at source (including PAYE).

Final payment (TMA 1970 s 59B, Sch 3ZA)

Balance of income tax due for a year of assessment (after deducting payments on account, tax deducted at source and credits in respect of dividends, etc) is due on:

31 January following end of year of assessment (TMA 1970 s 59B(4)).

Extended due dates:

    (a)   If a taxpayer has given notice of liability within 6 months of the end of the year of assessment , but a notice to make a return is not given until after 31 October following the end of the year of assessment, the due date is 3 months after the notice is given (TMA 1970 s 59B(3)).

    (b)   If tax is payable as a result of a taxpayer's notice of amendment, an HMRC notice of correction or an HMRC notice of closure following enquiry, in each case given less than 30 days before the due date (or the extended due date at (a) above), the due date is on or before the day following the end of a 30-day period beginning on the day on which the notice is given (TMA 1970 s 59B(5), Sch 3ZA).

    (c)   If an assessment other than a self-assessment is made, tax payable under the assessment is due on the day following the end of a 30-day period beginning on the day on which notice of the assessment is given (TMA 1970 s 59B(6)).

The extensions under (b) and (c) do *not* alter the due date for *interest purposes* (see p 5).

Interest on overdue tax see p 5.

Remission of tax see p 8.

Repayment supplement see p 8.

Inheritance tax

(IHTA 1984 s 226)

Chargeable transfers other than on death, made between:

6 April and 30 September	–	30 April in next year.
1 October and 5 April	–	6 months after end of month in which chargeable transfer is made.

Chargeable events following conditional exemption for heritage etc property and charge on disposal of trees or underwood before the second death:

– 6 months after end of month in which chargeable event occurs.

Transfers on death:

Earlier of (*a*) 6 months after end of month in which death occurs, and
(*b*) delivery of account by personal representatives.

Tax or extra tax becoming payable on death:
Chargeable transfers and potentially exempt transfers within 7 years of death.

– 6 months after end of month in which death occurs.

PAYE and national insurance

(SSCBA 1992 s 15, SI 2001/1004, SI 2003/2682)

Employer's tax and Class 1 national insurance payable under PAYE.	19 April following deduction year (extended to 22 April where payments are made by electronic means).
Class 1A national insurance.	19 July following year in which contributions due (extended to 22 July where payments are made by electronic means).
PAYE settlement agreement and Class 1B national insurance.	19 October following year to which agreement relates (extended to 22 October where payments are made by electronic means).
Class 2 national insurance.	From April 2011 due in 2 instalments on 31 July and 31 January.
Class 4 national insurance.	See under income tax on p 4.

Interest on overdue tax

FA 2009 ss 101–104, Schs 53–54A introduced provisions to harmonise interest regimes across all taxes and duties. Implementation will be staged over a number of years. The provisions apply to income and capital gains tax self-assessment from 31 October 2011 (SI 2011/701). For details of dates from which interest is payable see **harmonised interest regime** p 10. For amounts outstanding immediately prior to 31 October 2011 the old rules under TMA 1970 s 86 have effect up to and including 30 October 2011, and the new rules under FA 2009 ss 101 and 103 have effect thereafter.

Where the harmonised interest regime does not yet apply interest runs from the due date (see p 4) to the date of payment, on the amount outstanding.

Interest is payable gross and is not tax deductible.

Income tax, capital gains tax, NICs Class 1, 1A, 4 and (from 6.4.99) 1B, and (from 1.10.99) stamp duty, SDRT and (from 26.9.05) stamp duty land tax

Period	Rate
from 29 September 2009	3.0%
24 March 2009–28 September 2009	2.5%
27 January 2009–23 March 2009	3.5%
6 January 2009–26 January 2009	4.5%
6 December 2008–5 January 2009	5.5%

Period	Rate
6 November 2008–5 December 2008	6.5%
6 January 2008–5 November 2008	7.5%
6 August 2007–5 January 2008	8.5%
6 September 2006–5 August 2007	7.5%
6 September 2005–5 September 2006	6.5%
6 September 2004–5 September 2005	7.5%
6 December 2003–5 September 2004	6.5%
6 August 2003–5 December 2003	5.5%

Surcharge on unpaid income tax and capital gains tax before 1 April 2011 (TMA 1970 s 59C)

For tax years before 2010–11, where income tax or capital gains tax became payable and all or part of it remained unpaid the day following 28 days after the due date, the taxpayer was liable to a surcharge of 5% of the unpaid tax. A further surcharge of 5% was levied on any of the tax remaining unpaid six months and one day from the due date. Interest was payable on the surcharge from the expiry of 30 days beginning on the day on which the surcharge was imposed until the date of payment chargeable at the above rate. Penalties for late filing of returns and late payment of tax have been reformed. A new system has been introduced (see **penalties** p 14) and the previous rules have been repealed for tax years 2010–11 onwards. The new rules are to be phased in over several years. The penalties for late payment apply for PAYE including CIS and student loan deductions and pension schemes from 6 April 2010, and for bank payroll tax from 31 August 2010. They apply to IT and CGT from 6 April 2011 and to other taxes from a date to be determined (FA 2009 Sch 56 and F(No 3)A 2010 Sch 10).

Corporation tax

Interest runs from the due date (see p 4) to the date of payment. For instalment payments by large companies for accounting periods ending after 30 June 1999, a special rate of interest runs from the due date to the earlier of the date of payment and nine months after the end of the accounting period (after which the normal rate applies).

Corporation tax self-assessment (accounting periods ending after 30 June 1999)

Period	Normal rate
from 29 September 2009	**3.0%**
24 March 2009 to 28 September 2009	2.5%
27 January 2009–23 March 2009	3.5%
6 January 2009–26 January 2009	4.5%
6 December 2008–5 January 2009	5.5%
6 November 2008–5 December 2008	6.5%
6 January 2008–5 November 2008	7.5%
6 August 2007–5 January 2008	8.5%
6 September 2006–5 August 2007	7.5%
6 September 2005–5 September 2006	6.5%
6 September 2004–5 September 2005	7.5%
6 December 2003–5 September 2004	6.5%
6 August 2003–5 December 2003	5.5%
6 November 2001–5 August 2003	6.5%

Period	Special rate for instalment payments (except where still unpaid nine months after end of accounting period)
from 16 March 2009	**1.50%**
16 February 2009–15 March 2009	2.00%
19 January 2009–15 February 2009	2.50%
15 December 2008–18 January 2009	3.00%
17 November 2008–14 December 2008	4.00%
20 October 2008–16 November 2008	5.50%
21 April 2008–19 October 2008	6.00%
18 February 2008–20 April 2008	6.25%
17 December 2007–17 February 2008	6.50%
16 July 2007–16 December 2007	6.75%
21 May 2007–15 July 2007	6.50%
22 January 2007–20 May 2007	6.25%

Period	Special rate for instalment payments (except where still unpaid nine months after end of accounting period)
20 November 2006–21 January 2007	6.00%
14 August 2006–19 November 2006	5.75%
15 August 2005–13 August 2006	5.50%
16 August 2004–14 August 2005	5.75%
21 June 2004–15 August 2004	5.50%
17 May 2004–20 June 2004	5.25%
16 February 2004–16 May 2004	5.00%
17 November 2003–15 February 2004	4.75%
21 July 2003–16 November 2003	4.50%
17 February 2003–20 July 2003	4.75%
19 November 2001–16 February 2003	5.00%

Corporation tax pay and file (accounting periods ending after 30 September 1993)

Period	Rate
from 29 September 2009	3.0%
24 March 2009– 28 September 2009	1.75%
27 January 2009–23 March 2009	2.75%
6 January 2009–26 January 2009	3.50%
6 December 2008–5 January 2009	4.25%
6 November 2008–5 December 2008	5.00%
6 January 2008–5 November 2008	6.00%
6 August 2007–5 January 2008	6.75%
6 September 2006–5 August 2007	6.00%
6 September 2005–5 September 2006	5.25%
6 September 2004–5 September 2005	6.00%
6 December 2003–5 September 2004	5.25%[1]
6 August 2003–5 December 2003	4.25%
6 November 2001–5 August 2003	5.00%

[1] This rate was corrected by HMRC (see news release HMRC 27/05 of 6 September 2005) and is higher than that previously used (5%). No attempt will be made to recover any further interest which may be due unless, exceptionally, a liability is reviewed.

Income tax on company payments (due on or after 14 October 1999)

Period	Rate
from 29 September 2009	3.0%
24 March 2009– 28 September 2009	2.5%
27 January 2009–23 March 2009	3.5%
6 January 2009–26 January 2009	4.5%
6 December 2008–5 January 2009	5.5%
6 November 2008–5 December 2008	6.5%
6 January 2008–5 November 2008	7.5%
6 August 2007–5 January 2008	8.5%
6 September 2006–5 August 2007	7.5%
6 September 2005–5 September 2006	6.5%
6 September 2004–5 September 2005	7.5%
6 December 2003–5 September 2004	6.5%
6 August 2003–5 December 2003	5.5%
6 November 2001–5 August 2003	6.5%

Inheritance tax

Interest runs from the due date (see p 5) to the date of payment.

Period	Rate
from 29 September 2009	3%
24 March 2009–28 September 2009	0%
27 January 2009–23 March 2009	1%

Period	Rate
6 January 2009–26 January 2009	2%
6 November 2008–5 January 2009	3%
6 January 2008–5 November 2008	4%
6 August 2007–5 January 2008	5%
6 September 2006–5 August 2007	4%
6 September 2005–5 September 2006	3%
6 September 2004–5 September 2005	4%
6 December 2003–5 September 2004	3%
6 August 2003–5 December 2003	2%
6 November 2001–5 August 2003	3%

Remission of tax

By concession, arrears of tax may be waived if they result from HMRC's failure to make proper and timely use of information supplied by the taxpayer or, where it affects the taxpayer's coding, by his or her employer. The concession also applies to information supplied by the Department for Work and Pensions affecting the taxpayer's entitlement to a retirement, disability or widow's pension (see Concession A19). The concession only applies where the taxpayer could reasonably have believed that his or her affairs were in order and (unless the circumstances are exceptional) where the taxpayer is notified of the arrears more than 12 months after the end of the tax year in which HMRC received the information indicating that more tax was due.

Interest on overpaid tax

Income tax, capital gains tax, Class 1, 1A, 4 and (from 6.4.99) 1B national insurance contributions and (from 1.10.99) stamp duty and stamp duty reserve tax and (from 26.9.05) stamp duty land tax

FA 2009 ss 101–104, Schs 53–54A introduce provisions to harmonise interest regimes across all taxes and duties. Implementation will be staged over a number of years. The provisions will apply to income and capital gains tax self-assessment from 31 October 2011. For details of the periods for which interest is repayable see **harmonised interest regime** p 10. For amounts outstanding immediately prior to 31 October 2011 the old rules under TA 1988 s 824 and TCGA 1992 s 283 have effect up to and including 30 October 2011, and the new rules under FA 2009 ss 102 and 103 have effect thereafter.

Calculated as simple interest on the amount of tax repaid. The supplement is tax free.

Period	Rate
from 29 September 2009	**0.50%**
27 January 2009–28 September 2009	0.00%
6 January 2009–26 January 2009	0.75%
6 December 2008–5 January 2009	1.50%
6 November 2008–5 December 2008	2.25%
6 January 2008–5 November 2008	3.00%
6 August 2007–5 January 2008	4.00%
6 September 2006–5 August 2007	3.00%
6 September 2005–5 September 2006	2.25%
6 September 2004–5 September 2005	3.00%[1]
6 December 2003–5 September 2004	2.25%[1]
6 August 2003–5 December 2003	1.50%[1]
6 November 2001–5 August 2003	2.25%[1]

[1] These rates were corrected by HMRC (see HMRC 27/05, 6 September 2005) and are lower than those previously used. No attempt will be made to recover amounts overpaid by HMRC unless, exceptionally, a repayment is reviewed.

Income tax

(TA 1988 s 824; FA 1997 s 92; ITTOIA 2005 s 749, SI 2011/701)

From 1996–97 for amounts which become repayable up to and including 30 October 2011 (from 1997–98 for partnerships whose trade, profession or business commenced before 6 April 1994) repayment supplement applies to:
(a)   amounts paid on account of income tax
(b)   income tax paid by or on behalf of an individual
(c)   late payment penalties for income and capital gains tax self-assessment under FA 2009 Sch 56

(d)   penalties incurred by an individual under any provision of TMA 1970

but excluding amounts paid in excess of the maximum the taxpayer is required to pay.

Except for tax deducted at source, the repayment supplement runs *from* the date on which the tax or penalty was paid *to* the date on which the order for repayment is issued. For tax deducted at source, repayment supplement runs from 31 January after the end of the tax year for which the tax was deducted.

Capital gains tax

(TCGA 1992 s 283, SI 2011/701)

From 1996–97 for amounts which become repayable up to and including 30 October 2011 repayment supplement runs *from* the date on which the tax was paid *to* the date on which the order for repayment is issued.

Inheritance tax

(IHTA 1984 s 235)

Repayments of inheritance tax or interest paid carries interest *from* the date of payment *to* the date on which the order for repayment is issued. Before 29 September 2009, the prescribed rates for unpaid tax applied equally to repayment supplements. From 29 September 2009, the rate is 0.5%.

Companies

Corporation tax self-assessment (accounting periods ending after 30 June 1999)

Normal rates

Rates on overpaid corporation tax in respect of periods after normal due date (SI 1989/1297 reg 3BB).

Period	Rate
from 29 September 2009	**0.5%**
27 January 2009–28 September 2009	0%
6 January 2009–26 January 2009	1%
6 December 2008–5 January 2009	2%
6 November 2008–5 December 2008	3%
6 January 2008–5 November 2008	4%
6 August 2007–5 January 2008	5%
6 September 2006–5 August 2007	4%
6 September 2005–5 September 2006	3%
6 September 2004–5 September 2005	4%
6 December 2003–5 September 2004	3%
6 August 2003–5 December 2003	2%
6 November 2001–5 August 2003	3%

Special rates

For instalment payments by large companies and early payments by other companies, a special rate of interest runs from the date the excess arises (but not earlier than the due date of the first instalment) to the earlier of the date the repayment order is issued and nine months and one day after the end of the accounting period, after which the normal rate of interest (as above) applies.

Rates on overpaid instalment payments and on corporation tax paid early (but not due by instalments).

Period	Rate
from 21 September 2009	**0.5%**
16 March 2009–20 September 2009	0.25%
16 February 2009–15 March 2009	0.75%
19 January 2009–15 February 2009	1.25%
15 December 2008–18 January 2009	1.75%
17 November 2008–14 December 2008	2.75%
20 October 2008–16 November 2008	4.25%
21 April 2008–19 October 2008	4.75%
18 February 2008–20 April 2008	5.00%
17 December 2007–17 February 2008	5.25%
16 July 2007–16 December 2007	5.50%
21 May 2007–15 July 2007	5.25%
22 January 2007–20 May 2007	5.00%
20 November 2006–21 January 2007	4.75%
14 August 2006–19 November 2006	4.50%

Period	Rate
15 August 2005–13 August 2006	4.25%
16 August 2004–14 August 2005	4.50%
21 June 2004–15 August 2004	4.25%
17 May 2004–20 June 2004	4.00%
16 February 2004–16 May 2004	3.75%
17 November 2003–15 February 2004	3.50%
21 July 2003–16 November 2003	3.25%
17 February 2003–20 July 2003	3.50%
19 November 2001–16 February 2003	3.75%
15 October 2001–18 November 2001	4.25%
1 October 2001–14 October 2001	4.50%
13 August 2001–30 September 2001	4.75%
21 May 2001–12 August 2001	5.00%
16 April 2001–20 May 2001	5.25%
19 February 2001–15 April 2001	5.50%
21 February 2000–18 February 2001	5.75%
24 January 2000–20 February 2000	5.50%

Corporation tax pay and file (accounting periods ending before 1 July 1999)

Period	Rate
from 29 September 2009	0.50%
27 January 2009–28 September 2009	0.00%
6 January 2009–26 January 2009	0.50%
6 December 2008–5 January 2009	1.25%
6 November 2008–5 December 2008	2.00%
6 January 2008–5 November 2008	2.75%
6 August 2007–5 January 2008	3.50%
6 September 2006–5 August 2007	2.75%
6 September 2005–5 September 2006	2.00%
6 September 2004–5 September 2005	2.75%
6 December 2003–5 September 2004	2.00%
6 August 2003–5 December 2003	1.25%
6 November 2001–5 August 2003	2.00%

Harmonised interest regime

(FA 2009 ss 101–104, Schs 53–54A, SI 2011/701)

A harmonised interest regime is being phased in for all taxes and duties and applies to income and capital gains tax self-assessment from 31 October 2011. Planned implementation dates for other taxes and duties are not yet clear. For amounts outstanding immediately prior to 31 October 2011, the previous legislation for income and capital gains tax self-assessment (TMA 1970 s 86, TA 1988 s 824 and TCGA 1992 s 283) had effect up to and including 30 October 2011, and the new legislation applies thereafter. The measure provides for differential interest charged and paid by HMRC to be based around the Bank of England base rate. The current rates are as set out above – 3.0% for late payment interest and 0.5% for repayment interest.

Late payment interest runs from the start date to the date of payment. The start date is generally the date on which the amount becomes due and payable, but special rules apply as follows:

Where an amount is due as a result of—
(a) an amendment or correction to an assessment or self-assessment; or
(b) an HMRC assessment in place of, or in addition to, an assessment made by the taxpayer; or
(c) an HMRC assessment in place of an assessment which ought to have been made by the taxpayer,

the start date is the date it would have been if the original assessment or self-assessment had been complete and accurate and made on the date (if any) by which it was required to be made, and the tax had been due and payable as a result of the original assessment or self-assessment.

Repayment interest runs from the start date until the date the payment or repayment is made. The start date in the case of an amount paid to HMRC is the later of—
(i) the date the amount was paid to HMRC; and
(ii) the date on which the amount became due and payable to HMRC (in a case where the amount has been paid in connection with a liability to make a payment to HMRC, and it is to be repaid by them).

The start date, in the case of an amount which has not been paid to HMRC and which is payable by virtue of a return or a claim having been submitted, is the later of—

(1)   the date (if any) on which the return or claim was required to be submitted; and

(2)   the date on which the return or claim was submitted.

The start date in the case of the carry back of losses or averaging claims is 31 January following the *later* tax year in relation to the claim.

Special relief

(TMA 1970 Sch 1AB para 3A; FA 1998 Sch 18 para 51BA)

From 1 April 2011 a new statutory 'special relief' is available which allows HMRC to give effect to a claim for repayment or discharge of an amount of tax that a person is liable to pay, but which the person believes is not due or, if it has been paid, was not due, where the usual time limits for such relief have expired. Relief is only available to taxpayers in receipt of an income tax or corporation tax self-assessment determination made by HMRC in the absence of a self-assessment return being submitted, and where the following specific conditions are met: (a) it would be unconscionable for HMRC to seek to recover the amount or to refuse to repay it if it has already been paid; (b) that the person's tax affairs are otherwise up to date, or arrangements have been put in place to HMRC's satisfaction, to bring them up to date as far as possible; and (c) the person has not previously claimed special relief, or its concessionary predecessor equitable liability, whether or not such a claim was successful. This latter condition may be waived in exceptional circumstances. There is no time limit for claiming the relief.

Certificates of tax deposit

Certificates are not available for purchase for use against corporation tax or PAYE liabilities. Certificates are available to individuals, partnerships, individual partners, trustees, personal representatives and companies for the payment of income tax, Class 4 national insurance contributions, capital gains tax, inheritance tax, petroleum revenue tax or petroleum royalty. Minimum first deposit £500; subsequent deposits not less than £250 or amount required to bring total deposits up to £500 (ie where total deposits have fallen below that amount). Interest is paid gross and is chargeable to tax. It will only be paid for the first six years of a deposit. A deposit bears interest for the first year at the rate in force at the time of the deposit and for each subsequent year at the rate in force on the anniversary of the deposit.

Date	Amount	Held for (mths in yr)	Pay't of tax %	Cashed %
11.6.04–5.8.04	Under £100,000	no limit	1.00	0.50
	£100,000 or over	under 1	1.00	0.50
		1–under 3	3.75	1.75
		3–under 6	3.50	1.75
		6–12	3.75	1.75
6.8.04–4.8.05	Under £100,000	no limit	1.25	0.50
	£100,000 or over	under 1	1.25	0.50
		1–12	3.75	1.75
5.8.05–3.8.06	Under £100,000	no limit	1.00	0.50
	£100,000 or over	under 1	1.00	0.50
		1–under 3	3.50	1.75
		3–under 6	3.25	1.50
		6–12	3.00	1.50
4.8.06–9.11.06	Under £100,000	no limit	1.75	0.75
	£100,000 or over	under 1	1.75	0.75
		1–under 3	4.25	2.00
		3–under 6	4.25	2.00
		6–12	4.00	2.00
10.11.06–11.1.07	Under £100,000	no limit	1.50	0.75
	£100,000 or over	under 1	1.50	0.75
		1–under 3	4.00	2.00
		3–under 6	4.00	2.00
		6–12	3.75	1.75
12.1.07–10.5.07	Under £100,000	no limit	1.50	0.75
	£100,000 or over	under 1	1.50	0.75
		1–under 3	4.25	2.00
		3–under 6	4.00	2.00
		6–12	4.00	2.00
11.5.07–5.7.07	Under £100,000	no limit	2.00	1.00
	£100,000 or over	under 1	2.00	1.00
		1–under 3	4.75	2.25
		3–under 6	4.50	2.25

Date	Amount	Held for (mths in yr)	Pay't of tax %	Cashed %
		6–12	4.50	2.25
6.7.07–6.12.07	Under £100,000	no limit	2.25	1.10
	£100,000 or over	under 1	2.25	1.10
		1–under 3	5.00	2.50
		3–under 6	4.75	2.25
		6–12	4.75	2.25
7.12.07–7.02.08	Under £100,000	no limit	3.00	1.50
	£100,000 or over	under 1	3.00	1.50
		1–under 3	5.50	2.75
		3–under 6	5.00	2.50
		6–under 9	4.75	2.25
		9–12	4.50	2.25
8.02.08–10.04.08	Under £100,000	no limit	2.00	1.00
	£100,000 or over	under 1	2.00	1.00
		1–under 3	4.50	2.25
		3–under 6	4.25	2.00
		6–under 9	4.00	2.00
		9–12	3.75	1.50
11.04.08–8.10.08	Under £100,000	no limit	2.00	1.00
	£100,000 or over	Under 1	2.00	1.00
		1–under 3	4.75	2.25
		3–under 6	4.50	2.25
		6–under 9	4.25	2.00
		9–12	4.25	2.00
9.10.08–6.11.08	Under £100,000	No limit	2.50	1.25
	£100,000 or over	under 1	2.50	1.25
		1–under 3	5.25	2.50
		3–under 6	5.00	2.50
		6–under 9	5.00	2.50
		9–12	4.75	2.25
7.11.08–4.12.08	Under £100,000	No limit	1.75	0.75
	£100,000 or over	under 1	1.75	0.75
		1–under 3	4.50	2.25
		3–under 6	4.25	2.00
		6–under 9	4.25	2.00
		9–12	4.00	2.00
5.12.08–8.1.09	Under £100,000	No limit	0.00	0.00
	£100,000 or over	under 1	0.00	0.00
		1–under 3	2.50	1.25
		3–under 6	2.50	1.25
		6–under 9	2.50	1.25
		9–12	2.25	1.00
9.1.09–5.2.09	Under £100,000	No limit	0.00	0.00
	£100,000 or over	under 1	0.00	0.00
		1–under 3	1.50	0.75
		3–under 6	1.25	0.50
		6–under 9	1.25	0.50
		9–12	1.25	0.50
6.2.09–5.3.09	Under £100,000	No limit	0.00	0.00
	£100,000 or over	under 1	0.00	0.00
		1–under 3	1.00	0.50
		3–under 6	1.00	0.50
		6–under 9	1.00	0.50
		9–12	0.75	0.25
6.3.09–	Under £100,000	No limit	0.00	0.00
	£100,000 or over	under 1	0.00	0.00
		1–under 3	0.75	0.25
		3–under 6	0.75	0.25
		6–under 9	0.75	0.25
		9–12	0.75	0.25

Student loan deductions

	Percentage	Threshold
2012–13	9%	£15,795 per year £1,316.25 per month £303.75 per week
2005–06 to 2011–12	9%	£15,000 per year £1,250 per month £288.46 per week

Filing dates

Corporation tax

(FA 1998 Sch 18 paras 14, 15)

The return must be filed on the latest of the following dates—

(a) 12 months from the end of the period for which the return is made;

(b) where the company makes up its accounts for a period not exceeding 18 months, 12 months from the end of that period;

(c) where the company makes up its accounts for a period exceeding 18 months, 30 months from the start of that period;

(d) 3 months from the date of issue of the notice requiring the return.

From 1 April 2011 all company returns for accounting periods ending after 31 March 2010 must be filed online. Computations and, in most cases, accounts must be submitted in iXBRL format.

Income tax and capital gains tax

(TMA 1970 ss 8, 8A, 12AA)

Basic position for paper returns.	On or before 31 October following end of tax year.
Basic position for electronic returns.	On or before 31 January following end of tax year.
Paper return and notice to file return issued after 31 July but on or before 31 October following end of tax year.	Within 3 months of date of notice.
Electronic return and notice to file return issued after 31 July but on or before 31 October following end of tax year.	On or before 31 January following end of tax year.
Paper or electronic return and notice to file return issued after 31 October following end of tax year.	Within 3 months of date of notice.
Paper return and taxpayer wishes tax underpayment of less than £3,000[1] to be coded out.	On or before 31 October following end of tax year.
Electronic return and taxpayer wishes tax underpayment of less than £3,000[1] to be coded out.	On or before 31 December following end of tax year.

[1] Applies to self-assessment underpayments of less than £2,000 before 2011–12.

Penalties

Penalties — modernised penalty regime

A new modernised penalty regime is being rolled out to all taxes and duties with the exception of tax credits. The penalty regime in force in respect of various defaults is set out below, but further changes may occur during 2012 as more taxes and duties move to the modernised regime.

Inaccuracy in return or other document

Applies to	Commencement date	Penalty details
IT, CGT, CT, VAT, CIS, NIC Classes 1 and 4 (FA 2007 Sch 24)	Return periods starting 1 April 2008 where the return is due to be filed on or after 1 April 2009	Penalty based on potential lost revenue Careless inaccuracy — 30% Deliberate but not concealed — 70% Deliberate and concealed — 100%
IHT, all other taxes and duties (except tax credits)	Return periods starting 1 April 2009 where the return is due to be filed on or after 1 April 2010, or where the liability arises on or after 1 April 2010; for IHT in respect of deaths from 1 April 2009	*Reductions for disclosure* Unprompted disclosure minimum penalties nil, 20% and 30% Prompted disclosure minimum penalties 15%, 35% and 50%
Class 1A NIC	2010–11 returns	
Corporation tax credit, return by registered pension scheme	Return periods starting 1 April 2009 where the return is due to be filed on or after 1 April 2010	
IT, CGT but offshore matter (FA 2010 Sch 10)	6 April 2011	Penalties above are increased by either 0%, 50% or 100% depending on the territory concerned (see table below for a list of territories in each category)

Inaccuracy in return or other document as a result of third party providing incorrect (or withholding) information

Applies to	Commencement date	Penalty details
IT, CGT, CT, VAT, IHT, CIS, NIC Classes 1 and 4, all other taxes and duties (except tax credits) (FA 2007 Sch 24)	1 April 2009 where the return is due to be filed on or after 1 April 2010	100% of potential lost revenue Subject to reduction for disclosure as for inaccuracies above.
Class 1A NIC	2010–11 returns	

Failure to notify HMRC of an error in an assessment (within 30 days)

Applies to	Commencement date	Penalty details
IT, CGT, CT, VAT, CIS, NIC Classes 1 and 4 (FA 2007 Sch 24)	1 April 2008 where the return is due to be filed on or after 1 April 2009	30% of potential lost revenue *Reductions for disclosure* Unprompted disclosure minimum penalty nil Prompted disclosure minimum penalty 15%
IHT, SDLT, all other taxes and duties except tax credits	1 April 2009 where the return is due to be filed on or after 1 April 2010	
Class 1A NIC	2010–11 returns	

Failure to notify chargeability (includes failure to register for VAT)

Applies to	Commencement date	Penalty details
IT, CGT, NIC Class 4 (Class 2 similar provisions but in separate legislation) (FA 2008 Sch 41)	2009–10	Penalty based on potential lost revenue Failure to notify — 30% Deliberate but not concealed — 70% Deliberate and concealed — 100%
CT	Accounting periods ending on or after 31 March 2010	*Reductions for disclosure* Unprompted disclosure minimum penalties nil (within 12 months late), 10% (more than 12 months late), 20% and 30% Prompted disclosure minimum penalties 15%, 35%, 50%
All other taxes and duties	Obligations arising on or after 1 April 2010	
IT, CGT but offshore matter (FA 2010 Sch 10)	6 April 2011	Penalties above are increased by either 0%, 20% or 100% depending on the territory concerned (see table below for a list of territories in each category)

Failure to make returns on time

Applies to	Commencement date	Penalty details
Bank Payroll Tax	31 August 2010	Initial penalty £100 Failure continues for more than three months — with notice — £10 per day for up to 90 days Six months late — greater of 5% of the tax due and £300 12 months late — same penalty as for 6 months late unless deliberately withholding the return
IT, CGT, NIC Class 4 (FA 2009 Sch 55)	6 April 2011	Deliberate withholding of the return more than 12 months — 70% of tax due (minimum £300) Deliberate and concealed withholding of the return more than 12 months — 100% of tax due (minimum £300)
Return by Registered Pension scheme (FA 2009 Sch 55)	1 April 2011	*Reductions for disclosure* Unprompted disclosure minimum penalty 20% and 30% Prompted disclosure minimum penalties 35% and 50%
CIS returns (FA 2009 Sch 55)	6 October 2011	Initial penalty £100 After two months — £200 Six months late — greater of 5% of the tax due and £300 12 months late — same penalty as for 6 months late unless deliberately withholding the return Deliberate withholding of the return more than 12 months — 70% of tax due (minimum £1,500) Deliberate and concealed withholding of the return more than 12 months — 100% of tax due (minimum £3,000) *Reductions for disclosure* Unprompted disclosure minimum penalty 20% and 30% Prompted disclosure minimum penalties 35% and 50% Special rules apply to the first returns made on registration for CIS so that the maximum total penalty that can apply for the initial and second fixed penalties for all such returns is £3,000. Subsequent tax-geared penalties may still be incurred. Where a CIS return only relates to persons registered for 'gross payment' a tax-geared penalty after 6 months or 12 months cannot apply. In these cases the person is liable to the fixed amount penalty.
IT, CGT but offshore matter (FA 2010 Sch 10)	6 April 2011	Penalties above for a return later than 12 months which has been withheld are increased by either 0%, 50% or 100% depending on the territory concerned (see table below for a list of territories in each category)

Failure to pay tax on time

Applies to	Commencement date	Penalty details
PAYE, NIC Class 1, CIS, student loan deductions (FA 2009 Sch 56)	2010–11 liabilities (on a risk assessed basis at present)	Penalty based on number of late payments in a year applied to the amounts paid late 1 late payment — nil 2, 3, 4 late payments — 1% 5, 6, 7 late payments — 2% 8, 9, 10 late payments — 3% 11, 12 late payments — 4% Any amount paid 6 months late — 5% Any amount paid 12 months late — 5%
NIC Class 1A and 1B (SI 2001/1004 reg 67B)	2010–11	31 days late — 5% 6 months late — 5% 12 months late — 5%
Bank Payroll Tax	31 August 2010	5% 5 months late — 5% 11 months late — 5%
Tax due by Registered Pension schemes (FA 2009 Sch 56)	Payments due 30 September 2010	31 days late — 5% 6 months late — 5% 12 months late — 5%
IT, CGT payable under self-assessment	6 April 2011 for self-assessment for 2010–11 onwards	31 days late — 5% 6 months late — 5% 12 months late — 5%

Offshore penalties — territory categories

Category 1

Anguilla	Estonia	Japan	Portugal[4]
Aruba	Finland	Korea, South	Romania
Australia	France[2]	Latvia	Slovakia
Belgium	Germany	Lithuania	Slovenia
Bulgaria	Greece	Malta	Spain[5]
Canada	Guernsey[3]	Montserrat	Sweden
Cayman Islands	Hungary	Netherlands (not including Bonaire, Sint Eustatius and Saba)	USA (not including overseas territories and possessions)[6]
Cyprus	Ireland	New Zealand (not including Tokelau)	
Czech Republic	Isle of Man	Norway	
Denmark (not including Faroe Islands or Greenland)[1]	Italy	Poland	

[1] Faroe Islands and Greenland are in Category 2.
[2] Includes overseas Departments of France; the overseas collectivities of France are in Category 2.
[3] Includes Alderney and Sark.
[4] Includes Madeira and the Azores.
[5] Includes the Canary Islands and other overseas territories of Spain.
[6] The overseas territories and possessions of the USA are in Category 2.

Category 2

Territories not listed in Categories 1 or 3 (other than the UK) will be in Category 2. Crown Dependencies and Overseas Territories of the UK are, unless listed, in Category 2.

Category 3

Albania	Costa Rica	Kyrgyzstan	Saint Lucia
Algeria	Curaçao	Lebanon	Saint Vincent and the Grenadines
Andorra	Cuba	Macau[1]	San Marino
Antigua and Barbuda	Democratic People's Republic of Korea	Marshall Islands	Seychelles
Armenia	Dominica	Mauritius	Sint Maarten
Bahrain	Dominican Republic	Micronesia, Federated States of	Suriname
Barbados	Ecuador	Monaco	Syria
Belize	El Salvador	Nauru	Tokelau
Bonaire, Sint Eustatius and Saba	Gabon	Nicaragua	Tonga
Brazil	Grenada	Niue	Trinidad and Tobago
Cameroon	Guatemala	Palau	United Arab Emirates
Cape Verde	Honduras	Panama	Uruguay
Colombia	Iran	Paraguay	
Congo, Republic of the	Iraq	Peru	
Cook Islands	Jamaica	Saint Kitts and Nevis	

[1] China and Hong Kong are in Category 2.

Personal tax and corporation tax

Offence	Penalty
Failure to notify chargeability to income or capital gains tax within six months of tax year or to corporation tax within one year of accounting period (TMA 1970 s 7; FA 1998 Sch 18).	*Up to tax liability still unpaid after 31 January following tax year (IT or CGT) or one year after end of accounting period (CT).* **Repealed for failures on or after 1 April 2010.**
Failure to render return for income tax or capital gains tax (TMA 1970 ss 93, 93A).	*(a) Initial penalty of £100 (or tax due if less);*
	(b) upon direction by Commissioners, further penalty up to £60 for each day failure continues;
	(c) if failure continues after six months from filing date, and no penalty imposed under (b), a further penalty of £100 (or tax due if less);
	(d) if failure continues after one year from filing date, a further penalty up to amount of tax due. **Repealed and replaced by penalty under FA 2009 Sch 55 above for 2010–11 onwards.**
Failure to render return for corporation tax (FA 1998 Sch 18 paras 17, 18).	(a) £100 if up to three months late (£500 if previous two returns also late);
	(b) £200 if over three months late (£1,000 if previous two returns also late);
	(c) if failure continues, on final day for delivery of return or, if later, 18 months after return period, 10% of tax unpaid 18 months after return period (20% of tax unpaid at that date if return not made within two years of return period).
Failure to maintain records supporting personal and trustees' returns of partnership returns (TMA 1970 s 12B).	Up to £3,000.
Fraudulently or negligently making an incorrect statement in connection with a claim to reduce payments on account (TMA 1970 s 59A(6)).	Up to the amount (or additional amount) payable on account if a correct statement had been made.
Fraudulently or negligently delivering incorrect return or accounts or making an incorrect claim for an allowance, deduction or relief (TMA 1970 ss 95, 95A; FA 1998 Sch 18 para 89).	*Up to amount of tax underpaid by reason of incorrectness for (IT and CGT) the tax year (or following tax year and any preceding tax year) in which the return or claim is delivered, (CT) the accounting period(s) to which the return or claim relates.* **Repealed for returns or claims for periods to which penalty under FA 2007 Sch 24 applies (see p 14)**.

Offence	Penalty
Failure to notify within charge to corporation tax within three months after the beginning of the first accounting period and any subsequent accounting period not following on immediately from the end of a previous accounting period. With effect for accounting periods beginning on or after 22 July 2004 (FA 2004 s 55).	(a) *Initial penalty up to £300; and* (b) *a continuing penalty up to £60 for each day on which the failure continues.* **Repealed for accounting periods ending after 31 March 2010.**
Deliberately or recklessly failing to pay corporation tax due in respect of total liability of company for accounting period, or fraudulently or negligently making claim for repayment (TMA 1970 s 59E(4); SI 1998/3175 reg 13).	Penalty not exceeding twice amount of interest charged under SI 1998/3175 reg 7.
Failure to register as self-employed (and liable to Class 2 NIC) within three months after month in which self-employment begins (SI 2001/1004 reg 87).	*Up to £100.* **Repealed for obligations arising after 5 April 2009.**

PAYE

Offence	Penalty
Failure to submit return P9D or P11D (benefits in kind) by due date (6 July following subsequent tax years) (TMA 1970 s 98(1)).	(a) Initial penalty up to £300; and (b) continuing penalty up to £60 for each day on which the failure continues.
Fraudulently or negligently submitting incorrect return P9D or P11D (TMA 1970 s 98(2)).	*Penalty up to £3,000.* **Does not apply from 1 April 2009 when penalty for careless or deliberate error under FA 2007 Sch 24 applies.**
Failure to submit returns P14 (individual end of year summary), P35 (annual return), P38 or P38A (supplementary returns for employees not on P35) by due date (19 May following tax year) (TMA 1970 s 98A).	(a) First 12 months: penalty of £100 for each 50 employees (or part thereof) for each month the failure continues; (b) failures exceeding 12 months: penalty up to amount of PAYE or NIC due and unpaid after 19 April following tax year.
Fraudulently or negligently submitting incorrect forms P14, P35, P38 or P38A (TMA 1970 s 98A).	*Penalty up to the amount of tax due.* **Repealed from 1 April 2008 in relation to documents for tax periods commencing on or after that date.**
Failure to submit returns P11D(b) (Class 1A NIC returns) by due date (19 July following tax year) (SI 2001/1004 reg 81(2)).	(a) First 12 months: penalty of £100 for each 50 employees (or part thereof) for each month the failure continues (but total penalty not to exceed total Class 1A NIC due); (b) failures exceeding 12 months: a penalty not exceeding the amount of Class 1A NIC due and unpaid after 19 July following tax year.
Fraudulently or negligently submitting incorrect form P11D(b) (2001/1004 reg 81(1) before substitution by SI 2010/721).	*Up to the difference between the amount paid and the amount which should have been paid if the return had been correct.* **Does not apply from 2010–11 when FA 2007 Sch 24 applies.**
Failure to submit information in connection with mandatory e-filing from 2004–05 onwards (SI 2003/2682 as amended by 2009/2029 reg 14).	Penalty based on number of employees not exceeding £3,000 for 1,000 or more employees.

Inheritance tax returns and information

Offence	Penalty
Failure to deliver an account within 12 months of death (unless tax is less than £100 or there is a reasonable excuse) (IHTA 1984 s 245).	(a) Initial penalty of £100 (or the amount of tax payable if less); (b) further penalty up to £60 (where penalty determined by court or tribunal) for each day on which the failure continues; (c) if failure continues after six months after the date on which account is due, and proceedings not commenced, a further penalty of £100 (or amount of tax payable if less); and (d) if failure continues one year after end of the period in which account is due (where the account is due after 22 July 2004), and IHT is payable, a penalty not exceeding £3,000.

Offence	Penalty
Failure to submit account or notify HMRC under IHTA 1984 s 218A if a disposition on a death is varied within six months of the variation and additional tax is payable (IHTA 1984 s 245A(1A), (1B)).	(a) Initial penalty up to £100; (b) further penalty up to £60 (if determined by court or tribunal) for each day on which the failure continues; (c) up to £3,000 if failure continues after 12 months from date notification is due (where account due after 22 July 2004).
Failure to provide information etc under IHTA 1984 s 218 concerning a settlement by a UK-domiciled settlor with non-resident trustees (IHTA 1984 s 245A(1)).	(a) Initial penalty up to £300; and (b) further penalty up to £60 (where penalty determined by court or tribunal) for each day on which the failure continues.
Failure to provide documents etc under IHTA 1984 s 219A(1) or (4) (IHTA 1984 s 245A(3)).	(a) *Initial penalty up to £50; and* (b) *further penalty up to £30 (where penalty determined by court or tribunal) for each day on which the failure continues.* **Repealed with effect from 1 April 2010 and replaced by penalties under FA 2008 Sch 36 (see p 22).**
Taxpayer fraudulently or negligently delivering, furnishing or producing incorrect accounts, information or documents (IHTA 1984 s 247; FA 2004 s 295(4), (9)).	*(Accounts etc delivered after 22 July 2004)* *Penalty up to the amount of tax payable.* **Repealed for accounts etc to which penalty under FA 2007 Sch 24 applies (see p 14).** *(Accounts etc delivered on or before 22 July 2004)* (a) *in the case of fraud, penalty up to aggregate of £3,000 and the amount payable; and* (b) *in the case of negligence, penalty up to the aggregate of £1,500 and the amount of tax payable.*
Person other than the taxpayer fraudulently or negligently delivering, furnishing or producing incorrect accounts, information or documents (IHTA 1984 s 247(3); FA 2004 s 295(4), (9)).	*(Accounts etc delivered after 22 July 2004)* Up to £3,000. Accounts etc delivered on or before 22 July 2004 (a) in the case of fraud, penalty up to £3,000; and (b) in the case of negligence, penalty up to £1,500.
Incorrect return etc: Assisting in or inducing the delivery, furnishing or production of any account, information or document knowing it to be incorrect (IHTA 1984 s 247(4)).	Up to £3,000.

Special returns of information

Offence	Penalty
Failure to comply with a notice to deliver a return or other document, furnish particulars or make anything available for inspection under any of the provisions listed in column 1 of the table in TMA 1970 s 98.	(a) Initial penalty up to £300; (b) further penalty up to £60 for each day on which the failure continues.
Failure to furnish information, give certificates or produce documents or records under any of the provisions listed in column 2 of the table in TMA 1970 s 98.	(a) Initial penalty up to £300; and (b) further penalty up to £60 for each day on which the failure continues.
Fraudulently or negligently delivering any incorrect document, information etc required under the above provisions (TMA 1970 s 99).	Penalty up to £3,000.
Failure to deduct income tax at source from payments of interest or royalties under ITA 2007 Part 15 where the exemption does not apply and the company did not believe or could not reasonably have believed that it would apply (TMA 1970 s 98(4A)–(4E)).	(a) Initial penalty up to £3,000; and (b) further penalty up to £600 for each day on which the failure continues.
Advance pricing agreements: Fraudulently or negligently making a false or misleading statement in the preparation of, or application to enter into, any advance pricing agreement (TIOPA 2010 s 227).	Penalty up to £10,000.
Declaration of non-UK residence: Fraudulently or negligently making a false or misleading declaration of non-UK residence to a deposit-taker or building society under ITA 2007 ss 858-861 (TMA 1970 s 99B).	Penalty up to £3,000.

Other offences by taxpayers, agents etc

Offence	Penalty
Falsification of documents. Intentionally falsifying, concealing or destroying documents required under TMA 1970 ss 20A or 20BA (TMA 1970 s 20BB).	On summary conviction, a fine up to the statutory maximum (£5,000); on conviction on indictment, imprisonment for a term not exceeding two years or a fine or both.
Failure to produce documents etc for the purposes of an enquiry under TMA 1970 s 19A or under FA 1998 Sch 18 para 27 (TMA 1970 s 97AA; FA 1998 Sch 18 para 29).	(a) *Initial penalty of £50; and* (b) *further penalty up to £30 (if determined by HMRC) or £150 (if determined by tribunal) for each day on which failure continues.* ***Repealed on or after 1 April 2009.***
European Economic Interest Groupings– Offences in connection with the supply of information: (i) failure to supply information	Initial penalty up to £300 per member of the Grouping at the time of failure and after direction by the tribunal: continuing penalty up to £60 per member of the Grouping at the end of the day for each day on which the failure continues.
(ii) fraudulent or negligent delivery of an incorrect return, accounts or statement (TMA 1970 s 98B).	Up to £3,000 for each member of the Grouping at the time of delivery.
Assisting in the delivery of incorrect returns, accounts or information (TMA 1970 s 99).	Penalty up to £3,000.
Certificates of non-liability to income tax: Fraudulently or negligently giving such a certificate for the purposes of receiving interest gross on a bank or building society account, or failing to comply with an undertaking given in such a certificate (TMA 1970 s 99A).	Penalty up to £3,000.
Refusal to allow a deduction of income tax at source (TMA 1970 s 106).	£50.
Obstruction of officer in inspection of property to ascertain its market value (TMA 1970 s 111).	*Up to £50.* ***Repealed with effect from 1 April 2010 and replaced by penalties under FA 2008 Sch 36 (see below).***
Construction Industry Scheme: (pre 1 April 2007 scheme) Failure by contractor to check validity of registration card (TA 1988 s 566(2B)–(2E)).	Up to £3,000.
(pre 1 April 2007 scheme) Fraudulent attempt by sub-contractor to obtain or misuse a sub-contractor's certificate (TA 1988 s 561(10), (11)).	Up to £3,000.
Construction Industry Scheme: (post 31 March 2007 scheme) Making false statements etc for the purpose of obtaining a gross payment certificate (FA 2004 s 72).	Up to £3,000.
Fraudulent evasion of income tax (TMA 1970 s 106A).	On summary conviction, imprisonment for up to six months or a fine up to the statutory maximum (£5,000); on conviction on indictment, imprisonment for up to seven years or a fine or both.
Enterprise investment scheme relief: Issue by a company of a certificate of approval for such relief fraudulently or negligently or without the authority of HMRC (ITA 2007 s 207).	Not exceeding £3,000.
Treasury consent: Creation or transfer of shares or debentures in a non-resident subsidiary company without the consent of HM Treasury (TA 1988 s 766).	*On conviction on indictment—* (a) *imprisonment for not more than two years or a fine, or both; or* (b) *in the case of a UK company, a fine not exceeding the greater of £10,000, or three times the tax payable by the company attributable to income and gains arising in the previous 36 months.* ***Repealed with effect from 1 July 2009.***
Failure of a company to maintain records (other than those only required for claims, etc, or dividend vouchers and certificates of income tax deducted where other evidence is available) (FA 1998 Sch 18 para 23).	Penalty not exceeding £3,000.

Offence	Penalty
Failure to notify notifiable proposals or notifiable arrangements, or failure to notify the client of the relevant scheme reference number under the provisions of FA 2004 ss 306–319 (TMA 1970 s 98C).	(a) Up to 31 December 2010 an initial penalty not exceeding £5,000; (i) From 1 January 2011 in the case of provisions under FA 2004 ss 308(1) and (3), 309(1) and 310 up to £600 per day in 'initial period' (but a tribunal can determine a higher penalty up to £1 million); (ii) From 1 January 2011 in the case of provisions in FA 2004 ss 312(2), 312A(2), 313ZA, 313A, 313B, 313C an initial penalty up to £5,000. Where a disclosure order is made the amount in (i) above is increased up to £5,000 per day that failure continues from ten days after the order is made. (b) a continuing penalty not exceeding £600 for each day on which the failure continues after imposition of initial penalty. Where a disclosure order is made the amount is increased up to £5,000 per day that failure continues from ten days after the order is made.
Failure to notify scheme reference number etc under FA 2004 s 313(1); for second failure, occurring within three years from the date on which the first failure began; for subsequent failures, occurring within three years from the date on which the previous failure began. (TMA 1970 s 98C; FA 2004 s 315(1)).	Penalty of £100 in respect of each scheme to which the failure relates; penalty of £500 in respect of each scheme to which the failure relates; penalty of £1,000 in respect of each scheme to which the failure relates.
Failure to comply with HMRC investigatory powers under FA 2008 Sch 36. Failure to comply with an information notice within FA 2008 Sch 36 Pt 1 or deliberately obstructing an HMRC officer in the course of an inspection of business premises under FA 2008 Sch 36 Pt 2 which has been approved by the First-tier Tribunal. Applies to IT (including PAYE and CIS), CT, CGT, VAT and certain foreign taxes with effect from 1 April 2009. Extended to IHT, SDLT and other taxes from 1 April 2010 and to Bank Payroll Tax (BPT) from 31 August 2010.	(a) an initial penalty of £300; (b) if failure/obstruction continues, a further penalty up to £60 per day; (c) if failure/obstruction continues after penalty under (a) imposed, a tax-related amount determined by the Upper Tribunal.
Carelessly or deliberately providing inaccurate information or an inaccurate document in response to an information notice.	Up to £3,000 per inaccuracy.
Failure of a senior accounting officer to ensure a company maintains appropriate tax accounting arrangements (FA 2009 Sch 46).	£5,000.
Failure of a senior accounting officer to provide a certificate stating whether the company had appropriate tax accounting arrangements (FA 2009 Sch 46).	£5,000.
Failure to notify Commissioners of name of senior accounting officer (FA 2009 Sch 46).	£5,000.
Failure of a third party to notify the contact details of a debtor (FA 2009 Sch 49).	£300.

Mitigation of penalties

HMRC have discretion to mitigate or entirely remit any penalty or to stay or compound any penalty proceedings (TMA 1970 s 102).

Interest on penalties

Penalties under TMA 1970 Parts II (ss 7–12B), IV (ss 28A–43B), VA (ss 59A–59D) and X (ss 93–107), and FA 1998 Sch 18 carry interest at the prescribed rate (see p 5): TMA 1970 s 103A. For tax years before 2010–11, surcharges on unpaid income tax and capital gains tax carried interest under TMA 1970 s 59C. Surcharges have been replaced by a modernised penalty regime (see p 14).

Publishing details of deliberate tax defaulters

From 1 April 2010 HMRC have the power to publish the names and details of taxpayers who are penalised for deliberate defaults leading to a loss of tax of more than £25,000 (FA 2009 s 94).

Time limits for claims and elections

Whenever possible, a claim or election must be made on the tax return or by an amendment to the return (TMA 1970 s 42 and FA 1998 Sch 18 paras 9, 10, 67 and 79). Exceptions to this general rule are dealt with in TMA 1970 Sch 1A. Except where another period is expressly prescribed, a claim for relief in respect of income tax and capital gains tax must be made within four years after the end of the tax year (for claims made before 1 April 2010 such claims had to be made within five years from the 31 January following the year of assessment to which they related). (TMA 1970 s 43(1); FA 2008 Sch 39 para 12.) The time limit for claims by companies is four years from the end of the accounting period to which it relates (six years for claims made before 1 April 2010) (FA 1998 Sch 18 para 55; FA 2008 Sch 39 para 45).

The tables below set out some of the main exceptions to the general limits.

Income tax

Claim	Time limit
Trading losses: Loss sustained in a trade, profession or vocation to be set against other income of the year or the last preceding year. Extended to certain pre-trading expenditure by ITTOIA 2005 s 57 (ITA 2007 s 64).	One year after 31 January next following tax year in which loss arose.
Unrelieved trading losses to be set against capital gains (TCGA 1992 ss 261B, 261C).	One year after 31 January next following tax year in which loss arose.
Losses of new trade etc: Loss sustained in the first four years of a new trade, profession or vocation to be offset against other income arising in the three years immediately preceding the year of loss. Extended to certain pre-trading expenditure by ITTOIA 2005 s 57 (ITA 2007 s 72).	One year after 31 January next following tax year in which loss arose.
Property business losses: Claim for relief against total income (ITA 2007 s 124).	One year after 31 January next following tax year specified in claim.
Loss on disposal of unlisted shares: Loss on disposal of shares in an EIS company or a qualifying trading company to be offset against other income of the year of loss or the last preceding year (ITA 2007 s 132).	One year after 31 January next following tax year in which loss arose.
Gift aid: Election to treat donations to charity under gift aid made after 5 April 2003 as made in the previous tax year (ITA 2007 s 426).	On or before date on which donor delivers tax return for the previous tax year and not later than 31 January after that year.

Capital gains

Claim	Time limit
Assets of negligible value: Loss to be allowed where the value of an asset has become negligible (TCGA 1992 s 24(2)).	Two years after end of chargeable period of deemed sale (and reacquisition).
Assets held on 31 March 1982: Events occurring prior to 31 March 1982 to be ignored in computing gains arising after 5 April 1988 (TCGA 1992 s 35(5), (6) as amended).	*One year after 31 January next following tax year in which first relevant disposal made after 5.4.88 (**capital gains tax for tax years before 2008–09 only**)*; two years after end of accounting period in which first relevant disposal made after 31.3.88 (corporation tax).
Main residence: Determination of main residence for principal private residence exemption (TCGA 1992 s 222(5)(a)).	Two years after acquisition of second residence.
Relief for loans to traders: Losses on certain loans to traders to be allowed as capital losses at the time of claim or 'earlier time' (TCGA 1992 s 253(3A)).	Two years after the end of the tax year or accounting period of loss.
Relief for loans to traders (payments by guarantor): Losses arising from payments by guarantor of certain irrecoverable loans to traders to be allowed as capital losses at time of claim or 'earlier time' (TCGA 1992 s 253(4), (4A)).	Four years after the end of the tax year or accounting period in which payment made (for claims before 1 April 2010, five years after 31 January following tax year in which payment made (capital gains tax); six years after end of accounting period in which payment made (corporation tax)).
Election for valuation at 6 April 1965: Gain on a disposal of an asset held at 6 April 1965 to be computed as if the asset had been acquired on that date. An election once made is irrevocable (TCGA 1992 Sch 2 para 17).	*One year after 31 January following tax year in which disposal made (**capital gains tax for tax years before 2008–09 only**)*; two years after end of accounting period in which disposal made (corporation tax); or such further time as HMRC may allow.

Corporation tax

Claim	Time limit
Trading losses: Loss sustained by a company in a trade in an accounting period to be offset against profits of that accounting period and profits of the preceding year. Extended to certain pre-trading expenditure by CTA 2009 s 61 (CTA 2010 s 37(7)).	Two years or such further period as HMRC may allow.
Group relief: Group relief to be given for accounting periods ending after 30 June 1999. The surrendering company must consent to the claim (FA 1998 Sch 18 paras 66–77).	The last of: (a) one year from filing date of claimant company's return for accounting period for which claim is made; (b) 30 days after end of an enquiry into return; (c) if HMRC amend return after an enquiry, 30 days after issue of notice of amendment; (d) if an appeal is made against amendment, 30 days after determination of appeal; (or such later time as HMRC may allow).
Non-trading deficit on loan relationship: Claim for non-trading deficits on loan relationships (including non-trading debits on derivative contracts) in an accounting period to be: (a) offset against profits of same period or carried back (CTA 2009 s 460);	Two years after end of accounting period in which deficit arose (or such later time as HMRC may allow).
(b) treated as non-trading deficit of subsequent accounting period to be carried forward to succeeding accounting periods (CTA 2009 s 458).	Two years after end of that subsequent accounting period.
Intangible assets: Election to replace accounts depreciation with fixed writing-down allowance of 4% (CTA 2009 s 730).	Two years after end of the accounting period in which asset was created or acquired.
Research and development: Claim for tax relief to be made, amended or withdrawn in company tax return (or amended return) (FA 1998 Sch 18 paras 83E).	One year from the filing date for return or such later time as HMRC may allow.
UITF 40 spreading adjustment: Election to treat it as arising and charged in an accounting period rather than spreading it over three to six years (FA 2006 Sch 15 para 13).	One year from filing date for return.

Capital allowances

Claim	Time limit
Corporation tax claims: Claims, amended claims and withdrawals of claims in respect of corporation tax capital allowances (CAA 2001 s 3(2), (3)(b), FA 1998 Sch 18 para 82).	The last of: (a) one year after filing date of claimant company's return for accounting period for which claim is made; (b) 30 days after end of enquiry into return; (c) if HMRC amend the return after an enquiry, 30 days after issue of notice of amendment; (d) if appeal is made against amendment, 30 days after determination of appeal; (or such later time as HMRC may allow).
Short life assets: Plant or machinery to be treated as a short life asset (CAA 2001 s 85(2)).	One year after 31 January after tax year in which chargeable period ends (income tax); two years after end of chargeable period (corporation tax).
Connected persons: Succession to a trade between connected persons to be ignored in computing capital allowances (CAA 2001 s 266).	Two years after date of the succession.
Sales between persons under common control treated as made at the lower of open market value and tax written down value (CAA 2001 s 570(5)).	Two years after date of the disposal.

Exchanges

Recognised stock exchanges

The following is a list of countries with exchanges which have been designated as recognised stock exchanges under ITA 2007 s 1005; CTA 2010 s 1137. Unless otherwise specified, any stock exchange (or options exchange) in a country listed below is a recognised stock exchange provided it is recognised under the law of the country concerned relating to stock exchanges.

HMRC may make an order designating a market in the UK as a recognised stock exchange.

Country	Date of recognition
Australian Stock Exchange and its stock exchange subsidiaries	22 September 1988
Austria[3]	22 October 1970
Bahamas	
Bahamas International Securities Exchange	19 April 2010
Belgium[3]	22 October 1970
Bermuda	4 December 2007
Brazil	
Rio De Janeiro Stock Exchange	17 August 1995
São Paulo Stock Exchange	11 December 1995
Canada	
Any stock exchange prescribed for the purposes of the Canadian Income Tax Act	22 October 1970
Cayman Islands Stock Exchange	4 March 2004
China	
Hong Kong – Any stock exchange recognised under Section 2A(1) of the Hong Kong Companies Ordinance	26 February 1971
Cyprus	
Cyprus Stock Exchange	22 June 2009
Denmark	
Copenhagen Stock Exchange	22 October 1970
Estonia	
NASDAQ OMX Tallinn	5 May 2010
Finland	
Helsinki Stock Exchange	22 October 1970
France[3]	22 October 1970
Germany[3]	5 August 1971
Greece	
Athens Stock Exchange	14 June 1993
Guernsey[3]	10 December 2002
Iceland	31 March 2006
Irish Republic[3]	22 October 1970
Italy[3]	3 May 1972
Japan[3]	22 October 1970
Korea	10 October 1994
Lithuania	
NASDAQ OMX Vilnius	12 March 2012
Luxembourg[3]	21 February 1972
Malaysia	
Kuala Lumpur Stock Exchange	10 October 1994
Malta Stock Exchange	29 December 2005
Mauritius Stock Exchange	31 January 2011
Mexico	10 October 1994
Netherlands[3]	22 October 1970
New Zealand	22 September 1988
Norway[3]	22 October 1970
Poland	
Warsaw Stock Exchange	25 February 2010
Portugal[3]	21 February 1972
Russia	
MICEX Stock Exchange	5 January 2011
Singapore	30 June 1977
South Africa	
Bond Exchange of South Africa	16 April 2008

Country	Date of recognition
Johannesburg Stock Exchange	22 October 1970
Spain[3]	5 August 1971
Sri Lanka	
Colombo Stock Exchange	21 February 1972
Sweden	
Stockholm Stock Exchange	16 July 1985
Swiss Stock Exchange	12 May 1997
Thailand	10 October 1994
United Kingdom	
London Stock Exchange	19 July 2007
PLUS-listed Market	19 July 2007
LIFFE Administration and Management	26 September 2011
United States	
Any stock exchange registered with the SEC as a national securities exchange[1]	22 October 1970
Nasdaq Stock Market[2]	10 March 1992

[1] 'National securities exchange' does not include any local exchanges registered with Securities and Exchange Commission.

[2] As maintained through the facilities of the National Association of Securities Dealers Inc and its subsidiaries.

[3] i.e., a stock exchange according to the law of the country concerned relating to stock exchanges.

Recognised futures exchanges

The following is a list of exchanges which have been designated as recognised futures exchanges under TCGA 1992 s 288(6). By concession, those exchanges were recognised futures exchanges for the tax year of recognition onwards.

Recognised futures exchanges	Date of recognition
International Petroleum Exchange of London	6 August 1985
London Metal Exchange	6 August 1985
London Gold Market	12 December 1985
London Silver Market	12 December 1985
CME Group (formerly Chicago Mercantile Exchange and Chicago Board of Trade)	19 December 1986
New York Mercantile Exchange	19 December 1986
Philadelphia Board of Trade	19 December 1986
Mid America Commodity Exchange	29 July 1987
Montreal Exchange	29 July 1987
Hong Kong Futures Exchange	15 December 1987
Commodity Exchange (Comex)	25 August 1988
Sydney Futures Exchange	13 October 1988
Euronext (London International Financial Futures and Options Exchange)	22 March 1992
OM Stockholm	18 March 1992
OMLX (formerly OM London)	18 March 1992
New York Board of Trade	10 June 2004

Recognised investment exchanges and clearing houses

The following is a list of investment exchanges and clearing houses recognised as investment exchanges under the Financial Services and Markets Act 2000 and able to carry out investment business in the UK.

Recognised investment exchanges	Date of recognition
London Stock Exchange plc	22 November 2001
LIFFE Administration and Management	22 November 2001
The London Metal Exchange Ltd	22 November 2001
ICE Futures Europe	22 November 2001
EDX London Ltd[1]	1 July 2003
PLUS Stock Exchange plc	19 July 2007

[1] As of 1 May 2011 EDX London Ltd was absorbed into Turquoise Global Holdings Limited and is no longer a recognised investment exchange.

Recognised clearing houses	Date of recognition
LCH.Clearnet Ltd	22 November 2001
Euroclear UK & Ireland Ltd	23 November 2001
European Central Counterparty Ltd	27 March 2008
ICE Clear Europe Ltd	15 May 2008
CME Clearing Europe Ltd	15 December 2010

Recognised overseas investment exchanges and clearing houses

The following is a list of overseas investment exchanges and clearing houses recognised under the Financial Services and Markets Act 2000 and able to conduct investment business in the UK.

Recognised overseas investment exchange	Date of recognition
National Association of Securities Dealers Automated Quotations (NASDAQ)	23 November 2001
Australian Securities Exchange Ltd	30 January 2002
The Chicago Mercantile Exchange (CME)	23 November 2001
Chicago Board of Trade (CBOT)	23 November 2001
New York Mercantile Exchange Inc (NYMEX Inc)	23 November 2001
SIX Swiss Exchange AG	23 November 2001
EUREX (Zurich)	23 November 2001
ICE Futures US Inc	17 May 2007
NYSE LIFFE US	29 September 2009

Recognised clearing house	Date of recognition
SIX X-Clear	19 August 2004
Eurex Clearing AG	16 January 2007
The Chicago Mercantile Exchange (CME)	11 January 2008
ICE Clear US Inc	25 March 2008
European Multilateral Clearing Facility NV	29 January 2009
Cassa di Compensazione e Garanzia SpA	8 July 2009
LCH SA	18 May 2010

Alternative finance investment bonds

List of recognised stock exchanges designated solely for the purposes of ITA 2007 s 564G, TCGA 1992 s 151N, CTA 2009 s 507.

Recognised stock exchanges	Date of recognition
Abu Dhabi Securities Market	1 April 2007
Bahrain Stock Exchange	1 April 2007
Dubai Financial Market	1 April 2007
Dubai International Financial Exchange	1 April 2007
Labuan International Financial Exchange	1 April 2007
Saudi Stock Exchange (Tadawul)	1 April 2007
Surabaya Stock Exchange	1 April 2007

Applications for clearances and approvals

Clearance application	Address
Transfer of long-term insurance business (TCGA 1992 s 211, TA 1988 s 444AED)	CTIIA (Insurance Group), Mailstation E, 3rd Floor, 100 Parliament Street, London SW1A 2BQ
Demergers (CTA 2010 s 1091); Company purchase of own shares (CTA 2010 s 1044); Transactions in securities (CTA 2010 s 748; ITA 2007 s 701); Enterprise Investment Scheme – acquisition of shares by new company (ITA 2007 s 247(1)(f)); Share exchanges (TCGA 1992 ss 138, 139, 140B); and Intangible fixed assets (CTA 2009 s 831) Loan relationships transfers/mergers (CTA 2009 ss 426, 427, 438) Derivative contracts transfers/mergers (CTA 2009 ss 677, 686) Schemes converting income to capital (TCGA 1992 ss 184G–H) Assignment of lease granted at undervalue (CTA 2009 s 237; ITTOIA 2005 s 300) Transactions in land (CTA 2010 s 831; ITA 2007 s 770)	Clearance and Counteraction Team, Anti-Avoidance Group, First Floor, 22 Kingsway, London WC2B 6NR (Market sensitive applications to Team Leader– see note below.)[1]
Company migration (TMA 1970 s 109B–F, formerly FA 1988 s 130)	Neil Nagle, Business International, Transfer Pricing Team, 100 Parliament Street, London SW1A 2BQ
Advance pricing agreements (TIOPA 2010 Part 5)	APA Team Leader, HMRC, CTIAA, Transfer Pricing Team, 100 Parliament Street, London SW1A 2BQ
	For APAs involving oil, gas and mining taxation: Competent Authority, (APAs), Large Business Service Oil & Gas (APAs), 3rd Floor, 22 Kingsway, London WC2B 6NR
Controlled foreign companies (TA 1988 ss 747–756, Schs 24–26)	Mary Sharp, CTIIA, Business International, 100 Parliament Street, London SW1A 2BQ
Corporate Venturing Schemes (FA 2000 Sch 15)	Small Company Enterprise Centre, HMRC, 1st Floor, Fitzroy House, Castle Meadow Road, Nottingham NG2 1BD
Inward investment (in Statement of Practice 02/07)	Colin Miller, HMRC, CTIAA, Business International, Advance Agreements Unit, 100 Parliament Street, London, SW1A 2BQ
IHT clearance for business owners	See www.hmrc.gov.uk/cap/clearanceiht.htm

Approval application	Address
Pensions (formerly TA 1988 ss 590, 591)	Registration of a pension scheme from 6 April 2006 must be done online, but HMRC can be contacted at Pension Schemes Services, Fitzroy House, Castle Meadow Road, Nottingham, NG2 1BD
Employee share schemes (ITEPA 2003 Schs 2, 3, 4)	HMRC Employee Shares & Securities Unit, Nottingham Team, 1st Floor, Fitzroy House, Castle Meadow Road, Nottingham NG2 1BD Questions on EMI: Small Company Enterprise Centre, 1st Floor, Fitzroy House, Castle Meadow Road, Nottingham NG2 1BD Questions on share valuation: Shares and Assets Valuation, Ferrers House, PO Box 38, Castle Meadow Road, Nottingham NG2 1BB
Qualifying life assurance policies (TA 1988 Sch 15)	Claire Ritchie, CTIIA (Insurance Group), 3rd Floor, 100 Parliament Street, London SW1A 2BQ
Professional bodies (relief for subscriptions) (ITEPA 2003 s 343)	A list of approved professional bodies and learned societies is available on the HMRC website (at www.hmrc.gov.uk/list3/list3.htm)

Confirmation or pre-transaction or general advice	Address
Funding issues (in Statement of Practice 04/07)	Miles Nelson, HMRC, CTIAA, Business International, Financial Transfer Pricing Team, 100 Parliament Street, London SW1A 2BQ
Non-statutory clearances	Large businesses should contact their client relationship manager. All other businesses and their agents should send applications to HMRC Clearances Team, Alexander House, 21 Victoria Avenue, Southend-on-Sea, Essex SS99 1BD[2] or email hmrc.southendteam@hmrc.gsi.gov.uk
HMRC advice on non-business activities	See www.hmrc.gov.uk/cap/cap1.htm
General enquiries on IR35	Telephone 0845 303 3535
CGT post-transaction value checks	Complete form CG34
General advice on specialist technical issues	See www.hmrc.gov.uk/cap/gen-advice.htm
SDLT transactions	See www.hmrc.gov.uk/sdlt/calculate/advance-approval.htm

[1]   Where clearance is sought under any one or more of the sections handled by the Clearance and Counteraction Team, clearance applications may be sent in a single letter to the above London address for clearances under those sections. The letter should make clear what clearance is required. E-mail applications can be sent to reconstructions@hmrc.gsi.gov.uk and fax applications to 020 7438 4409. For market sensitive information, call Team Leader on 020 7438 7215 before sending an e-mail or fax. A reply by e-mail should be requested if required. General enquiries can be made on 020 7438 7474.

[2]   Non-statutory clearances: Businesses may apply for a non-statutory clearance where there is material uncertainty and the issue is commercially significant.

Capital allowances

Rates

Agricultural buildings for periods before April 2011

	Expenditure incurred after	% Rate
Initial allowance	31 October 1992[1]	20
	31 October 1993	Nil
Writing-down allowance	31 March 1986 and before 6 April 2011 (1 April 2011 for companies)	4[2, 3]

[1] Initial allowances were temporarily reintroduced for 1 year in respect of capital expenditure on agricultural buildings or works. The allowances applied to buildings or works constructed under a contract entered into between 1 November 1992 and 31 October 1993, and brought into use for the purposes of the farming trade by 31 December 1994. See CAA 1990 s 124A.

[2] Agricultural buildings allowances are abolished for income tax purposes for 2011/12 onwards and for corporation tax purposes for the financial year beginning 1 April 2011 onwards. (FA 2008, s 84.)

[3] As a transitional measure, writing-down allowances were stepped down over the three financial or tax years prior to abolition. For 2008–09 (for corporation tax, the financial year beginning 1 April 2008) only 75% of the allowance was given. For 2009–10 (or financial year beginning 1 April 2009) only 50% was given and for 2010–11 (or financial year beginning 1 April 2010) only 25%. Where a chargeable period falls in more than one tax or financial year, time apportionment applies to determine the amount of the allowance. (FA 2008, s 85.)

Note: For balancing events on or after 21 March 2007, no election for a balancing adjustment can be made so that the new holder of the relevant interest will, in all cases, calculate writing-down allowances based on the previous owner's balance of qualifying expenditure (cost less allowances claimed).

Dredging

	Expenditure incurred after	% Rate
Writing-down allowance	5 November 1962	4

Industrial buildings and structures for periods before April 2011

Initial allowance	Expenditure[1] incurred after	% Rate
Generally:	31 October 1992	20
	31 October 1993	Nil
Exception: Enterprise zones	within 10 years of site being included in zone[2]	100
Writing-down allowance		
Generally:	5 April 1946	2
	5 November 1962[3] and before 6 April 2011 (1 April 2011 for companies)[4, 5]	4
Exception: Enterprise zones	within 10 years of site being included in zone[2, 4]	25

[1] The amount qualifying for allowance is the price paid for the relevant interest *minus* (i) the value of the land element and (ii) any value attributable to elements over and above those which would feature in a normal commercial lease negotiated in the open market: FA 1995 s 100 confirming previous practice.

[2] CAA 2001 s 306, 310. Includes expenditure on qualifying hotels. See p 36 for enterprise zones.

[3] Includes expenditure on qualifying hotels (other than in an enterprise zone).
Also includes expenditure on the construction of toll roads incurred for accounting periods or basis periods ending after 5 April 1991.

[4] Industrial buildings allowances and allowances for buildings in enterprise zones are abolished for income tax purposes for 2011–12 onwards and for corporation tax purposes for the financial year beginning 1 April 2011 onwards. (FA 2008, ss 84, 86.)

[5] As a transitional measure, writing-down allowances (other than those on enterprise zones) were stepped down over the three financial or tax years prior to abolition. For 2008–09 (for corporation tax, the financial year beginning 1 April 2008) only 75% of the allowance was given. For 2009–10 (or financial year beginning 1 April 2009) only 50% was given and for 2010–11 (or financial year beginning 1 April 2010) only 25%. Where a chargeable period falls in more than one tax or financial year, time apportionment applies to determine the amount of the allowance. (FA 2008, ss 85, 87.)

Note: For balancing events on or after 21 March 2007, no balancing adjustment will arise and the new holder of the relevant interest will calculate writing-down allowances based on the previous owner's balance of qualifying expenditure (cost less allowances claimed).

Flat conversions

Initial allowance	Expenditure incurred	% Rate
	10 May 2001 to 1 or 6 April 2013	100

Applies to expenditure incurred on renovating or converting vacant or storage space above commercial properties to provide low value flats for rent. A writing-down allowance is given at 25% (on a straight-line basis) on unrelieved expenditure. (CAA 2001 ss 393A–393W; FA 2001 s 67, Sch 19.)

This relief will be withdrawn for expenditure incurred on or after 1 April 2013 (corporation tax) and on or after 6 April 2013 (income tax). The entitlement to claim writing down allowance on any outstanding residue of qualifying expenditure will also cease with effect from the same dates.

Know-how

Expenditure incurred after 31 March 1986: annual 25% writing-down allowance (reducing balance basis).

Plant and machinery

	Expenditure incurred after	Expenditure incurred before	Up to pa
Annual investment allowance[1]			
for income tax purposes	5 April 2012		£25,000
	5 April 2010	6 April 2012	£100,000
	5 April 2008	6 April 2010	£50,000
for corporation tax purposes	31 March 2012		£25,000
	31 March 2010	1 April 2012	£100,000
	31 March 2008	1 April 2010	£50,000
First-year allowance (FYA)[13]			
General[12]			**% Rate**
for income tax purposes	5 April 2009	6 April 2010	40
for corporation tax purposes	31 March 2009	1 April 2010	40
Small and medium-sized businesses[2]			
for income tax purposes	1 July 1998	6 April 2008	40
for corporation tax purposes	1 July 1998	1 April 2008	40
	1 July 1997	2 July 1998	50
in Northern Ireland *only*	11 May 1998	12 May 2002	100
Small businesses[3]			
for income tax purposes	5 April 2006	6 April 2008	50
	5 April 2004	6 April 2005	50
for corporation tax purposes	31 March 2006	1 April 2008	50
	31 March 2004	1 April 2005	50
ICT	31 March 2000	1 April 2004	100
Energy-saving plant or machinery[4]	31 March 2001		100
New low-emission cars and refuelling equipment[5]	16 April 2002	1 April 2015	100
Environmentally beneficial plant or machinery[6]	31 March 2003		100
Zero-emission goods vehicles[7]			
for income tax purposes	5 April 2010	6 April 2015	100
for corporation tax purposes	31 March 2010	1 April 2015	100
Enterprise zones[18]	31 March 2012	1 April 2017	100
Writing-down allowance (WDA)[8]			
Foreign leased assets[11]	9 March 1982	1 April 2006	10
	Chargeable period beginning on or after		
Long life assets[8, 9]			
for income tax purposes	6 April 2012		8
for corporation tax purposes	1 April 2012		8
	Chargeable period ending before		
for income tax purposes	6 April 2012		10
for corporation tax purposes	1 April 2012		10
for income tax purposes	6 April 2008		6
for corporation tax purposes	1 April 2008		6

Integral features[8, 10]	Chargeable period beginning on or after	
for income tax purposes	6 April 2012	8
for corporation tax purposes	1 April 2012	8
	Chargeable period ending before	
for income tax purposes	6 April 2012	10
for corporation tax purposes	1 April 2012	10
Thermal insulation[8, 15]	Chargeable period beginning on or after	
for income tax purposes	6 April 2012	8
for corporation tax purposes	1 April 2012	8
	Chargeable period ending before	
for income tax purposes	6 April 2012	10
for corporation tax purposes	1 April 2012	10
Certain cars[8, 14]	Chargeable period beginning on or after	
for income tax purposes	6 April 2012	8
for corporation tax purposes	1 April 2012	8
	Chargeable period ending before	
for income tax purposes	6 April 2012	10
for corporation tax purposes	1 April 2012	10
Solar panels[8, 17]	Chargeable period beginning on or after	
for income tax purposes	6 April 2012	8
for corporation tax purposes	1 April 2012	8
Cushion gas[8, 16]	Chargeable period beginning on or after	
for income tax purposes	6 April 2012	8
for corporation tax purposes	1 April 2012	8
	Chargeable period ending before	
for income tax purposes	6 April 2012	10
for corporation tax purposes	1 April 2012	10
Generally	Chargeable periods beginning on or after	
for income tax purposes	6 April 2012	18
for corporation tax purposes	1 April 2012	18
	Chargeable period ending before	
for income tax purposes	6 April 2012	20
for corporation tax purposes	1 April 2012	20
for income tax purposes	6 April 2008	25
for corporation tax purposes	1 April 2008	25
	Chargeable periods straddling	
for income tax purposes	6 April 2012	Hybrid rate[8, 9]
for corporation tax purposes	1 April 2012	Hybrid rate[8, 9]
for income tax purposes	6 April 2008	Hybrid rate[8, 9]
for corporation tax purposes	1 April 2008	Hybrid rate[8, 9]

1   **Annual investment allowance:** Applies from April 2008. The first £25,000 (£100,000 for expenditure incurred before 6 April 2012 but after 5 April 2010 (income tax) or before 1 April 2012 but after 31 March 2010 (corporation tax)) of qualifying expenditure incurred in a chargeable period qualifies for the annual investment allowance at 100%. The limit is proportionately increased or decreased where the chargeable period is longer or shorter than a year. A group of companies (defined as for company law purposes) can only receive a single allowance. This restriction also applies to certain related businesses or companies. Expenditure on cars does not qualify. (CAA 2001 ss 38A, 38B, 51A–51N; FA 2011 s 11).

2   **Small and medium-sized businesses:** The allowance did not apply to certain expenditure including that on plant and machinery for leasing, motor cars, ships, railway assets or long-life assets. After the first year, allowances revert to the normal WDA. The rate of 50% applied only for expenditure incurred during the year ended 1 July 1998 when a 12% FYA applied to long-life assets. (See notes 4 and 11 below.) Small and medium-sized businesses are, broadly, those satisfying any two of the following conditions: (a) turnover £22,800,000 or less (b) assets £11,400,000 or less (c) not more than 250 employees (CAA 1990 ss 22(3C), (6B), 22A, 44, 46–49). For accounting periods ending before 30 January 2004, the thresholds were: (a) turnover £11,200,000 or less (b) assets £5,600,000 or less.

3   **Small businesses:** See note 2 above for conditions for relief. Small businesses are, broadly, those satisfying any two of the following conditions: (a) turnover £5,600,000 or less (b) assets £2,800,000 or less (c) not more than 50 employees. For accounting periods ending before 30 January 2004, the

thresholds were: (a) turnover £2,800,000 or less (b) assets £1,400,000 or less (FA 2004 s 142).

4   **Energy-saving plant or machinery:** The allowances are available for investment by *any* business in designated energy-saving plant and machinery in accordance with the Government's Energy Technology Product List. 100% first-year allowances are not available for expenditure incurred on or after 1 April 2012 (corporation tax) or 6 April 2012 (income tax) on plant or machinery to generate renewable electricity or heat where tariff payments are received under either of the renewable energy schemes introduced by the Department of Energy and Climate Change. The restriction applies from April 2014 for combined heat and power equipment (CAA 2001 ss 45A–45C, 46; FA 2001 s 65, Sch 17; SI 2001/2541; SI 2005/1114). The product lists are available at www.eca.gov.uk.

5   **Low-emission cars:** The allowance is given on (a) new cars which are either electrically propelled or emit not more than 110g/km of CO_2 (120g/km for expenditure incurred before 1 April 2008), registered after 16 April 2002 and (b) new plant and machinery to refuel vehicles in a gas refuelling station with natural gas, hydrogen fuels, or (for expenditure on or after 1 April 2008) biogas (CAA 2001 ss 45D, 45E, 46). **Legislation will be introduced in Finance Bill 2013 to extend the 100% first-year allowance for two years to 31 March 2015. The qualifying threshold will also be reduced to 95g/km of CO_2 from the same date.**

6   **Environmentally beneficial plant or machinery:** Allowances are available for expenditure by *any* business on new and unused designated technologies and products which satisfy the relevant environmental criteria in accordance with the Government's technologies or products lists (CAA 2001 ss 45H–45J, 46; FA 2003 s 167, Sch 30; SI 2003/2076). The product lists are available at www.eca.gov.uk.

7   **Zero-emission goods vehicles:** The allowance is given on new (and not second hand) vehicles which cannot under any circumstances produce CO_2 emissions when driven and which are of a design primarily suited to the conveyance of goods or burden. The expenditure must be incurred before 1 April 2015 (corporation tax) or 6 April 2015 (income tax) and is limited to expenditure of 85 million euros per undertaking (as defined) over the five years (CAA 2001 ss 45DA-45DB, 212T).

8   **WDAs** are calculated on a reducing balance basis. For chargeable periods beginning before 6 April 2012 and ending on or after that date (or, for corporation tax purposes, beginning before 1 April 2012 and ending on or after that date) a hybrid rate of WDAs applies, calculated by time apportionment of the 20% and 18% rates, or, for the special rate expenditure, the 10% and 8% rates. For chargeable periods beginning on or after 6 April 2008 (1 April 2008 for corporation tax purposes), a WDA of up to £1,000 can be claimed in respect of the main pool and/or the special rate pool where the unrelieved expenditure in the pool concerned is £1,000 or less.

9   **Long-life assets:** Applies to plant or machinery with an expected working life, when new, of 25 years or more. Applies where expenditure on long-life assets in a year is £100,000 or more (in the case of companies the de minimis limit is £100,000 divided by one plus the number of associated companies). Transitional provisions apply to maintain a 25% allowance for expenditure incurred before 1 January 2001 under a contract entered into before 26 November 1996 and to expenditure on second-hand plant or machinery if old rules applied to vendor. It does not apply to plant or machinery in a building used wholly or mainly as, or for purposes ancillary to, a dwelling-house, retail shop, showroom, hotel or office, cars, or sea-going ships and railway assets acquired before 1 January 2011. Expenditure on or after 1 or 6 April 2008 qualifies, as special rate expenditure, for a writing down allowance of 8% (10% for periods before 1 or 6 April 2012, see note 8 above) reducing balance. The balance of the long-life asset pool at 1 or 6 April 2008 was also transferred into the special rate pool. The rate applying for chargeable periods beginning before 1 or 6 April 2008 was 6% and a hybrid rate applied for chargeable periods spanning those dates calculated by a time apportionment of the 6% and 10% rates (CAA 2001 ss 90–104, Sch 3 para 20).

10   **Integral features** of a building are electrical systems (including lighting systems); cold water systems; space or water heating systems, powered ventilation systems, air cooling or purification and any floor or ceiling comprised in such systems; lifts, escalators and moving walkways and external solar shading. Applies to expenditure incurred on or after 1 April 2008 (corporation tax) and 6 April 2008 (income tax). They all fall into the special rate pool and qualify for a 8% (10% for periods before 1 or 6 April 2012, see note 8 above) writing down allowance (CAA 2001 ss 33A, 104A).

11   **Foreign leased assets:** The relief applies only to leases finalised before 1 April 2006 (CAA 2001 s 109; FA 2006 Sch 9 para 13).

12   **First-year tax credits:** For expenditure incurred on or after 1 April 2008, a company can surrender a tax loss attributable to first-year allowances for energy saving or environmentally friendly equipment in exchange for a cash payment from the Government. The cash payment is equal to 19% of the loss surrendered, subject to an upper limit of the greater of £250,000 and the company's PAYE and NIC liability for the period concerned. (CAA 2001 Sch A1). **Legislation will be introduced in Finance Bill 2013 to extend the availability of first-year tax credits for a further five years from 1 April 2013.**

13   **First year allowances**, where applicable, are available on expenditure over the annual investment allowance level or on which annual investment allowance has not been claimed, which would otherwise qualify for writing down allowance at 18% in the general plant and machinery pool.

14   **Cars:** For expenditure on and after 1 April 2009 for companies, 6 April 2009 for unincorporated businesses, the regime for cars costing £12,000 is abolished. Cars with CO_2 emissions exceeding 160gm/km will be allocated to the special rate pool. All other cars will go into the general pool. **Legislation will be introduced in Finance Bill 2013 to reduce the threshold for a main rate car to 130gm/km**.

15   **Thermal insulation** Expenditure on thermal insulation incurred on or after 1 April 2008 (corporation tax) and 6 April 2008 (income tax) falls into the special rate pool and qualifies for a 8% (10% for periods before 1 or 6 April 2012, see note 8 above) writing down allowance (CAA 2001 ss 28, 104A).

16   **Cushion gas** Expenditure on cushion gas incurred on or after 1 April 2010 falls into the special rate pool and qualifies for a 8% (10% for periods before 1 or 6 April 2012, see note 8 above) writing down allowance (CAA 2001 ss 70J, 104A).

17   **Solar panels** Expenditure on solar panels incurred on or after 1 April 2012 (corporation tax) and 6 April 2012 (income tax) falls into the special rate pool and qualifies for a 8% writing down allowance (CAA 2001 s 104A).

¹⁸ **Enterprise zones** For expenditure incurred for the purpose of a qualifying activity in the five year period from 1 April 2012 to 31 March 2017 inclusive 100% first-year allowances will be available for companies chargeable to corporation tax which invest in unused (not second hand) plant or machinery for use primarily in designated assisted areas within certain enterprise zones. Expenditure must be incurred for the purposes of broadly a new or expanding business carried on by the company, must not be replacement expenditure and is limited to 125 million euros per single investment projectg (as defined) over the five years. A full list of current zones and designated assisted areas delineated by maps will be published on the Treasury website in due course.

Cars: Car hire p 78.

Mineral extraction

First-year allowance: 100% FYA is available for certain expenditure incurred after 16 April 2002 wholly for the purposes of a North Sea Oil ring-fence trade or on plant and machinery used in such a trade.

Writing-down allowance: for expenditure incurred after 31 March 1986, 10% for expenditure on the acquisition of a mineral asset and certain pre-trading expenditure, otherwise 25% (on reducing balance basis). (CA 2001 s 418.)

Motor cars

Expenditure on or after 1 April 2009 (corporation tax) or 6 April 2009 (income tax) on cars is allocated to the special rate (currently 8%) plant and machinery pool if the car's CO_2 emissions exceed 160g/km and otherwise to the (currently 18%) main pool. (CAA 2001 ss 104AA, 104F, 208A, 268A-268D.) The position for expenditure before 1 April 2009 (for companies) or 6 April 2009 (for unincorporated businesses) is as follows. Legislation will be introduced in Finance Bill 2013 to reduce the threshold for a main rate car to 130g/km.

		% Rate[1]
Writing-down allowance (WDA)	Chargeable period ending before 1 April 2008 for corporation tax and 5 April 2008 for income tax	25%
	Chargeable period straddling 1 April 2008 for corporation tax and 6 April 2008 for income tax	hybrid rate
	Chargeable period ending before 1 April 2012 for corporation tax or 6 April 2012 income tax	20%
	Chargeable period straddling 1 April 2012 for corporation tax and 6 April 2012 for income tax	**hybrid rate**
	Chargeable period beginning on or after 1 April 2012 for corporation tax or 6 April 2012 for income tax	**18%**

[1] Restricted to £3,000 for cars costing more than £12,000 and bought outright, on hire purchase or by way of a lease with an option to purchase (CAA 2001 ss 74, 75).

[2] See also note 5, p 34 and Car hire, p 78.

[3] Cars that have an element of non-business use will still be dealt with in a single asset pool, but the rate of WDA will depend on the emissions.

Patent rights

Writing-down allowance

Expenditure incurred after 31 March 1986: annual 25% writing-down allowance (reducing balance basis). (CAA 2001 s 472.)

Research and development (formerly scientific research)

	Expenditure incurred after	% Rate
Allowance in year 1	5 November 1962	**100**

Note: Land and houses are excluded from 1 April 1985.

Disadvantaged areas

Renovation of business premises

	Expenditure incurred on or after	% Rate
First-year allowance	11 April 2007	**100**

The expenditure must be incurred on renovating or converting vacant business properties in Northern Ireland or the designated disadvantaged areas in the UK that have been vacant for at least a year, to bring the property back into business use. (Premises refurbished by or used by businesses in the following trades are excluded from the scheme: fisheries and aquaculture, shipbuilding, the coal or steel industries, synthetic fibres, primary production of certain agricultural products and the manufacture of products which imitate or substitute for milk or milk products.) The enhanced rate will apply to any expenditure currently qualifying for plant and machinery, industrial buildings or agricultural buildings allowances and also to expenditure on commercial buildings (such as shops and offices). A writing-down allowance is given at 25% (on a straight-line basis) on unrelieved expenditure. (FA 2005 s 92, Sch 6; SI 2012/868)

Enterprise zones

Before 1 April 2011 (corporation tax) or 6 April 2011 (income tax) an initial allowance of 100% was available for expenditure on industrial or commercial building by businesses within enterprise zones. Where the initial allowance was not or was only partially claimed a 25% writing-down allowance on cost, on a straight-line basis, applied to the unclaimed balance. There was no phasing out of the allowance between 2008 and 2011.

For 100% first-year allowances available for companies investing in plant or machinery for use primarily in designated assisted areas within certain Enterprise Zones see under **plant and machinery**.

Capital gains

Annual exemption

Individuals[a], personal representatives[b] and certain trusts[c]

[a] For 2008–09 onwards, an individual who claims to use the remittance basis for a tax year is not entitled to the capital gains tax annual exemption for that year. This does not apply if the individual's unremitted foreign income and gains for the year are less than £2,000.
[b] Year of death and following two years (maximum).
[c] Trusts for mentally disabled persons and those in receipt of attendance allowance or disability living allowance. Exemption divided by number of qualifying settlements created (after 9 March 1981) by one settlor, subject to a minimum of one-tenth.

Exempt amount of net gains	2007–08	2008–09	2009–10	2010–11	2011–12	2012–13
	£9,200	£9,600	£10,100	£10,100	£10,600	**£10,600**

Trusts[a] generally

Exempt amount of net gains	2007–08	2008–09	2009–10	2010–11	2011–12	2012–13
	£4,600	£4,800	£5,050	£5,050	£5,300	**£5,300**

[a] Exemption divided by number of qualifying settlements created (after 6 June 1978) by one settlor, subject to a minimum of one-fifth.

Chattel exemption

	Disposals exemption	Marginal relief: Maximum chargeable gain
From 1989–90 onwards	£6,000	$5/3$ excess over £6,000

Rates of tax

2012–13	*Individuals*	• to income tax basic rate limit £34,370	**18%**
		• above income tax basic rate limit £34,370	**28%**
	Trusts and personal representatives		**28%**
2011–12	*Individuals*	• to income tax basic rate limit £35,000	18%
		• above income tax basic rate limit £35,000	28%
	Trusts and personal representatives		28%
2010–11	*Individuals*	*gains before 23 June 2010*	18%
		gains on or after 23 June 2010	
		• to income tax basic rate limit £37,400	18%
		• above income tax basic rate limit £37,400	28%
	Trusts and personal representatives		
		gains before 23 June 2010	18%
		gains on or after 23 June 2010	28%
2008–09 to 2009–10	*Individuals, trusts and personal representatives*		18%
2007–08	*Individuals*	• to income tax starting rate limit £2,230	10%
		• from £2,231 to income tax basic rate limit £34,600	20%
		• above income tax basic rate limit £34,600	40%
	Trusts and personal representatives		40%
2006–07	*Individuals*	• to income tax starting rate limit £2,150	10%
		• from £2,151 to income tax basic rate limit £33,300	20%
		• above income tax basic rate limit £33,300	40%
	Trusts and personal representatives		40%
2004–05 to 2005–06	*Individuals*	• to income tax starting rate limit	10%
		• above starting rate limit to income tax basic rate limit	20%
		• above income tax basic rate limit	40%
	Trusts and personal representatives		40%

For 2007–08 and earlier years, gains are taxed on individuals as the top slice of income. For gains arising on or after 23 June 2010, the rate of tax for an individual is determined by treating gains as the top slice of income. Also for gains arising on or after 23 June 2010, a rate of 10% applies where entrepreneurs' relief is claimed — see p 40.

Trusts for vulnerable persons: From 2004–05 onwards, gains taxed at beneficiary's rates (on beneficiary if UK resident or on trustees if beneficiary not UK-resident).

Indexation allowance – individuals

(TCGA 1992 ss 53–57, 109.)

Indexation allowance is abolished for disposals on or after 6 April 2008 by individuals, trustees and personal representatives (but not companies). For disposals before that date by such persons, an indexation allowance is given up to April 1998 and taper relief applies thereafter on disposals made after 5 April 1998 (see below). Indexation allowance is deducted before applying taper relief. The indexation allowance is calculated by multiplying each item of allowable expenditure by:

$$\frac{RD - RI}{RI}$$

where:

RD is the retail prices index figure for month of disposal;

RI is the retail prices index for month of expenditure (or March 1982 if later).

See pp 46–61 for indexation allowances applicable for corporation tax and pp 62–63 for RPI values.

For disposals after 31 March 1998 of assets acquired on or before that date the factors below can be used to calculate the indexation allowance available to April 1998 for acquisitions in the month shown.

	Jan	Feb	Mar	Apr	May	Jun	Jul	Aug	Sept	Oct	Nov	Dec
1982	–	–	1·047	1·006	0·992	0·987	0·986	0·985	0·987	0·977	0·967	0·971
1983	0·968	0·960	0·956	0·929	0·921	0·917	0·906	0·898	0·889	0·883	0·876	0·871
1984	0·872	0·865	0·859	0·834	0·828	0·823	0·825	0·808	0·804	0·793	0·788	0·789
1985	0·783	0·769	0·752	0·716	0·708	0·704	0·707	0·703	0·704	0·701	0·695	0·693
1986	0·689	0·683	0·681	0·665	0·662	0·663	0·667	0·662	0·654	0·652	0·638	0·632
1987	0·626	0·620	0·616	0·597	0·596	0·596	0·597	0·593	0·588	0·580	0·573	0·574
1988	0·574	0·568	0·562	0·537	0·531	0·525	0·524	0·507	0·500	0·485	0·478	0·474
1989	0·465	0·454	0·448	0·423	0·414	0·409	0·408	0·404	0·395	0·384	0·372	0·369
1990	0·361	0·353	0·339	0·300	0·288	0·283	0·282	0·269	0·258	0·248	0·251	0·252
1991	0·249	0·242	0·237	0·222	0·218	0·213	0·215	0·213	0·208	0·204	0·199	0·198
1992	0·199	0·193	0·189	0·171	0·167	0·167	0·171	0·171	0·166	0·162	0·164	0·168
1993	0·179	0·171	0·167	0·156	0·152	0·153	0·156	0·151	0·146	0·147	0·148	0·146
1994	0·151	0·144	0·141	0·128	0·124	0·124	0·129	0·124	0·121	0·120	0·119	0·114
1995	0·114	0·107	0·102	0·091	0·087	0·085	0·091	0·085	0·080	0·085	0·085	0·079
1996	0·083	0·078	0·073	0·066	0·063	0·063	0·067	0·062	0·057	0·057	0·057	0·053
1997 ·	0·053	0·049	0·046	0·040	0·036	0·032	0·032	0·026	0·021	0·019	0·019	0·016
1998	0·019	0·014	0·011	–	–	–	–	–	–	–	–	–

Losses. For disposals after 30 November 1993, indexation allowance can only be used to reduce or extinguish a gain. It cannot be used to create or increase a capital loss.

Share identification rules

(TCGA 1992 ss 104–106A; FA 2006 s 74)

For disposals on or after 6 April 2008 by individuals, trustees or personal representatives, shares and securities of the same class in the same company are identified with acquisitions in the following order:
- acquisitions on the same day as the disposal;
- acquisitions within 30 days after the day of disposal;
- shares comprised in a single pool incorporating all other shares of the same class, whenever acquired.

For acquisitions after 5 April 1998 and before 5 April 2008 for individuals, trustees and personal representatives, disposals are identified with acquisitions in the following order:
- same day acquisitions (subject to special rules distinguishing shares acquired after 5 April 2002 from approved employee share option schemes from other shares acquired on the same day);
- acquisitions within the following 30 days[1] (thus countering 'bed and breakfasting');
- previous acquisitions after 5 April 1998 on a last in/first out basis;
- shares acquired after 5 April 1982 in the pool at 5 April 1998 (the 'section 104 holding');
- shares acquired before 6 April 1982 (the '1982 holding');
- any shares acquired on or before 6 April 1965 on a last in/first out basis;
- if any shares disposed of are still not fully matched, shares acquired subsequent to the disposal (beyond the above mentioned 30-day period).

For the purposes of corporation tax on chargeable gains, disposals of shares etc are identified with acquisitions in the following order:
- same day acquisitions;
- acquisitions within the previous nine days on a first in/first out basis;
- the pool of shares acquired after 31 March 1982;
- any shares held at 31 March 1982;
- any shares acquired on or before 6 April 1965 on a last in/first out basis;
- (if shares disposed of still not fully matched) subsequent acquisitions.

These rules are modified for disposals of shares before 5 December 2005 if the company acquired shares of the same class within a short period and held not less than 2% of the number issued.

[1] The 30-day matching rule does not apply in relation to acquisitions after 21 March 2006 where the individual making the disposal is not (or is not treated as) resident or ordinarily resident in the UK at the time of the acquisition.

Entrepreneurs' relief

(TCGA 1992 ss 169H–169S; FA 2008 s 9, Sch 3)

Entrepreneurs' relief applies to disposals by an individual on or after 6 April 2008 of:
- all or part of a trade carried on alone or in partnership;
- assets of such a trade following cessation; or
- shares or securities in the individual's 'personal trading company' (as defined).

Where a disposal of shares or of an interest in the assets of a partnership qualifies for relief, an associated disposal of assets owned by the individual and used by the company or partnership also qualifies for relief.

Trustees can claim relief where a qualifying beneficiary has an interest in the business concerned.

The relief is available where the relevant conditions are met throughout a period of one year. For gains arising on or after 23 June 2010, the relief operates by charging qualifying net gains to CGT at 10%. Previously, it operated by reducing the amount of qualifying net gains by four-ninths (so that the gains were effectively charged to CGT at 10%). Relief is subject to a lifetime limit of gains of £10 million (£5 million for disposals before 6 April 2011; £2 million for disposals before 23 June 2010; £1 million for disposals before 6 April 2010), but disposals before 6 April 2008 do not count towards the limit. Relief given to trustees counts towards the limit of the qualifying beneficiary.

Transitional rules apply to allow relief to be claimed in certain circumstances where a gain made before 6 April 2008 is deferred and becomes chargeable on or after that date.

Taper relief

(TCGA 1992 s 2A, Sch A1; FA 2000 ss 66, 67; FA 2002 ss 46, 47, Sch 10; FA 2003 s 160)

Taper relief is abolished for gains accruing, or treated as accruing, on or after 6 April 2008. (FA 2008 Sch 2 para 25.) Taper relief was available for disposals made after 5 April 1998 by individuals, trustees and personal representatives. The chargeable gain is reduced according to the number of complete years for which the asset has been held (counting from 6 April 1998). Non-business assets acquired before 17 March 1998 qualify for an addition of one year to the period for which they are held after 5 April 1998. Business assets acquired before 17 March 1998 also qualify for the one-year addition but only if disposed of before 6 April 2000.

Taper relief applies to gains after all deductions and before the annual exemption. Losses are set against pre-tapered gains in the most beneficial way possible. Where applicable, the combined period of holding by spouses is taken into account.

Business assets			
Disposals from 6 April 2002 to 5 April 2008		Disposals from 6 April 2000 to 5 April 2002	
No of complete yrs from 6.4.98 for which asset held	% of gain chargeable	No of complete yrs from 6.4.98 for which asset held	% of gain chargeable
		0	100
0	100	1	87.5
1	50	2	75
2 or more	25	3	50
		4 or more	25

Non-business assets			
No of complete yrs from 6.4.98 for which asset held	% of gain chargeable	No of complete yrs from 6.4.98 for which asset held	% of gain chargeable
0	100	6	80
1	100	7	75
2	100	8	70
3	95	9	65
4	90	10 or more	60
5	85		

Business assets. A 'business asset' is one of the following:
- an asset used for the purposes of a trade carried on (alone or in partnership) by the taxpayer or, after 5 April 2004, any individual, trustee or personal representative; *or*
- an asset used for the purposes of a trade carried on by a 'qualifying company' (alone or, after 4 April 2004, in partnership); *or*
- shares or securities in a 'qualifying company'; *or*
- from 6 April 2000, an asset used for the purpose of any office or employment (full-time or part-time) held by the taxpayer with a person carrying on a trade; or
- before 6 April 2000, an asset held for the purposes of a qualifying office or employment to which the taxpayer is required to devote substantially the whole of his time.

Qualifying company. From 6 April 2000, a *'qualifying company'*, by reference to an individual, is a trading company (or holding company of a trading group), where one or more of the following conditions is met:
- the company is unlisted (including an AIM company); *or*
- the taxpayer is an employee (full-time or part-time) of the company or a fellow group company (in which case the requirement that the company be a trading company etc is dropped, provided the taxpayer's interest in the company, including connected person holdings, is no more than 10%); *or*
- the taxpayer can exercise at least 5% of the voting rights.

Leases

Depreciation table (TCGA 1992 Sch 8 para 1)

Yrs	%	Yrs	%	Yrs	%	Yrs	%
50 (or more)	100	37	93·497	24	79·622	11	50·038
49	99·657	36	92·761	23	78·055	10	46·695
48	99·289	35	91·981	22	76·399	9	43·154
47	98·902	34	91·156	21	74·635	8	39·399
46	98·490	33	90·280	20	72·770	7	35·414
45	98·059	32	89·354	19	70·791	6	31·195
44	97·595	31	88·371	18	68·697	5	26·722
43	97·107	30	87·330	17	66·470	4	21·983
42	96·593	29	86·226	16	64·116	3	16·959
41	96·041	28	85·053	15	61·617	2	11·629
40	95·457	27	83·816	14	58·971	1	5·983
39	94·842	26	82·496	13	56·167	0	0
38	94·189	25	81·100	12	53·191		

Formula: Fraction of expenditure disallowed—

$$\frac{AE - D}{AE}$$

Where:

AE is the percentage for duration of lease at acquisition or expenditure; and
D is the percentage for duration of lease at disposal.

Fractions of years: Add one-twelfth of the difference between the percentage for the whole year and the next higher percentage for each additional month. Odd days under 14 are not counted; 14 odd days or more count as a month.

Short leases: premiums treated as rent (TCGA 1992 Sch 8 para 5; ITTOIA 2005 ss 277–281A; CTA 2009 s 217–221A) Part of premium for grant of a short lease which is chargeable to income tax as property income:

$$P - (2\% \times (n - 1) \times P)$$

Where:

P is the amount of premium;
n is the number of complete years which lease has to run when granted.

Length of lease (complete years)	Amount chargeable to CGT %	In-come tax charge %	Length of lease (complete years)	Amount chargeable to CGT %	In-come tax charge %	Length of lease (complete years)	Amount chargeable to CGT %	In-come tax charge %
Over 50	100	0	34	66	34	17	32	68
50	98	2	33	64	36	16	30	70
49	96	4	32	62	38	15	28	72
48	94	6	31	60	40	14	26	74
47	92	8	30	58	42	13	24	76
46	90	10	29	56	44	12	22	78
45	88	12	28	54	46	11	20	80
44	86	14	27	52	48	10	18	82
43	84	16	26	50	50	9	16	84
42	82	18	25	48	52	8	14	86
41	80	20	24	46	54	7	12	88
40	78	22	23	44	56	6	10	90
39	76	24	22	42	58	5	8	92
38	74	26	21	40	60	4	6	94
37	72	28	20	38	62	3	4	96
36	70	30	19	36	64	2	2	98
35	68	32	18	34	66	1 or less	0	100

Reliefs

The following is a summary of the other main capital gains tax reliefs and exemptions.

Charities

Gains accruing to charities which are both applicable and applied for charitable purposes are exempt. The exemption also applies from 6 April 2002 to donations to Community Amateur Sports Clubs (CASCs).

Individuals

Compensation (injury to person, profession or vocation)	Exempt.
Decorations for valour (acquired otherwise than for money or money's worth)	Gain exempt.
Enterprise Investment Scheme (see p 91)	Gain on disposal after relevant three-year period exempt to extent full relief given on shares.
Entrepreneurs' relief (see p 40)	Gains on specified assets chargeable at 10% rate up to lifetime limit. (Before 23 June 2010, five ninths of qualifying gains chargeable at 18% (an effective rate of 10%) up to lifetime limit.)
Foreign currency acquired for personal expenditure	Gain exempt.
Gifts for public benefit, works of art, historic buildings etc	No chargeable gain/allowable loss.
Gifts of pre-eminent objects	Donors who gift pre-eminent objects to the nation will receive a reduction in their UK tax liability of 30% (20% for companies) of the value of the object they are donating. The tax reduction can be against income or capital gains tax and can be spread forward across a period of up to five years starting with the tax year in which the object is offered. Applies from a date to be appointed.
Gilt-edged stock	No chargeable gain/allowable loss.
Hold-over relief for gifts	Restricted to:
	(1) gifts of business assets (including unquoted shares in trading companies and holding companies of trading groups). Relief is not available on the transfer of shares or securities to a company made after 8 November 1999 (other than transfers between 6.4.03 and 20.10.03);
	(2) gifts of heritage property;
	(3) gifts to heritage maintenance funds;
	(4) gifts to political parties; and
	(5) gifts which are chargeable transfers for inheritance tax.
	Where available, transferee's acquisition cost treated as reduced by held-over gain.
Married persons or civil partners living together	No chargeable gain/allowable loss on transfers between spouses or civil partners.
Motor vehicles	Gain exempt.
Principal private residence	Gain exempt.
If residence is partly let, exemption for the let part is limited to the smaller of–	(1) exemption on owner-occupied part; and
	(2) £40,000.
Qualifying corporate bonds	No chargeable gain (for loans made before 17 March 1998, allowable loss in certain cases if all or part of loss is irrecoverable).
Seed enterprise investment scheme (see p 91)	Individuals may claim capital gains reinvestment relief where they realise capital gains on disposals of assets in the tax year 2012-13 and in the same year make investments that qualify for the main seed enterprise investment scheme (SEIS) relief from income tax. The maximum exemption is £100,000 of gains. A disposal of shares on which SEIS income tax relief has been given and not withdrawn is exempt.
Venture capital trusts (see p 92)	Gain on disposal of shares by original investor exempt if company still a venture capital trust. Exemption applies only to shares acquired up to the permitted maximum of £200,000 per year of assessment (£100,000 for shares acquired before 6 April 2004). Deferral relief was available on gains on assets where the disposal proceeds were reinvested in VCT shares issued before 6 April 2004 and within one year before or after the disposal. This relief is withdrawn for shares issued after that date.

Businesses

Roll-over relief for replacement of business assets

Qualifying assets:
- Buildings and land both occupied and used for the purposes of the trade.
- Fixed plant and machinery.
- Ships, aircraft and hovercraft.
- Satellites, space stations and spacecraft.
- Goodwill*.
- Milk and potato quotas*.
- Ewe and suckler cow premium quotas*.
- Fish quotas (from 29 March 1999)*.
- UK oil licences (from 1 July 1999).
- Payment entitlement under farmers' single payment scheme (from 22 March 2005).

The 'replacement' assets must be acquired within 12 months before or three years after the disposal of the old asset. Both assets must be within any of the above classes. Holdover relief is available where the new asset is a depreciating asset (having a predictable useful life not exceeding 60 years).

* From 1 April 2002 onwards, subject to transitional rules, these items are removed from the list for companies only (as they fall within the intangible assets regime from that date (FA 2002 Sch 29 para 132(5)).

Personal representatives

Allowable expenses

Expenses allowable for the costs of establishing title in computing chargeable gains on disposal of assets in a deceased person's estate: deaths occurring after 5 April 2004 (SP 2/04). (HMRC accepts computations based either on the scale or on the actual allowable expenditure incurred.)

Gross value of estate	Allowable expenditure
Up to £50,000	1.8% of the probate value of the assets sold by the personal representatives.
Between £50,001 and £90,000	£900, to be divided between all the assets of the estate in proportion to the probate values and allowed in those proportions on assets sold by the personal representatives.
Between £90,001 and £400,000	1% of the probate value of the assets sold.
Between £400,001 and £500,000	£4,000, to be divided between all the assets of the estate in proportion to the probate values and allowed in those proportions on assets sold by the personal representatives.
Between £500,001 and £1,000,000	0.8% of the probate value of the assets sold.
Between £1,000,001 and £5,000,000	£8,000 to be divided between all the assets of the estate in proportion to the probate values and allowed in those proportions on assets sold by the personal representatives.
Exceeding £5,000,000	0.16% of the probate value of the assets sold subject to a maximum of £10,000.

Trustees

Allowable expenses

Expenses allowable in computing chargeable gains of corporate trustees in the administration of trusts and estates: acquisition, disposals and deemed disposals after 5 April 2004 (SP 2/04). (HMRC accepts computations based either on the scale or on the actual allowable expenditure incurred.)

Transfers of assets to beneficiaries etc	
(a) Quoted stocks and shares	
(i) One beneficiary	£25 per holding.
(ii) More than one beneficiary	£25 per holding, divided equally between the beneficiaries.
(b) Unquoted shares	As (a) above, plus any exceptional expenditure.
(c) Other assets	As (a) above, plus any exceptional expenditure.
Actual disposals and acquisitions	
(a) Quoted stocks and shares	Investment fee as charged by the trustees (where a comprehensive annual management fee is charged, the investment fee is taken to be £0.25 per £100 of the sale or purchase moneys).
(b) Unquoted shares	As (a) above, plus actual valuation costs.
(c) Other assets	Investment fee (as (a) above), subject to a maximum of £75, plus actual valuation costs.
Deemed disposals by trustees	
(a) Quoted stocks and shares	£8 per holding.
(b) Unquoted shares	Actual valuation costs.
(c) Other assets	Actual valuation costs.

Indexation allowance – corporation tax on capital gains

For corporation tax purposes, an indexation allowance is given as a deduction in calculating gains on disposals from the amount realised (or deemed to be realised) on disposal. The indexation allowance is calculated by multiplying each item of allowable expenditure by:

$$\frac{RD - RI}{RI}$$

Where:
    RD is the retail prices index figure for month of disposal;
    RI is the retail prices index for month of expenditure (or March 1982 if later).

See ante for indexation allowances up to April 1998 and taper relief which applies thereafter on disposals made after 5 April 1998 and before 6 April 2008 by individuals, trustees and personal representatives. See post for RPI values. The factors below can be used to calculate the indexation allowance for corporation tax purposes.

MONTH OF DISPOSAL

	2009				2010										
1982	Sept	Oct	Nov	Dec	Jan	Feb	Mar	Apr	May	June	July	Aug	Sept	Oct	Nov
Mar	1·710	1·719	1·727	1·744	1·743	1·759	1·778	1·805	1·815	1·821	1·815	1·826	1·836	1·842	1·855
Apr	1·657	1·665	1·673	1·690	1·689	1·705	1·723	1·749	1·759	1·765	1·759	1·770	1·780	1·786	1·799
May	1·638	1·646	1·654	1·671	1·670	1·686	1·704	1·730	1·739	1·746	1·739	1·750	1·760	1·766	1·779
June	1·630	1·639	1·646	1·663	1·662	1·678	1·696	1·722	1·732	1·738	1·732	1·743	1·753	1·759	1·771
July	1·630	1·638	1·645	1·663	1·661	1·677	1·696	1·721	1·731	1·737	1·731	1·742	1·752	1·758	1·770
Aug	1·629	1·637	1·645	1·662	1·661	1·676	1·695	1·720	1·730	1·736	1·730	1·741	1·751	1·757	1·769
Sept	1·630	1·639	1·646	1·663	1·662	1·678	1·696	1·722	1·732	1·738	1·732	1·743	1·753	1·759	1·771
Oct	1·617	1·626	1·633	1·650	1·649	1·665	1·683	1·709	1·718	1·724	1·718	1·729	1·739	1·745	1·757
Nov	1·605	1·613	1·620	1·637	1·636	1·652	1·670	1·695	1·705	1·711	1·705	1·716	1·726	1·732	1·744
Dec	1·609	1·618	1·625	1·642	1·641	1·657	1·675	1·700	1·710	1·716	1·710	1·721	1·731	1·737	1·749
1983	Sept	Oct	Nov	Dec	Jan	Feb	Mar	Apr	May	June	July	Aug	Sept	Oct	Nov
Jan	1·606	1·615	1·622	1·639	1·638	1·653	1·672	1·697	1·707	1·713	1·707	1·718	1·727	1·733	1·745
Feb	1·595	1·603	1·611	1·628	1·626	1·642	1·660	1·685	1·695	1·701	1·695	1·706	1·176	1·722	1·734
Mar	1·590	1·599	1·606	1·623	1·622	1·637	1·655	1·681	1·690	1·696	1·690	1·701	1·711	1·717	1·729
Apr	1·554	1·563	1·570	1·586	1·585	1·601	1·619	1·643	1·653	1·659	1·653	1·664	1·673	1·679	1·691
May	1·544	1·552	1·559	1·576	1·574	1·590	1·608	1·632	1·642	1·648	1·642	1·652	1·662	1·668	1·680
June	1·538	1·546	1·553	1·569	1·568	1·584	1·601	1·626	1·636	1·641	1·636	1·646	1·656	1·661	1·673
July	1·524	1·532	1·539	1·556	1·555	1·570	1·587	1·612	1·621	1·627	1·621	1·632	1·641	1·647	1·659
Aug	1·513	1·521	1·528	1·544	1·543	1·558	1·576	1·600	1·610	1·616	1·610	1·620	1·630	1·635	1·647
Sept	1·502	1·510	1·517	1·533	1·532	1·547	1·565	1·589	1·598	1·604	1·598	1·609	1·618	1·624	1·635
Oct	1·493	1·501	1·508	1·524	1·523	1·538	1·556	1·580	1·589	1·595	1·589	1·600	1·609	1·615	1·626
Nov	1·484	1·492	1·499	1·515	1·514	1·529	1·547	1·571	1·580	1·586	1·580	1·590	1·600	1·605	1·617
Dec	1·478	1·486	1·493	1·509	1·508	1·523	1·540	1·564	1·573	1·579	1·573	1·584	1·593	1·599	1·610
1984	Sept	Oct	Nov	Dec	Jan	Feb	Mar	Apr	May	June	July	Aug	Sept	Oct	Nov
Jan	1·479	1·487	1·494	1·510	1·509	1·524	1·541	1·566	1·575	1·580	1·575	1·585	1·594	1·600	1·612
Feb	1·469	1·477	1·484	1·500	1·499	1·514	1·531	1·555	1·564	1·570	1·564	1·575	1·584	1·589	1·601
Mar	1·461	1·469	1·476	1·492	1·491	1·506	1·523	1·547	1·556	1·562	1·556	1·566	1·576	1·581	1·593
Apr	1·429	1·437	1·443	1·459	1·459	1·473	1·490	1·513	1·522	1·528	1·522	1·533	1·542	1·547	1·559
May	1·420	1·428	1·434	1·450	1·449	1·464	1·481	1·504	1·513	1·519	1·513	1·523	1·532	1·538	1·549
June	1·414	1·421	1·428	1·444	1·443	1·457	1·474	1·498	1·507	1·512	1·507	1·517	1·526	1·531	1·543
July	1·414	1·424	1·431	1·447	1·446	1·460	1·477	1·501	1·510	1·515	1·510	1·520	1·529	1·534	1·545
Aug	1·394	1·402	1·408	1·424	1·423	1·437	1·454	1·477	1·486	1·492	1·486	1·496	1·505	1·511	1·511
Sept	1·389	1·397	1·404	1·419	1·418	1·432	1·449	1·472	1·481	1·487	1·481	1·491	1·500	1·506	1·517
Oct	1·374	1·382	1·389	1·404	1·403	1·418	1·434	1·457	1·466	1·472	1·466	1·476	1·485	1·490	1·501
Nov	1·367	1·375	1·382	1·397	1·396	1·410	1·427	1·450	1·458	1·464	1·458	1·468	1·477	1·483	1·494
Dec	1·369	1·377	1·384	1·399	1·398	1·412	1·429	1·452	1·461	1·466	1·461	1·470	1·479	1·485	1·496
1985	Sept	Oct	Nov	Dec	Jan	Feb	Mar	Apr	May	June	July	Aug	Sept	Oct	Nov
Jan	1·361	1·368	1·375	1·390	1·389	1·403	1·420	1·443	1·452	1·457	1·452	1·462	1·470	1·476	1·487
Feb	1·342	1·349	1·356	1·371	1·370	1·384	1·401	1·423	1·432	1·437	1·432	1·442	1·451	1·456	1·467
Mar	1·320	1·328	1·334	1·349	1·348	1·362	1·378	1·401	1·409	1·415	1·409	1·419	1·428	1·433	1·444
Apr	1·272	1·279	1·285	1·300	1·299	1·313	1·329	1·351	1·359	1·364	1·359	1·369	1·377	1·382	1·393
May	1·261	1·269	1·275	1·290	1·289	1·302	1·318	1·340	1·349	1·354	1·349	1·358	1·366	1·372	1·382
June	1·257	1·264	1·270	1·285	1·284	1·297	1·313	1·335	1·344	1·349	1·344	1·353	1·361	1·367	1·377
July	1·261	1·268	1·274	1·289	1·288	1·302	1·317	1·339	1·348	1·353	1·348	1·357	1·366	1·371	1·381
Aug	1·255	1·262	1·268	1·283	1·282	1·296	1·311	1·333	1·342	1·347	1·342	1·351	1·359	1·365	1·375
Sept	1·256	1·256	1·270	1·284	1·283	1·297	1·313	1·335	1·343	1·348	1·343	1·352	1·361	1·366	1·376
Oct	1·252	1·260	1·266	1·281	1·280	1·293	1·309	1·331	1·339	1·344	1·339	1·349	1·357	1·362	1·373
Nov	1·245	1·252	1·258	1·273	1·272	1·285	1·301	1·323	1·331	1·336	1·331	1·341	1·349	1·354	1·364
Dec	1·242	1·249	1·255	1·270	1·269	1·282	1·298	1·320	1·328	1·333	1·328	1·337	1·346	1·351	1·361

MONTH OF DISPOSAL

	2010	2011												2012	
1982	Dec	Jan	Feb	Mar	Apr	May	June	July	Aug	Sept	Oct	Nov	Dec	Jan	Feb
Mar	1·875	1·883	1·912	1·927	1·951	1·961	1·961	1·954	1·972	1·995	1·996	2·002	2·014	1·996	2·020
Apr	1·818	1·826	1·854	1·869	1·892	1·902	1·902	1·896	1·913	1·936	1·937	1·943	1·954	1·937	1·960
May	1·798	1·806	1·834	1·848	1·872	1·882	1·882	1·875	1·893	1·915	1·916	1·922	1·933	1·916	1·939
June	1·790	1·798	1·826	1·841	1·864	1·874	1·874	1·867	1·885	1·907	1·908	1·914	1·925	1·908	1·931
July	1·790	1·797	1·825	1·840	1·863	1·873	1·873	1·867	1·884	1·906	1·907	1·913	1·924	1·907	1·930
Aug	1·789	1·796	1·824	1·839	1·862	1·872	1·872	1·853	1·883	1·905	1·906	1·912	1·923	1·906	1·929
Sept	1·790	1·798	1·826	1·841	1·864	1·874	1·874	1·866	1·885	1·907	1·908	1·914	1·925	1·908	1·931
Oct	1·777	1·784	1·812	1·827	1·850	1·859	1·859	1·853	1·870	1·892	1·893	1·899	1·910	1·893	1·917
Nov	1·763	1·770	1·798	1·813	1·836	1·845	1·845	1·839	1·856	1·878	1·879	1·885	1·896	1·879	1·902
Dec	1·768	1·775	1·803	1·818	1·841	1·851	1·851	1·845	1·861	1·883	1·885	1·891	1·901	1·885	1·908
1983	Dec	Jan	Feb	Mar	Apr	May	June	July	Aug	Sep	Oct	Nov	Dec	Jan	Feb
Jan	1·765	1·772	1·800	1·814	1·837	1·847	1·847	1·841	1·858	1·880	1·881	1·887	1·898	1·881	1·904
Feb	1·753	1·760	1·788	1·802	1·825	1·835	1·835	1·829	1·846	1·867	1·869	1·875	1·886	1·869	1·892
Mar	1·748	1·755	1·783	1·797	1·820	1·830	1·830	1·824	1·841	1·862	1·863	1·869	1·880	1·863	1·886
Apr	1·710	1·717	1·744	1·759	1·781	1·791	1·791	1·785	1·801	1·823	1·824	1·830	1·840	1·824	1·846
May	1·699	1·706	1·733	1·747	1·769	1·779	1·779	1·773	1·790	1·811	1·812	1·818	1·828	1·812	1·834
June	1·692	1·699	1·726	1·740	1·763	1·772	1·772	1·766	1·783	1·804	1·805	1·811	1·822	1·805	1·828
July	1·678	1·685	1·712	1·726	1·748	1·757	1·757	1·752	1·768	1·789	1·790	1·796	1·807	1·790	1·812
Aug	1·666	1·673	1·700	1·714	1·736	1·745	1·745	1·739	1·756	1·777	1·778	1·784	1·794	1·778	1·800
Sept	1·654	1·661	1·688	1·702	1·724	1·733	1·733	1·727	1·743	1·764	1·766	1·771	1·782	1·766	1·788
Oct	1·645	1·652	1·678	1·692	1·714	1·723	1·723	1·718	1·734	1·755	1·756	1·762	1·772	1·756	1·778
Nov	1·635	1·642	1·669	1·683	1·705	1·714	1·714	1·708	1·724	1·745	1·746	1·752	1·762	1·746	1·768
Dec	1·628	1·635	1·662	1·676	1·698	1·707	1·707	1·701	1·717	1·738	1·739	1·745	1·755	1·739	1·761
1984	Dec	Jan	Feb	Mar	Apr	May	June	July	Aug	Sept	Oct	Nov	Dec	Jan	Feb
Jan	1·630	1·637	1·663	1·677	1·699	1·708	1·708	1·703	1·719	1·739	1·741	1·746	1·757	1·741	1·762
Feb	1·619	1·626	1·653	1·666	1·688	1·697	1·697	1·692	1·708	1·728	1·729	1·735	1·745	1·729	1·751
Mar	1·611	1·618	1·644	1·658	1·680	1·689	1·689	1·683	1·699	1·720	1·721	1·726	1·737	1·721	1·742
Apr	1·577	1·583	1·609	1·623	1·644	1·653	1·653	1·648	1·663	1·684	1·685	1·691	1·701	1·685	1·706
May	1·567	1·574	1·600	1·613	1·634	1·643	1·643	1·638	1·654	1·674	1·675	1·681	1·691	1·675	1·696
June	1·560	1·567	1·593	1·606	1·628	1·637	1·637	1·631	1·647	1·667	1·668	1·674	1·684	1·668	1·689
July	1·563	1·570	1·596	1·609	1·631	1·640	1·640	1·634	1·650	1·670	1·671	1·677	1·687	1·671	1·692
Aug	1·540	1·546	1·572	1·585	1·606	1·615	1·615	1·610	1·625	1·645	1·646	1·652	1·662	1·646	1·667
Sept	1·535	1·541	1·567	1·580	1·601	1·610	1·610	1·604	1·620	1·640	1·641	1·647	1·657	1·641	1·662
Oct	1·519	1·526	1·551	1·564	1·585	1·594	1·594	1·588	1·604	1·624	1·625	1·630	1·640	1·625	1·646
Nov	1·511	1·518	1·543	1·556	1·577	1·586	1·586	1·581	1·596	1·616	1·617	1·622	1·632	1·617	1·638
Dec	1·513	1·520	1·545	1·558	1·579	1·588	1·588	1·583	1·598	1·618	1·619	1·624	1·634	1·619	1·640
1985	Dec	Jan	Feb	Mar	Apr	May	June	July	Aug	Sept	Oct	Nov	Dec	Jan	Feb
Jan	1·504	1·511	1·536	1·549	1·570	1·579	1·579	1·573	1·589	1·608	1·610	1·615	1·625	1·610	1·630
Feb	1·484	1·491	1·516	1·529	1·550	1·558	1·558	1·553	1·568	1·588	1·589	1·594	1·604	1·589	1·609
Mar	1·461	1·468	1·492	1·505	1·526	1·534	1·534	1·529	1·544	1·564	1·565	1·570	1·580	1·565	1·585
Apr	1·410	1·416	1·440	1·453	1·473	1·482	1·482	1·476	1·491	1·510	1·511	1·516	1·526	1·511	1·531
May	1·399	1·405	1·429	1·442	1·462	1·470	1·470	1·465	1·480	1·499	1·500	1·505	1·514	1·500	1·520
June	1·394	1·400	1·424	1·437	1·457	1·465	1·465	1·460	1·475	1·493	1·494	1·500	1·509	1·494	1·514
July	1·398	1·405	1·429	1·441	1·461	1·470	1·470	1·464	1·479	1·498	1·499	1·504	1·514	1·499	1·519
Aug	1·392	1·398	1·422	1·435	1·455	1·463	1·463	1·458	1·473	1·491	1·492	1·498	1·507	1·492	1·512
Sept	1·393	1·399	1·424	1·436	1·456	1·464	1·464	1·459	1·474	1·493	1·494	1·499	1·508	1·494	1·514
Oct	1·389	1·396	1·420	1·432	1·452	1·461	1·461	1·455	1·470	1·489	1·490	1·495	1·504	1·490	1·510
Nov	1·381	1·387	1·411	1·424	1·444	1·452	1·452	1·447	1·461	1·480	1·481	1·486	1·496	1·481	1·501
Dec	1·378	1·384	1·408	1·421	1·441	1·449	1·449	1·444	1·458	1·477	1·478	1·483	1·493	1·478	1·498

	2009				2010										
1986	Sept	Oct	Nov	Dec	Jan	Feb	Mar	Apr	May	June	July	Aug	Sept	Oct	Nov
Jan	1·237	1·244	1·250	1·265	1·264	1·277	1·293	1·315	1·323	1·328	1·323	1·333	1·341	1·346	1·346
Feb	1·229	1·236	1·242	1·257	1·256	1·269	1·285	1·306	1·315	1·320	1·315	1·324	1·332	1·337	1·348
Mar	1·226	1·233	1·239	1·254	1·253	1·266	1·282	1·303	1·312	1·317	1·312	1·321	1·329	1·334	1·345
Apr	1·204	1·212	1·218	1·232	1·231	1·244	1·260	1·281	1·289	1·295	1·289	1·299	1·307	1·312	1·322
May	1·200	1·208	1·214	1·228	1·227	1·240	1·256	1·277	1·285	1·290	1·285	1·294	1·303	1·308	1·318
June	1·202	1·209	1·215	1·229	1·228	1·241	1·257	1·278	1·286	1·292	1·286	1·296	1·304	1·309	1·319
July	1·208	1·215	1·221	1·236	1·235	1·248	1·263	1·285	1·293	1·298	1·293	1·302	1·310	1·316	1·326
Aug	1·201	1·208	1·214	1·229	1·228	1·241	1·256	1·278	1·286	1·291	1·286	1·295	1·303	1·308	1·319
Sept	1·190	1·197	1·203	1·218	1·217	1·230	1·245	1·266	1·275	1·280	1·275	1·284	1·292	1·297	1·307
Oct	1·187	1·194	1·200	1·214	1·213	1·226	1·242	1·263	1·271	1·276	1·271	1·280	1·288	1·293	1·304
Nov	1·168	1·175	1·181	1·196	1·195	1·208	1·223	1·244	1·252	1·257	1·252	1·261	1·269	1·274	1·284
Dec	1·161	1·168	1·174	1·188	1·187	1·200	1·215	1·237	1·245	1·250	1·245	1·254	1·262	1·267	1·277
1987	Sept	Oct	Nov	Dec	Jan	Feb	Mar	Apr	May	June	July	Aug	Sept	Oct	Nov
Jan	1·153	1·160	1·166	1·180	1·179	1·192	1·207	1·228	1·236	1·241	1·236	1·245	1·253	1·258	1·268
Feb	1·144	1·151	1·157	1·171	1·170	1·183	1·198	1·219	1·227	1·232	1·227	1·236	1·244	1·249	1·259
Mar	1·140	1·147	1·153	1·167	1·166	1·179	1·194	1·215	1·223	1·228	1·223	1·232	1·240	1·245	1·254
Apr	1·115	1·122	1·128	1·141	1·140	1·153	1·168	1·189	1·196	1·201	1·196	1·205	1·213	1·218	1·228
May	1·113	1·120	1·126	1·139	1·138	1·151	1·166	1·186	1·194	1·199	1·194	1·203	1·211	1·216	1·226
June	1·113	1·120	1·126	1·139	1·138	1·151	1·166	1·186	1·194	1·199	1·194	1·203	1·211	1·216	1·226
July	1·115	1·122	1·128	1·141	1·140	1·153	1·168	1·189	1·196	1·201	1·196	1·205	1·213	1·218	1·228
Aug	1·109	1·116	1·121	1·135	1·134	1·147	1·162	1·182	1·190	1·195	1·190	1·199	1·207	1·212	1·221
Sept	1·103	1·109	1·115	1·129	1·128	1·141	1·155	1·176	1·184	1·188	1·184	1·192	1·200	1·205	1·215
Oct	1·092	1·099	1·105	1·119	1·118	1·130	1·145	1·165	1·173	1·178	1·173	1·182	1·190	1·194	1·204
Nov	1·082	1·089	1·095	1·108	1·107	1·120	1·134	1·155	1·162	1·167	1·162	1·171	1·179	1·184	1·193
Dec	1·084	1·091	1·097	1·110	1·109	1·122	1·136	1·157	1·165	1·169	1·165	1·173	1·181	1·186	1·196
1988	Sept	Oct	Nov	Dec	Jan	Feb	Mar	Apr	May	June	July	Aug	Sept	Oct	Nov
Jan	1·084	1·091	1·097	1·110	1·109	1·122	1·136	1·157	1·165	1·169	1·165	1·173	1·181	1·186	1·196
Feb	1·076	1·083	1·089	1·102	1·101	1·114	1·128	1·149	1·156	1·161	1·156	1·165	1·173	1·177	1·187
Mar	1·068	1·075	1·081	1·094	1·093	1·106	1·120	1·140	1·148	1·153	1·148	1·157	1·164	1·169	1·179
Apr	1.035	1.042	1.047	1.060	1.060	1.072	1.086	1.106	1.113	1.118	1.113	1.122	1.129	1.134	1.144
May	1.027	1.034	1.040	1.053	1.052	1.064	1.078	1.098	1.105	1.110	1.105	1.114	1.121	1.126	1.136
June	1.020	1.026	1.032	1.045	1.044	1.056	1.070	1.090	1.098	1.102	1.098	1.106	1.114	1.118	1.128
July	1.018	1.024	1.030	1.043	1.042	1.054	1.068	1.088	1.096	1.100	1.096	1.104	1.112	1.116	1.126
Aug	·995	1·002	1·007	1·020	1·019	1·032	1·045	1·065	1·072	1·077	1·072	1·081	1·088	1·093	1·102
Sept	·986	·993	·998	1·011	1·010	1·022	1·036	1·055	1·063	1·067	1·063	1·071	1·078	1·083	1·092
Oct	·966	·973	·978	·991	·990	1·002	1·016	1·035	1·042	1·047	1·042	1·050	1·058	1·062	1·071
Nov	·957	·964	·969	·982	·981	·993	1·006	1·025	1·033	1·037	1·033	1·041	1·048	1·053	1·062
Dec	·952	·958	·964	·976	·976	·987	1·001	1·020	1·027	1·032	1·027	1·035	1·043	1·047	1·056
1989	Sept	Oct	Nov	Dec	Jan	Feb	Mar	Apr	May	June	July	Aug	Sept	Oct	Nov
Jan	·940	·946	·951	·964	·963	·975	·988	1·007	1·014	1·019	1·014	1·023	1·030	1·034	1·043
Feb	·926	·932	·937	·950	·949	·961	·974	·993	1·000	1·004	1·000	1·008	1·015	1·020	1·029
Mar	·917	·923	·929	·941	·940	·952	·965	·984	·991	·996	·991	·999	1·006	1·011	1·020
Apr	·884	·890	·895	·907	·906	·918	·931	·949	·956	·961	·956	·964	·971	·976	·984
May	·872	·878	·883	·896	·895	·906	·919	·937	·944	·949	·944	·952	·959	·963	·972
June	·866	·872	·877	·889	·888	·899	·912	·931	·938	·942	·938	·945	·952	·957	·965
July	·864	·870	·875	·887	·887	·898	·911	·929	·936	·940	·936	·944	·951	·955	·964
Aug	·859	·865	·870	·883	·882	·893	·906	·924	·931	·935	·931	·939	·946	·950	·959
Sept	·846	·852	·858	·870	·869	·880	·893	·911	·918	·922	·918	·925	·932	·937	·945
Oct	·832	·838	·843	·855	·854	·866	·878	·896	·903	·907	·903	·911	·917	·922	·930
Nov	·817	·823	·828	·840	·839	·850	·862	·880	·887	·891	·887	·895	·901	·905	·914
Dec	·812	·818	·823	·835	·834	·845	·858	·875	·882	·886	·882	·890	·896	·901	·909

MONTH OF DISPOSAL

	2010	2011												2012	
1986	Dec	Jan	Feb	Mar	Apr	May	June	July	Aug	Sept	Oct	Nov	Dec	Jan	Feb
Jan	1·373	1·379	1·403	1·416	1·435	1·444	1·444	1·438	1·453	1·472	1·473	1·478	1·487	1·473	1·493
Feb	1·364	1·371	1·394	1·407	1·426	1·435	1·435	1·430	1·444	1·463	1·464	1·469	1·478	1·464	1·483
Mar	1·361	1·367	1·391	1·404	1·423	1·432	1·432	1·426	1·441	1·459	1·460	1·466	1·475	1·460	1·480
Apr	1·339	1·345	1·368	1·381	1·400	1·408	1·408	1·403	1·417	1·436	1·437	1·442	1·451	1·437	1·456
May	1·334	1·340	1·364	1·376	1·396	1·404	1·404	1·399	1·413	1·431	1·432	1·438	1·447	1·432	1·452
June	1·336	1·342	1·365	1·377	1·397	1·405	1·405	1·400	1·414	1·433	1·434	1·439	1·448	1·434	1·453
July	1·342	1·348	1·372	1·384	1·404	1·412	1·412	1·407	1·421	1·440	1·441	1·446	1·455	1·441	1·460
Aug	1·335	1·341	1·365	1·377	1·396	1·404	1·404	1·399	1·414	1·432	1·433	1·438	1·447	1·433	1·452
Sept	1·323	1·330	1·353	1·365	1·384	1·393	1·393	1·388	1·402	1·420	1·421	1·426	1·435	1·417	1·440
Oct	1·320	1·326	1·349	1·362	1·381	1·389	1·389	1·384	1·398	1·416	1·417	1·422	1·432	1·417	1·437
Nov	1·300	1·306	1·330	1·342	1·361	1·369	1·369	1·364	1·378	1·396	1·397	1·402	1·411	1·397	1·416
Dec	1·293	1·299	1·322	1·334	1·353	1·361	1·361	1·356	1·370	1·388	1·389	1·394	1·403	1·389	1·408

1987	Dec	Jan	Feb	Mar	Apr	May	June	July	Aug	Sept	Oct	Nov	Dec	Jan	Feb
Jan	1·284	1·290	1·313	1·325	1·344	1·352	1·352	1·347	1·361	1·379	1·380	1·385	1·394	1·380	1·399
Feb	1·275	1·281	1·304	1·316	1·335	1·343	1·343	1·338	1·352	1·370	1·371	1·375	1·384	1·371	1·389
Mar	1·270	1·276	1·299	1·311	1·330	1·338	1·338	1·333	1·347	1·365	1·366	1·371	1·380	1·366	1·385
Apr	1·244	1·250	1·272	1·284	1·303	1·310	1·310	1·306	1·319	1·337	1·338	1·343	1·352	1·338	1·357
May	1·241	1·247	1·270	1·282	1·300	1·308	1·308	1·303	1·317	1·335	1·336	1·341	1·349	1·336	1·354
June	1·241	1·247	1·270	1·282	1·300	1·308	1·308	1·303	1·317	1·335	1·336	1·341	1·349	1·336	1·354
July	1·244	1·250	1·272	1·284	1·303	1·310	1·310	1·306	1·319	1·337	1·338	1·343	1·352	1·338	1·357
Aug	1·237	1·243	1·265	1·277	1·296	1·304	1·304	1·299	1·312	1·330	1·331	1·336	1·345	1·331	1·350
Sept	1·230	1·236	1·259	1·271	1·289	1·297	1·297	1·292	1·306	1·323	1·324	1·329	1·338	1·324	1·343
Oct	1·220	1·225	1·248	1·259	1·278	1·286	1·286	1·281	1·294	1·312	1·313	1·318	1·327	1·313	1·331
Nov	1·209	1·215	1·237	1·249	1·267	1·275	1·275	1·270	1·283	1·301	1·302	1·307	1·315	1·302	1·320
Dec	1·211	1·217	1·239	1·251	1·269	1·277	1·277	1·272	1·286	1·303	1·304	1·309	1·318	1·304	1·322

1988	Dec	Jan	Feb	Mar	Apr	May	June	July	Aug	Sept	Oct	Nov	Dec	Jan	Feb
Jan	1·211	1·217	1·239	1·251	1·269	1·277	1·277	1·272	1·286	1·303	1·304	1·309	1·318	1·304	1·322
Feb	1·203	1·208	1·230	1·242	1·260	1·268	1·268	1·263	1·277	1·294	1·295	1·300	1·309	1·295	1·313
Mar	1·194	1·200	1·222	1·233	1·252	1·259	1·259	1·255	1·268	1·285	1·286	1·291	1·300	1·286	1·305
Apr	1.159	1.164	1.186	1.198	1.216	1.223	1.223	1.218	1.232	1.249	1.250	1.254	1.263	1.250	1.267
May	1.151	1.156	1.178	1.189	1.207	1.215	1.215	1.210	1.223	1.240	1.241	1.246	1.254	1.241	1.259
June	1.143	1.148	1.170	1.181	1.199	1.206	1.206	1.202	1.215	1.232	1.233	1.237	1.246	1.233	1.250
July	1.141	1.146	1.168	1.179	1.197	1.204	1.204	1.200	1.213	1.230	1.231	1.235	1.244	1.231	1.248
Aug	1·117	1·122	1·144	1·155	1·172	1·180	1·180	1·175	1·188	1·205	1·206	1·210	1·219	1·206	1·223
Sept	1·107	1·113	1·134	1·145	1·162	1·170	1·170	1·165	1·178	1·195	1·196	1·200	1·208	1·196	1·213
Oct	1.086	1.091	1.112	1.123	1.141	1.148	1.148	1.143	1.156	1.173	1.174	1.178	1.186	1.174	1.191
Nov	1.076	1.082	1.103	1.114	1.131	1.138	1.138	1.134	1.146	1.163	1.164	1.168	1.176	1.164	1.181
Dec	1.071	1.076	1.097	1.108	1.125	1.132	1.132	1.128	1.141	1.158	1.158	1.162	1.170	1.158	1.175

1989	Dec	Jan	Feb	Mar	Apr	May	June	July	Aug	Sept	Oct	Nov	Dec	Jan	Feb
Jan	1.058	1.063	1.084	1.095	1.112	1.119	1.119	1.114	1.127	1.143	1.144	1.149	1.157	1.144	1.161
Feb	1.043	1.048	1.069	1.080	1.097	1.104	1.104	1.099	1.112	1.128	1.129	1.133	1.141	1.129	1.146
Mar	1.034	1.039	1.060	1.070	1.087	1.094	1.094	1.090	1.102	1.118	1.119	1.124	1.132	1.119	1.136
Apr	·998	1·003	1·024	1·034	1·051	1·058	1·058	1·053	1·066	1·081	1·082	1·087	1·094	1·082	1·099
May	·986	·991	1·011	1·022	1·038	1·045	1·045	1·041	1·053	1·069	1·070	1·074	1·082	1·070	1·086
June	·979	·984	1·004	1·015	1·031	1·038	1·038	1·034	1·046	1·062	1·062	1·067	1·075	1·062	1·079
July	·977	·983	1·003	1·013	1·029	1·036	1·036	1·032	1·044	1·060	1·061	1·065	1·073	1·061	1·077
Aug	·972	·978	·997	1·008	1·024	1·031	1·031	1·027	1·039	1·054	1·055	1·060	1·067	1·055	1·072
Sept	·959	·964	·984	·994	1·010	1·017	1·017	1·013	1·025	1·040	1·041	1·045	1·053	1·041	1·057
Oct	·944	·949	·969	·979	·995	1·002	1·002	·997	1·009	1·025	1·026	1·030	1·037	1·026	1·042
Nov	·927	·932	·952	·962	·978	·985	·985	·981	·992	1·008	1·008	1·013	1·020	1·008	1·024
Dec	·923	·928	·947	·957	·973	·980	·980	·976	·987	1·003	1·003	1·008	1·015	1·003	1·019

MONTH OF DISPOSAL

1990	2009				2010										
	Sept	Oct	Nov	Dec	Jan	Feb	Mar	Apr	May	June	July	Aug	Sept	Oct	Nov
Jan	·802	·808	·813	·824	·823	·834	·847	·864	·871	·875	·871	·879	·885	·890	·898
Feb	·791	·797	·802	·814	·813	·824	·836	·854	·860	·864	·860	·868	·874	·879	·887
Mar	·773	·779	·784	·796	·795	·806	·818	·835	·842	·846	·842	·849	·856	·860	·868
Apr	·721	·727	·731	·743	·742	·752	·764	·781	·787	·791	·787	·795	·801	·805	·813
May	·706	·712	·716	·727	·727	·737	·749	·765	·772	·776	·772	·779	·785	·789	·797
June	·699	·705	·710	·721	·720	·730	·742	·758	·765	·769	·765	·772	·778	·782	·790
July	·698	·703	·708	·719	·718	·729	·741	·757	·763	·767	·763	·771	·777	·781	·789
Aug	·681	·686	·691	·702	·701	·711	·723	·739	·746	·749	·746	·753	·759	·763	·770
Sept	·665	·665	·675	·686	·685	·695	·707	·723	·729	·733	·729	·736	·742	·746	·754
Oct	·652	·658	·662	·673	·672	·682	·694	·710	·716	·720	·716	·723	·729	·733	·741
Nov	·656	·662	·666	·677	·676	·686	·698	·714	·720	·724	·720	·727	·733	·737	·745
Dec	·657	·663	·667	·678	·677	·687	·699	·715	·721	·725	·721	·728	·734	·738	·746

1991	Sept	Oct	Nov	Dec	Jan	Feb	Mar	Apr	May	June	July	Aug	Sept	Oct	Nov
Jan	·654	·659	·664	·674	·674	·684	·695	·711	·717	·721	·717	·724	·730	·734	·742
Feb	·645	·650	·655	·665	·665	·675	·686	·702	·708	·712	·708	·715	·721	·725	·733
Mar	·639	·644	·648	·659	·658	·668	·680	·696	·702	·705	·702	·709	·715	·718	·726
Apr	·618	·623	·627	·638	·637	·647	·658	·674	·680	·684	·680	·687	·693	·696	·704
May	·613	·618	·622	·633	·632	·642	·653	·669	·675	·679	·675	·682	·688	·691	·699
June	·599	·611	·615	·626	·625	·635	·646	·661	·667	·671	·667	·674	·680	·684	·691
July	·606	·614	·619	·629	·629	·638	·649	·665	·671	·675	·671	·678	·684	·688	·695
Aug	·609	·611	·615	·626	·625	·635	·646	·661	·667	·671	·667	·674	·680	·684	·691
Sept	·600	·605	·609	·620	·619	·629	·640	·655	·661	·665	·661	·668	·674	·678	·685
Oct	·594	·599	·603	·614	·613	·623	·634	·649	·655	·659	·655	·662	·668	·671	·679
Nov	·588	·593	·597	·608	·607	·617	·628	·643	·649	·653	·649	·656	·662	·665	·673
Dec	·587	·592	·596	·606	·606	·615	·626	·642	·648	·651	·648	·654	·660	·664	·671

1992	Sept	Oct	Nov	Dec	Jan	Feb	Mar	Apr	May	June	July	Aug	Sept	Oct	Nov
Jan	·588	·593	·597	·608	·607	·617	·628	·643	·649	·653	·649	·656	·662	·665	·673
Feb	·580	·585	·589	·599	·599	·608	·619	·635	·640	·644	·640	·647	·653	·657	·664
Mar	·575	·580	·584	·595	·594	·604	·614	·630	·636	·639	·636	·642	·648	·652	·659
Apr	·551	·556	·561	·571	·570	·579	·590	·605	·611	·615	·611	·617	·623	·627	·634
May	·539	·551	·555	·565	·564	·574	·584	·599	·605	·609	·605	·612	·617	·621	·628
June	·546	·551	·555	·565	·564	·574	·584	·599	·605	·609	·605	·612	·617	·621	·628
July	·546	·556	·561	·571	·570	·579	·590	·605	·611	·615	·611	·617	·623	·627	·634
Aug	·550	·555	·559	·569	·569	·578	·589	·604	·610	·613	·610	·616	·622	·626	·633
Sept	·544	·549	·554	·564	·563	·572	·583	·598	·604	·608	·604	·610	·616	·620	·627
Oct	·539	·544	·548	·558	·558	·567	·578	·593	·598	·602	·598	·605	·610	·614	·621
Nov	·541	·546	·550	·560	·560	·569	·580	·595	·601	·604	·601	·607	·613	·616	·623
Dec	·547	·552	·556	·566	·565	·575	·585	.601	.606	.610	·606	·613	·619	·622	.629

1993	Sept	Oct	Nov	Dec	Jan	Feb	Mar	Apr	May	June	July	Aug	Sept	Oct	Nov
Jan	·561	·566	·571	·581	·580	·590	·600	·616	·621	·625	·621	·628	·634	·637	·645
Feb	·551	·556	·561	·571	·570	·579	·590	·605	·611	·615	·611	·617	·623	·627	·634
Mar	·546	·551	·555	·565	·564	·574	·584	·599	·605	·609	·605	·612	·617	·621	·628
Apr	·531	·536	·541	·550	·550	·559	·570	·585	·590	·594	·590	·597	·602	·606	·613
May	·526	·531	·535	·545	·544	·554	·564	·579	·585	·588	·585	·591	·597	·600	·607
June	·527	·532	·536	·546	·545	·555	·565	·580	·586	·589	·586	·592	·598	·601	·609
July	·530	·535	·539	·549	·549	·558	·569	·584	·589	·593	·589	·596	·601	·605	·612
Aug	·524	·529	·533	·543	·542	·551	·562	·577	·582	·586	·582	·589	·594	·598	·605
Sept	·517	·522	·526	·536	·536	·545	·555	·570	·576	·579	·576	·582	·588	·591	·598
Oct	·518	·523	·528	·537	·537	·546	·556	·571	·577	·580	·577	·583	·589	·592	·599
Nov	·520	·525	·530	·540	·539	·548	·559	·573	·579	·583	·579	·585	·591	·595	·602
Dec	·517	·522	·526	·536	·536	·545	·555	·570	·576	·579	·576	·582	·588	·591	·598

MONTH OF DISPOSAL

	2010	2011												2012	
1990	Dec	Jan	Feb	Mar	Apr	May	June	July	Aug	Sept	Oct	Nov	Dec	Jan	Feb
Jan	·911	·916	·936	·946	·962	·968	·968	·964	·976	·991	·992	·996	1·003	·992	1·008
Feb	·900	·905	·924	·934	·950	·957	·957	·953	·964	·979	·980	·984	·992	·980	·996
Mar	·881	·886	·905	·915	·931	·937	·937	·933	·945	·960	·960	·965	·972	·960	·976
Apr	·826	·831	·849	·859	·874	·880	·880	·876	·887	·902	·902	·906	·914	·902	·918
May	·810	·815	·833	·842	·857	·864	·864	·860	·871	·885	·886	·890	·897	·886	·901
June	·803	·807	·826	·835	·850	·856	·856	·852	·863	·878	·878	·882	·890	·878	·893
July	·801	·806	·824	·834	·849	·855	·855	·851	·862	·876	·877	·881	·888	·877	·892
Aug	·783	·788	·806	·815	·830	·836	·836	·832	·843	·857	·858	·862	·869	·858	·873
Sept	·766	·771	·789	·798	·813	·819	·819	·815	·826	·840	·841	·845	·852	·841	·855
Oct	·753	·757	·775	·784	·799	·805	·805	·801	·812	·826	·827	·830	·837	·827	·841
Nov	·757	·762	·779	·788	·803	·809	·809	·805	·816	·830	·831	·835	·842	·831	·845
Dec	·758	·763	·781	·790	·804	·811	·811	·807	·818	·831	·832	·836	·843	·832	·847
1991	Dec	Jan	Feb	Mar	Apr	May	June	July	Aug	Sept	Oct	Nov	Dec	Jan	Feb
Jan	·754	·759	·776	·786	·800	·806	·806	·803	·813	·827	·828	·832	·839	·828	·843
Feb	·745	·749	·767	·776	·791	·797	·797	·793	·804	·817	·818	·822	·829	·818	·833
Mar	·738	·743	·760	·769	·784	·790	·790	·786	·797	·811	·811	·815	·822	·811	·826
Apr	·716	·721	·738	·747	·761	·767	·767	·763	·774	·787	·788	·792	·799	·788	·802
May	·711	·715	·733	·742	·756	·762	·762	·758	·769	·782	·783	·787	·793	·783	·797
June	·703	·708	·725	·734	·748	·754	·754	·750	·761	·774	·775	·779	·785	·775	·789
July	·707	·712	·729	·738	·752	·758	·758	·754	·765	·778	·779	·783	·789	·779	·793
Aug	·703	·708	·725	·734	·748	·754	·754	·750	·761	·774	·775	·779	·785	·775	·789
Sept	·697	·701	·718	·727	·741	·747	·747	·744	·754	·767	·768	·772	·779	·768	·782
Oct	·691	·695	·712	·721	·735	·741	·741	·737	·748	·761	·762	·765	·772	·762	·776
Nov	·684	·689	·706	·715	·729	·735	·735	·731	·741	·754	·755	·759	·765	·755	·769
Dec	·683	·688	·704	·713	·727	·733	·733	·730	·740	·753	·754	·758	·764	·754	·768
1992	Dec	Jan	Feb	Mar	Apr	May	June	July	Aug	Sept	Oct	Nov	Dec	Jan	Feb
Jan	·684	·689	·706	·715	·729	·735	·735	·731	·741	·754	·755	·759	·765	·755	·769
Feb	·676	·680	·697	·706	·720	·726	·726	·722	·732	·745	·746	·750	·756	·746	·760
Mar	·671	·675	·692	·701	·715	·721	·721	·717	·727	·740	·741	·745	·751	·741	·755
Apr	·646	·650	·666	·675	·689	·695	·695	·691	·701	·714	·705	·718	·725	·715	·728
May	·640	·644	·660	·669	·683	·688	·688	·685	·695	·708	·709	·712	·719	·709	·722
June	·640	·644	·660	·669	·683	·688	·688	·685	·695	·708	·709	·712	·719	·709	·722
July	·646	·650	·666	·675	·689	·695	·695	·691	·701	·714	·715	·718	·725	·715	·728
Aug	·644	·649	·665	·674	·688	·693	·693	·690	·700	·713	·713	·717	·724	·713	·727
Sept	·638	·643	·659	·668	·681	·687	·687	·684	·694	·707	·707	·711	·717	·707	·721
Oct	·633	·637	·653	·662	·675	·681	·681	·678	·688	·701	·701	·705	·711	·701	·715
Nov	.635	.639	.656	.664	.678	.684	.684	.680	.690	.703	.704	.707	.714	.704	.717
Dec	.641	.645	.662	.670	.684	.690	.690	.686	.696	.709	.710	.713	.720	.710	.723
1993	Dec	Jan	Feb	Mar	Apr	May	June	July	Aug	Sept	Oct	Nov	Dec	Jan	Feb
Jan	·656	·661	·677	·686	·700	·706	·706	·702	·712	·725	·726	·730	·736	·726	·740
Feb	·646	·650	·666	·675	·689	·695	·695	·691	·701	·714	·715	·718	·725	·715	·728
Mar	·640	·644	·660	·669	·683	·688	·688	·685	·695	·708	·709	·712	·719	·709	·722
Apr	·624	·629	·645	·654	·667	·673	·673	·669	·679	·692	·693	·696	·703	·693	·706
May	·619	·623	·639	·648	·661	·667	·667	·663	·673	·686	·687	·690	·697	·687	·700
June	·620	·624	·640	·649	·662	·668	·668	·665	·674	·687	·688	·691	·698	·688	·701
July	·623	·628	·644	·652	·666	·672	·672	·668	·678	·691	·692	·695	·701	·692	·705
Aug	·616	·621	·637	·645	·659	·665	·665	·661	·671	·684	·684	·688	·694	·684	·698
Sept	·610	·614	·630	·638	·652	·658	·658	·654	·664	·677	·677	·681	·687	·677	·691
Oct	·611	·615	·631	·640	·653	·659	·659	·655	·665	·678	·678	·682	·688	·678	·692
Nov	·613	·617	·633	·642	·655	·661	·661	·657	·667	·680	·681	·684	·691	·681	·694
Dec	·610	·614	·630	·638	·652	·658	·658	·654	·664	·677	·677	·681	·687	·677	·691

MONTH OF DISPOSAL

	2009				2010										
1994	Sept	Oct	Nov	Dec	Jan	Feb	Mar	Apr	May	June	July	Aug	Sept	Oct	Nov
Jan	·524	·529	·533	·543	·542	·551	·562	·577	·582	·586	·582	·589	·594	·598	·605
Feb	·515	·520	·524	·534	·533	·543	·553	·568	·574	·577	·574	·580	·586	·589	·596
Mar	·511	·516	·520	·530	·529	·538	·549	·564	·569	·573	·569	·575	·581	·585	·592
Apr	·493	·498	·502	·512	·511	·520	·531	·545	·551	·554	·551	·557	·562	·566	·573
May	·488	·493	·497	·507	·506	·515	·525	·540	·545	·549	·545	·551	·557	·560	·567
June	·488	·493	·497	·507	·506	·515	·525	·540	·545	·549	·545	·551	·557	·560	·567
July	·495	·500	·504	·514	·513	·522	·533	·547	·553	·556	·553	·559	·565	·568	·575
Aug	·488	·493	·497	·507	·506	·515	·525	·540	·545	·549	·545	·551	·557	·560	·567
Sept	·485	·490	·494	·503	·503	·512	·522	·537	·542	·546	·542	·548	·554	·557	·564
Oct	·483	·488	·492	·501	·501	·510	·520	·534	·540	·543	·540	·546	·552	·555	·562
Nov	·482	·487	·491	·500	·500	·509	·519	·533	·539	·542	·539	·545	·551	·554	·561
Dec	·475	·479	·484	·493	·492	·501	·512	·526	·532	·535	·532	·538	·543	·547	·553
1995	Sept	Oct	Nov	Dec	Jan	Feb	Mar	Apr	May	June	July	Aug	Sept	Oct	Nov
Jan	·475	·479	·484	·493	·492	·501	·512	·526	·532	·535	·532	·538	·543	·547	·553
Feb	·466	·470	·474	·484	·483	·492	·502	·517	·522	·526	·522	·528	·534	·537	·544
Mar	·460	·464	·468	·478	·477	·486	·496	·511	·516	·519	·516	·522	·527	·531	·538
Apr	·445	·450	·454	·463	·462	·471	·481	·495	·501	·504	·501	·507	·512	·515	·522
May	·439	·444	·448	·457	·457	·465	·475	·489	·495	·498	·495	·501	·506	·509	·516
June	·437	·442	·446	·455	·455	·463	·473	·487	·493	·496	·493	·499	·504	·507	·514
July	·444	·449	·453	·462	·461	·470	·480	·494	·500	·503	·500	·506	·511	·514	·521
Aug	·436	·441	·445	·454	·454	·462	·472	·486	·492	·495	·492	·498	·503	·506	·513
Sept	·430	·434	·438	·448	·447	·456	·465	·479	·485	·488	·485	·491	·496	·499	·506
Oct	·437	·442	·446	·455	·455	·463	·473	·487	·493	·496	·493	·499	·504	·507	·514
Nov	·437	·442	·446	·455	·455	·463	·473	·487	·493	·496	·493	·499	·504	·507	·514
Dec	·429	·433	·437	·447	·446	·455	·464	·478	·484	·487	·484	·490	·495	·498	·505
1996	Sept	Oct	Nov	Dec	Jan	Feb	Mar	Apr	May	June	July	Aug	Sept	Oct	Nov
Jan	·433	·438	·442	·451	·451	·459	·469	·483	·489	·492	·489	·495	·500	·503	·510
Feb	·427	·431	·435	·445	·444	·453	·463	·476	·482	·485	·482	·488	·493	·496	·503
Mar	·421	·426	·430	·439	·438	·447	·457	·471	·476	·479	·476	·482	·487	·490	·497
Apr	·411	·415	·419	·429	·428	·436	·446	·460	·465	·469	·465	·471	·476	·480	·486
May	·408	·413	·417	·426	·425	·434	·443	·457	·462	·466	·462	·468	·474	·477	·483
June	·407	·412	·416	·425	·424	·433	·442	·456	·461	·465	·461	·467	·473	·476	·482
July	·413	·417	·421	·430	·430	·438	·448	·462	·467	·470	·467	·473	·478	·482	·488
Aug	·406	·411	·415	·424	·423	·432	·442	·455	·460	·464	·460	·466	·472	·475	·481
Sept	·400	·404	·408	·417	·417	·425	·435	·449	·454	·457	·454	·460	·465	·468	·475
Oct	·400	·404	·408	·417	·417	·425	·435	·449	·454	·457	·454	·460	·465	·468	·475
Nov	·399	·404	·407	·417	·416	·424	·434	·448	·453	·456	·453	·459	·464	·467	·474
Dec	·394	·399	·403	·412	·411	·420	·429	·443	·448	·451	·448	·454	·459	·462	·469
1997	Sept	Oct	Nov	Dec	Jan	Feb	Mar	Apr	May	June	July	Aug	Sept	Oct	Nov
Jan	·394	·399	·403	·412	·411	·420	·429	·443	·448	·451	·448	·454	·459	·462	·469
Feb	·389	·394	·397	·406	·406	·414	·424	·437	·443	·446	·443	·448	·454	·457	·463
Mar	·385	·390	·394	·403	·402	·411	·420	·434	·439	·442	·439	·445	·450	·453	·459
Apr	·377	·382	·386	·395	·394	·402	·412	·425	·431	·434	·431	·436	·441	·445	·451
May	·372	·377	·380	·389	·389	·397	·407	·420	·425	·428	·425	·431	·436	·439	·446
June	·367	·371	·375	·384	·383	·392	·401	·415	·420	·423	·420	·425	·430	·434	·440
July	·367	·371	·375	·384	·383	·392	·401	·415	·420	·423	·420	·425	·430	·434	·440
Aug	·358	·363	·367	·375	·375	·383	·392	·406	·411	·414	·411	·416	·421	·425	·431
Sept	·352	·356	·360	·368	·368	·376	·385	·399	·404	·407	·404	·409	·414	·417	·424
Oct	·350	·354	·358	·367	·366	·374	·384	·397	·402	·405	·402	·408	·413	·416	·422
Nov	·349	·353	·357	·366	·365	·373	·383	·396	·401	·404	·401	·407	·412	·415	·421
Dec	·346	·350	·354	·363	·362	·370	·379	·393	·398	·401	·398	·403	·408	·411	·418

MONTH OF DISPOSAL

	2010	2011												2012	
1994	Dec	Jan	Feb	Mar	Apr	May	June	July	Aug	Sept	Oct	Nov	Dec	Jan	Feb
Jan	·616	·621	·637	·645	·659	·665	·665	·661	·671	·684	·684	·688	·694	·684	·698
Feb	·607	·612	·628	·636	·650	·655	·655	·652	·662	·674	·675	·678	·685	·675	·688
Mar	·603	·607	·623	·632	·645	·651	·651	·647	·657	·669	·670	·674	·680	·670	·684
Apr	·584	·588	·604	·612	·626	·631	·631	·628	·637	·650	·650	·654	·660	·650	·664
May	·578	·583	·598	·607	·620	·625	·625	·622	·632	·644	·645	·648	·654	·645	·658
June	·578	·583	·598	·607	·620	·625	·625	·622	·632	·644	·645	·648	·654	·645	·658
July	·586	·590	·606	·615	·628	·633	·633	·630	·640	·652	·653	·656	·663	·653	·666
Aug	·578	·583	·598	·607	·620	·625	·625	·622	·632	·644	·645	·648	·654	·645	·658
Sept	·575	·579	·595	·603	·617	·622	·622	·619	·628	·641	·641	·645	·651	·641	·654
Oct	·573	·577	·593	·601	·614	·620	·620	·616	·626	·638	·639	·643	·649	·639	·652
Nov	·572	·576	·592	·600	·613	·619	·619	·615	·625	·637	·638	·641	·648	·638	·651
Dec	·564	·568	·584	·592	·605	·611	·611	·608	·617	·629	·630	·634	·640	·630	·643
1995	Dec	Jan	Feb	Mar	Apr	May	June	July	Aug	Sept	Oct	Nov	Dec	Jan	Feb
Jan	·564	·568	·584	·592	·605	·611	·611	·608	·617	·629	·630	·634	·640	·630	·643
Feb	·555	·559	·575	·583	·596	·601	·601	·598	·607	·619	·620	·624	·630	·620	·633
Mar	·548	·553	·568	·576	·589	·595	·595	·591	·601	·613	·614	·617	·623	·614	·626
Apr	·533	·537	·552	·560	·573	·579	·579	·575	·585	·597	·597	·601	·607	·597	·610
May	·527	·531	·546	·554	·567	·572	·572	·569	·578	·590	·591	·594	·600	·591	·604
June	·525	·529	·544	·552	·565	·570	·570	·567	·576	·588	·589	·592	·598	·589	·601
July	·532	·536	·551	·559	·572	·577	·577	·574	·584	·596	·596	·600	·606	·596	·609
Aug	·524	·528	·543	·551	·564	·569	·569	·566	·575	·587	·588	·591	·597	·588	·600
Sept	·517	·521	·536	·544	·556	·562	·562	·558	·568	·580	·580	·584	·590	·580	·593
Oct	·525	·529	·544	·552	·565	·570	·570	·567	·576	·588	·588	·592	·598	·589	·601
Nov	·525	·529	·544	·552	·565	·570	·570	·567	·576	·588	·589	·592	·598	·589	·601
Dec	·516	·520	·535	·543	·555	·561	·561	·557	·567	·579	·579	·583	·589	·579	·592
1996	Dec	Jan	Feb	Mar	Apr	May	June	July	Aug	Sept	Oct	Nov	Dec	Jan	Feb
Jan	·521	·525	·540	·548	·561	·566	·566	·563	·572	·584	·585	·588	·594	·585	·597
Feb	·514	·518	·533	·541	·553	·559	·559	·555	·565	·577	·577	·581	·586	·577	·590
Mar	·508	·512	·527	·535	·547	·552	·552	·549	·558	·570	·571	·574	·580	·571	·583
Apr	·497	·501	·516	·524	·536	·541	·541	·538	·547	·559	·560	·563	·569	·560	·572
May	·494	·498	·513	·521	·533	·538	·538	·535	·544	·556	·557	·560	·566	·557	·569
June	·493	·497	·512	·520	·532	·537	·537	·534	·543	·555	·556	·559	·565	·556	·568
July	·499	·503	·518	·526	·538	·543	·543	·540	·549	·561	·562	·565	·571	·562	·574
Aug	·492	·496	·511	·519	·531	·536	·536	·533	·542	·554	·555	·558	·564	·555	·567
Sept	·485	·489	·504	·512	·524	·529	·529	·526	·535	·547	·547	·551	·557	·547	·560
Oct	·485	·489	·504	·512	·524	·529	·529	·526	·535	·547	·547	·551	·557	·547	·560
Nov	·484	·488	·503	·511	·523	·528	·528	·525	·534	·546	·546	·550	·556	·546	·559
Dec	·479	·483	·498	·506	·518	·523	·523	·520	·529	·541	·541	·545	·551	·541	·554
1997	Dec	Jan	Feb	Mar	Apr	May	June	July	Aug	Sept	Oct	Nov	Dec	Jan	Feb
Jan	·479	·483	·498	·506	·518	·523	·523	·520	·529	·541	·541	·545	·551	·541	·554
Feb	·474	·477	·492	·500	·512	·517	·517	·514	·523	·535	·535	·539	·545	·535	·548
Mar	·470	·474	·488	·496	·508	·514	·514	·510	·519	·531	·532	·535	·541	·532	·544
Apr	·461	·465	·480	·488	·500	·505	·505	·502	·511	·522	·523	·526	·532	·523	·535
May	·456	·460	·474	·482	·494	·499	·499	·496	·505	·516	·517	·520	·526	·517	·529
June	·450	·454	·469	·476	·488	·493	·493	·490	·499	·510	·511	·514	·520	·511	·523
July	·450	·454	·469	·476	·488	·493	·493	·490	·499	·510	·511	·514	·520	·511	·523
Aug	·441	·445	·459	·467	·479	·484	·484	·481	·490	·501	·502	·505	·510	·502	·514
Sept	·434	·438	·452	·460	·471	·476	·476	·473	·482	·493	·494	·497	·503	·494	·506
Oct	·432	·436	·450	·458	·470	·475	·475	·471	·480	·492	·492	·495	·501	·492	·504
Nov	·431	·435	·449	·457	·469	·474	·474	·471	·479	·491	·491	·494	·500	·491	·503
Dec	·428	·431	·446	·453	·465	·470	·470	·467	·476	·487	·488	·491	·496	·488	·499

MONTH OF DISPOSAL

1998	2009				2010										
	Sept	Oct	Nov	Dec	Jan	Feb	Mar	Apr	May	June	July	Aug	Sept	Oct	Nov
Jan	·350	·354	·358	·367	·366	·374	·384	·397	·402	·405	·402	·408	·413	·416	·422
Feb	·343	·347	·351	·360	·359	·367	·377	·390	·395	·398	·395	·400	·405	·409	·415
Mar	·339	·343	·347	·356	·355	·363	·373	·386	·391	·394	·391	·396	·401	·404	·410
Apr	·324	·328	·332	·341	·340	·348	·357	·370	·375	·378	·375	·381	·386	·389	·395
May	·317	·321	·325	·333	·333	·341	·350	·363	·368	·371	·368	·373	·378	·381	·387
June	·318	·322	·326	·334	·334	·341	·351	·364	·368	·371	·368	·374	·379	·382	·388
July	·321	·325	·329	·337	·337	·345	·354	·367	·372	·375	·372	·377	·382	·385	·391
Aug	·315	·319	·323	·332	·331	·339	·348	·361	·366	·369	·366	·371	·376	·379	·385
Sept	·310	·314	·318	·326	·325	·333	·342	·355	·360	·363	·360	·366	·370	·373	·380
Oct	·309	·313	·317	·325	·325	·333	·342	·354	·359	·362	·359	·365	·370	·373	·379
Nov	·310	·314	·318	·326	·325	·333	·342	·355	·360	·363	·360	·366	·370	·373	·380
Dec	·310	·314	·318	·326	·325	·333	·342	·355	·360	·363	·360	·366	·370	·373	·380

1999	Sept	Oct	Nov	Dec	Jan	Feb	Mar	Apr	May	June	July	Aug	Sept	Oct	Nov
Jan	·318	·322	·326	·334	·334	·341	·351	·364	·368	·371	·368	·374	·379	·382	·388
Feb	·315	·319	·323	·332	·331	·339	·348	·361	·366	·369	·366	·371	·376	·379	·385
Mar	·312	·316	·320	·328	·328	·336	·345	·358	·363	·366	·363	·368	·373	·376	·382
Apr	·303	·308	·311	·320	·319	·327	·336	·349	·354	·357	·354	·359	·364	·367	·373
May	·300	·304	·308	·316	·316	·324	·333	·345	·350	·353	·350	·356	·361	·364	·370
June	·300	·304	·308	·316	·316	·324	·333	·345	·350	·353	·350	·356	·361	·364	·370
July	·304	·308	·312	·320	·320	·328	·337	·349	·354	·357	·354	·360	·365	·368	·374
Aug	·301	·305	·309	·317	·317	·324	·334	·346	·351	·354	·351	·356	·361	·364	·370
Sept	·295	·300	·303	·312	·311	·319	·328	·341	·345	·348	·345	·351	·356	·359	·365
Oct	·293	·297	·301	·309	·309	·317	·326	·338	·343	·346	·343	·348	·353	·356	·362
Nov	·251	·296	·299	·308	·307	·315	·324	·337	·341	·344	·341	·347	·352	·355	·361
Dec	·250	·291	·295	·303	·302	·310	·319	·332	·337	·340	·337	·342	·347	·350	·356

2000	Sept	Oct	Nov	Dec	Jan	Feb	Mar	Apr	May	June	July	Aug	Sept	Oct	Nov
Jan	·292	·297	·300	·309	·308	·316	·325	·337	·342	·345	·342	·348	·352	·355	·361
Feb	·285	·290	·293	·301	·301	·309	·318	·330	·335	·338	·335	·340	·345	·348	·354
Mar	·279	·283	·286	·295	·294	·302	·311	·323	·328	·331	·328	·333	·338	·341	·347
Apr	·266	·270	·273	·282	·281	·289	·297	·310	·315	·317	·315	·320	·325	·327	·333
May	·261	·265	·269	·277	·277	·284	·293	·305	·310	·313	·310	·315	·320	·323	·329
June	·258	·262	·266	·274	·274	·281	·290	·302	·307	·310	·307	·312	·317	·320	·326
July	·263	·267	·270	·279	·278	·286	·294	·307	·311	·314	·311	·317	·321	·324	·330
Aug	·263	·267	·270	·279	·278	·286	·294	·307	·311	·314	·311	·317	·321	·324	·330
Sept	·254	·258	·262	·270	·269	·277	·285	·298	·302	·305	·302	·308	·312	·315	·321
Oct	·255	·259	·262	·270	·270	·277	·286	·298	·303	·306	·303	·308	·313	·316	·322
Nov	·251	·255	·259	·267	·266	·274	·282	·295	·299	·302	·299	·304	·309	·312	·318
Dec	·250	·254	·258	·266	·265	·273	·282	·294	·298	·301	·298	·304	·308	·311	·317

2001	Sept	Oct	Nov	Dec	Jan	Feb	Mar	Apr	May	June	July	Aug	Sept	Oct	Nov
Jan	·258	·262	·266	·274	·274	·281	·290	·302	·307	·310	·307	·312	·317	·320	·326
Feb	·252	·256	·259	·267	·267	·274	·283	·295	·300	·303	·300	·305	·310	·313	·319
Mar	·250	·254	·258	·266	·265	·273	·282	·294	·298	·301	·298	·304	·308	·311	·317
Apr	·244	·248	·251	·259	·259	·266	·275	·287	·292	·295	·292	·297	·302	·304	·310
May	·236	·240	·243	·251	·251	·258	·267	·279	·284	·286	·284	·289	·293	·296	·302
June	·235	·239	·242	·250	·249	·257	·265	·278	·282	·285	·282	·287	·292	·295	·300
July	·242	·246	·250	·258	·257	·265	·274	·286	·290	·293	·290	·295	·300	·303	·309
Aug	·237	·241	·245	·253	·252	·260	·268	·280	·285	·288	·285	·290	·295	·298	·303
Sept	·233	·237	·241	·249	·248	·255	·264	·276	·281	·284	·281	·286	·290	·293	·299
Oct	·235	·239	·243	·251	·250	·258	·266	·278	·283	·286	·283	·288	·293	·295	·301
Nov	·240	·244	·248	·256	·255	·263	·271	·283	·288	·291	·288	·293	·298	·301	·306
Dec	·242	·246	·249	·257	·257	·264	·273	·285	·290	·292	·290	·295	·299	·302	·308

MONTH OF DISPOSAL

	2010	2011												2012	
1998	Dec	Jan	Feb	Mar	Apr	May	June	July	Aug	Sept	Oct	Nov	Dec	Jan	Feb
Jan	·432	·436	·450	·458	·470	·475	·475	·471	·480	·492	·492	·495	·501	·492	·504
Feb	·425	·429	·443	·450	·462	·467	·467	·464	·473	·484	·485	·488	·493	·485	·497
Mar	·420	·424	·438	·446	·458	·463	·463	·460	·468	·479	·480	·483	·489	·480	·492
Apr	·405	·408	·423	·430	·442	·446	·446	·443	·452	·463	·464	·467	·472	·464	·475
May	·397	·401	·415	·422	·434	·439	·439	·435	·444	·455	·456	·459	·464	·456	·467
June	·398	·401	·416	·423	·435	·439	·439	·436	·445	·456	·457	·460	·465	·457	·468
July	·401	·405	·419	·426	·438	·443	·443	·440	·448	·460	·460	·463	·469	·460	·472
Aug	·395	·399	·413	·420	·432	·437	·437	·434	·442	·453	·454	·457	·462	·454	·465
Sept	·389	·393	·407	·414	·426	·431	·431	·428	·436	·447	·448	·451	·456	·448	·459
Oct	·388	·392	·406	·413	·425	·430	·430	·427	·435	·446	·447	·450	·455	·447	·458
Nov	·389	·393	·407	·414	·426	·431	·431	·428	·436	·447	·448	·451	·456	·448	·459
Dec	·389	·393	·407	·414	·426	·431	·431	·428	·436	·447	·448	·451	·456	·448	·459
1999	Dec	Jan	Feb	Mar	Apr	May	June	July	Aug	Sept	Oct	Nov	Dec	Jan	Feb
Jan	·398	·401	·416	·423	·435	·439	·439	·436	·445	·456	·457	·460	·465	·457	·468
Feb	·395	·399	·413	·420	·432	·437	·437	·434	·442	·453	·454	·457	·462	·454	·465
Mar	·392	·395	·410	·417	·428	·433	·433	·430	·439	·450	·450	·453	·459	·450	·462
Apr	·383	·386	·400	·407	·419	·424	·424	·421	·429	·440	·441	·444	·449	·441	·452
May	·379	·383	·397	·404	·415	·420	·420	·417	·426	·437	·437	·440	·446	·437	·449
June	·379	·383	·397	·404	·415	·420	·420	·417	·426	·437	·437	·440	·446	·437	·449
July	·383	·387	·401	·408	·420	·425	·425	·422	·430	·441	·442	·445	·450	·442	·453
Aug	·380	·384	·398	·405	·416	·421	·421	·418	·427	·437	·438	·441	·447	·438	·450
Sept	·374	·378	·392	·399	·410	·415	·415	·412	·421	·431	·432	·435	·440	·432	·443
Oct	·372	·375	·389	·396	·408	·413	·413	·410	·418	·429	·429	·432	·438	·429	·441
Nov	·370	·374	·388	·395	·406	·411	·411	·408	·416	·427	·428	·431	·436	·428	·439
Dec	·365	·369	·383	·390	·401	·406	·406	·403	·411	·422	·423	·426	·431	·423	·434
2000	Dec	Jan	Feb	Mar	Apr	May	June	July	Aug	Sept	Oct	Nov	Dec	Jan	Feb
Jan	·371	·375	·388	·396	·407	·412	·412	·409	·417	·428	·429	·432	·437	·429	·440
Feb	·364	·367	·381	·388	·399	·404	·404	·401	·410	·420	·421	·424	·429	·421	·432
Mar	·356	·360	·374	·381	·392	·397	·397	·394	·402	·413	·413	·416	·422	·413	·425
Apr	·343	·346	·360	·367	·378	·383	·383	·380	·388	·399	·399	·402	·407	·399	·410
May	·338	·342	·355	·362	·373	·378	·378	·375	·383	·394	·394	·397	·402	·394	·405
June	·335	·338	·352	·359	·370	·375	·375	·372	·380	·390	·391	·394	·399	·391	·402
July	·340	·343	·357	·364	·375	·379	·379	·377	·385	·395	·396	·399	·404	·396	·407
Aug	·340	·343	·357	·364	·375	·379	·379	·377	·385	·395	·396	·399	·404	·396	·407
Sept	·330	·334	·347	·354	·365	·370	·370	·367	·375	·386	·386	·389	·394	·386	·397
Oct	·331	·334	·348	·355	·366	·371	·371	·368	·376	·386	·387	·390	·395	·387	·398
Nov	·327	·331	·344	·351	·362	·367	·367	·364	·372	·382	·383	·386	·391	·383	·394
Dec	·326	·330	·343	·350	·361	·366	·366	·363	·371	·382	·382	·385	·390	·382	·393
2001	Dec	Jan	Feb	Mar	Apr	May	June	July	Aug	Sept	Oct	Nov	Dec	Jan	Feb
Jan	·335	·338	·352	·359	·370	·375	·375	·372	·380	·390	·391	·394	·399	·391	·402
Feb	·328	·331	·345	·352	·363	·367	·367	·365	·373	·383	·384	·387	·392	·384	·395
Mar	·326	·330	·343	·350	·361	·366	·366	·363	·371	·382	·382	·385	·390	·382	·393
Apr	·319	·323	·336	·343	·354	·359	·359	·356	·364	·374	·375	·378	·383	·375	·386
May	·311	·315	·328	·335	·346	·350	·350	·347	·355	·366	·366	·369	·374	·366	·377
June	·310	·313	·326	·333	·344	·349	·349	·346	·354	·364	·365	·368	·373	·365	·376
July	·318	·321	·335	·342	·353	·357	·357	·354	·362	·373	·373	·376	·381	·373	·384
Aug	·313	·316	·329	·336	·347	·352	·352	·349	·357	·367	·368	·371	·376	·368	·379
Sept	·308	·312	·325	·332	·342	·347	·347	·344	·352	·363	·363	·366	·371	·363	·374
Oct	·310	·314	·327	·334	·345	·349	·349	·347	·355	·365	·365	·368	·373	·365	·376
Nov	·316	·319	·332	·339	·350	·355	·355	·352	·360	·370	·371	·374	·379	·371	·382
Dec	·317	·321	·334	·341	·352	·356	·356	·354	·362	·372	·373	·375	·381	·373	·384

MONTH OF DISPOSAL

	2009				2010										
2002	Sept	Oct	Nov	Dec	Jan	Feb	Mar	Apr	May	June	July	Aug	Sept	Oct	Nov
Jan	·242	·246	·250	·258	·257	·265	·274	·286	·290	·293	·290	·295	·300	·303	·309
Feb	·239	·243	·246	·254	·254	·261	·270	·282	·287	·289	·287	·292	·296	·299	·305
Mar	·234	·238	·241	·249	·249	·256	·265	·277	·281	·284	·281	·287	·291	·294	·300
Apr	·225	·229	·233	·241	·240	·248	·256	·268	·273	·275	·273	·278	·282	·285	·291
May	·222	·226	·229	·237	·237	·244	·253	·264	·269	·272	·269	·274	·279	·281	·287
June	·222	·226	·229	·237	·237	·244	·253	·264	·269	·272	·269	·274	·279	·281	·287
July	·224	·228	·231	·239	·239	·246	·255	·267	·271	·274	·271	·276	·281	·284	·289
Aug	·221	·224	·228	·236	·235	·243	·251	·263	·268	·270	·268	·273	·277	·280	·286
Sept	·212	·216	·220	·227	·227	·234	·243	·255	·259	·262	·259	·264	·269	·271	·277
Oct	·210	·214	·218	·225	·225	·232	·241	·252	·257	·260	·257	·262	·266	·269	·275
Nov	·208	·212	·215	·223	·223	·230	·238	·250	·255	·258	·255	·260	·264	·267	·273
Dec	·206	·210	·213	·221	·221	·228	·236	·248	·253	·255	·253	·258	·262	·265	·271
2003	Sept	Oct	Nov	Dec	Jan	Feb	Mar	Apr	May	June	July	Aug	Sept	Oct	Nov
Jan	·207	·211	·214	·222	·221	·229	·237	·249	·253	·256	·253	·258	·263	·266	·271
Feb	·201	·205	·208	·216	·215	·223	·231	·243	·247	·250	·247	·252	·257	·259	·265
Mar	·197	·201	·204	·212	·211	·218	·227	·238	·243	·246	·243	·248	·252	·255	·261
Apr	·188	·192	·195	·203	·203	·210	·218	·230	·234	·237	·234	·239	·243	·246	·252
May	·186	·190	·193	·201	·201	·208	·216	·228	·232	·235	·232	·237	·241	·244	·250
June	·188	·191	·195	·202	·202	·209	·217	·229	·233	·236	·233	·238	·243	·245	·251
July	·188	·191	·195	·202	·202	·209	·217	·229	·233	·236	·233	·238	·243	·245	·251
Aug	·186	·189	·193	·200	·200	·207	·215	·227	·231	·234	·231	·236	·241	·243	·249
Sept	·180	·184	·187	·195	·194	·201	·209	·221	·225	·228	·225	·230	·235	·237	·243
Oct	·179	·183	·186	·194	·193	·200	·209	·220	·225	·227	·225	·229	·234	·237	·242
Nov	·178	·182	·186	·193	·193	·200	·208	·219	·224	·227	·224	·229	·233	·236	·241
Dec	·173	·177	·180	·188	·187	·195	·203	·214	·219	·221	·219	·223	·228	·231	·236
2004	Sept	Oct	Nov	Dec	Jan	Feb	Mar	Apr	May	June	July	Aug	Sept	Oct	Nov
Jan	·176	·180	·183	·191	·190	·197	·205	·217	·221	·224	·221	·226	·230	·233	·239
Feb	·171	·175	·178	·186	·186	·193	·201	·212	·217	·219	·217	·221	·226	·229	·234
Mar	·166	·170	·173	·181	·180	·187	·196	·207	·211	·214	·211	·216	·220	·223	·229
Apr	·159	·163	·166	·174	·173	·180	·188	·200	·204	·207	·204	·209	·213	·216	·221
May	·154	·158	·161	·169	·168	·175	·183	·195	·199	·202	·199	·204	·208	·211	·216
June	·153	·156	·160	·167	·168	·173	·181	·193	·197	·200	·197	·202	·206	·209	·214
July	·153	·156	·160	·167	·168	·173	·181	·193	·197	·200	·197	·202	·206	·209	·214
Aug	·149	·153	·156	·163	·163	·170	·178	·189	·193	·196	·193	·198	·202	·205	·210
Sept	·145	·148	·152	·159	·158	·165	·173	·184	·189	·191	·189	·194	·198	·200	·206
Oct	·142	·145	·148	·156	·155	·162	·170	·181	·186	·188	·186	·190	·195	·197	·203
Nov	·139	·143	·146	·153	·153	·160	·168	·179	·183	·186	·183	·188	·192	·195	·200
Dec	·134	·137	·141	·148	·147	·154	·162	·173	·177	·180	·177	·182	·186	·189	·194
2005	Sept	Oct	Nov	Dec	Jan	Feb	Mar	Apr	May	June	July	Aug	Sept	Oct	Nov
Jan	·140	·143	·147	·154	·154	·160	·168	·179	·184	·186	·184	·188	·193	·195	·201
Feb	·136	·139	·142	·150	·149	·156	·164	·175	·179	·182	·179	·184	·188	·191	·196
Mar	·130	·134	·137	·144	·144	·151	·159	·170	·174	·176	·174	·178	·183	·185	·191
Apr	·124	·127	·130	·138	·137	·144	·152	·163	·167	·170	·167	·172	·176	·178	·184
May	·121	·125	·128	·135	·135	·142	·149	·160	·165	·167	·165	·169	·173	·176	·181
June	·120	·124	·127	·134	·134	·140	·148	·159	·163	·166	·163	·168	·172	·175	·180
July	·120	·124	·127	·134	·134	·140	·148	·159	·163	·166	·163	·168	·172	·175	·180
Aug	·118	·121	·125	·132	·131	·138	·146	·157	·161	·164	·161	·166	·170	·172	·178
Sept	·115	·119	·122	·129	·128	·135	·143	·154	·158	·161	·158	·163	·167	·169	·175
Oct	·114	·117	·121	·128	·127	·134	·142	·153	·157	·159	·157	·161	·166	·168	·173
Nov	·112	·116	·119	·126	·126	·132	·140	·151	·155	·158	·155	·160	·164	·166	·171
Dec	·109	·113	·116	·123	·123	·129	·137	·148	·152	·155	·152	·157	·161	·163	·168

MONTH OF DISPOSAL

	2010	2011												2012	
2002	Dec	Jan	Feb	Mar	Apr	May	June	July	Aug	Sept	Oct	Nov	Dec	Jan	Feb
Jan	·318	·321	·335	·342	·353	·357	·357	·354	·362	·373	·373	·376	·381	·373	·384
Feb	·314	·318	·331	·338	·349	·353	·353	·350	·358	·369	·369	·372	·377	·369	·380
Mar	·309	·312	·326	·332	·343	·348	·348	·345	·353	·363	·364	·367	·372	·364	·375
Apr	·300	·303	·316	·323	·334	·339	·339	·336	·344	·354	·355	·357	·63	·355	·365
May	·296	·300	·313	·320	·330	·335	·335	·332	·340	·350	·351	·354	·359	·351	·362
June	·296	·300	·313	·320	·330	·335	·335	·332	·340	·350	·351	·354	·359	·351	·362
July	·298	·302	·315	·322	·333	·337	·337	·334	·342	·352	·353	·356	·361	·353	·364
Aug	·295	·298	·311	·318	·329	·333	·333	·330	·338	·349	·349	·352	·357	·349	·360
Sept	·286	·289	·302	·309	·320	·324	·324	·322	·329	·340	·340	·343	·348	·340	·351
Oct	·284	·287	·300	·307	·318	·322	·322	·319	·327	·337	·338	·341	·346	·338	·349
Nov	·282	·285	·298	·305	·315	·320	·320	·317	·325	·335	·336	·338	·343	·336	·346
Dec	·280	·283	·296	·303	·313	·318	·318	·315	·323	·333	·333	·336	·341	·333	·344
2003	Dec	Jan	Feb	Mar	Apr	May	June	July	Aug	Sept	Oct	Nov	Dec	Jan	Feb
Jan	·280	·284	·297	·303	·314	·318	·318	·316	·323	·334	·334	·337	·342	·334	·345
Feb	·274	·277	·290	·297	·307	·312	·312	·309	·317	·327	·327	·330	·335	·327	·338
Mar	·270	·273	·286	·292	·303	·307	·307	·305	·312	·322	·323	·326	·331	·323	·334
Apr	·260	·264	·276	·283	·294	·298	·298	·295	·303	·313	·313	·316	·321	·313	·324
May	·258	·262	·274	·281	·291	·296	·296	·293	·301	·311	·311	·314	·319	·311	·322
June	·260	·263	·276	·282	·293	·297	·297	·295	·302	·312	·313	·315	·320	·313	·323
July	·260	·263	·276	·282	·293	·297	·297	·295	·302	·312	·313	·315	·320	·313	·323
Aug	·258	·261	·274	·280	·291	·295	·295	·292	·300	·310	·311	·313	·318	·311	·321
Sept	·252	·255	·267	·274	·284	·289	·289	·286	·294	·304	·304	·307	·312	·304	·315
Oct	·251	·254	·267	·273	·284	·288	·288	·285	·293	·303	·303	·306	·311	·303	·314
Nov	·250	·253	·266	·273	·283	·287	·287	·285	·292	·302	·303	·305	·310	·303	·313
Dec	·245	·248	·260	·267	·277	·282	·282	·279	·287	·296	·297	·300	·305	·297	·307
2004	Dec	Jan	Feb	Mar	Apr	May	June	July	Aug	Sept	Oct	Nov	Dec	Jan	Feb
Jan	·247	·251	·263	·270	·280	·285	·285	·282	·289	·299	·300	·303	·307	·300	·310
Feb	·243	·246	·258	·265	·275	·280	·280	·277	·285	·294	·295	·298	·303	·295	·305
Mar	·237	·241	·253	·259	·270	·274	·274	·271	·279	·289	·289	·292	·297	·289	·300
Apr	·230	·233	·246	·252	·262	·267	·267	·264	·71	·281	·282	·284	·289	·282	·292
May	·225	·228	·240	·247	·257	·261	·261	·258	·266	·276	·276	·279	·284	·276	·286
June	·223	·226	·238	·245	·255	·259	·259	·256	·264	·274	·274	·277	·282	·274	·284
July	·223	·226	·238	·245	·255	·259	·259	·256	·264	·274	·274	·277	·282	·274	·284
Aug	·219	·222	·234	·241	·251	·255	·255	·252	·260	·269	·270	·273	·277	·270	·280
Sept	·214	·217	·230	·236	·246	·250	·250	·248	·248	·265	·265	·268	·273	·265	·275
Oct	·211	·214	·226	·233	·243	·247	·247	·244	·244	·261	·262	·265	·269	·262	·272
Nov	·208	·212	·224	·230	·240	·244	·244	·242	·242	·259	·259	·262	·267	·259	·269
Dec	·203	·206	·218	·224	·234	·239	·239	·236	·236	·253	·253	·256	·261	·253	·263
2005	Dec	Jan	Feb	Mar	Apr	May	June	July	Aug	Sept	Oct	Nov	Dec	Jan	Feb
Jan	·209	·212	·224	·231	·241	·245	·245	·242	·250	·259	·260	·263	·267	·260	·270
Feb	·205	·208	·220	·226	·236	·241	·241	·238	·245	·255	·255	·258	·263	·255	·265
Mar	·199	·202	·214	·220	·230	·235	·235	·232	·239	·249	·249	·252	·257	·249	·259
Apr	·192	·195	·207	·213	·223	·228	·228	·225	·232	·242	·242	·245	·249	·242	·252
May	·190	·193	·205	·211	·221	·225	·225	·222	·230	·239	·240	·242	·247	·240	·249
June	·188	·191	·203	·210	·220	·224	·224	·221	·228	·238	·238	·241	·246	·238	·248
July	·188	·191	·203	·210	·220	·224	·224	·221	·228	·238	·238	·241	·246	·238	·248
Aug	·186	·189	·201	·207	·217	·221	·221	·219	·226	·235	·236	·238	·243	·236	·246
Sept	·183	·186	·198	·204	·214	·218	·218	·215	·223	·232	·233	·235	·240	·233	·242
Oct	·182	·185	·197	·203	·213	·217	·217	·214	·221	·231	·231	·234	·238	·231	·241
Nov	·180	·183	·195	·201	·211	·215	·215	·212	·220	·229	·229	·232	·237	·229	·239
Dec	·177	·180	·192	·198	·208	·212	·212	·209	·216	·226	·226	·229	·233	·226	·236

MONTH OF DISPOSAL

	2009				2010										
2006	Sept	Oct	Nov	Dec	Jan	Feb	Mar	Apr	May	June	July	Aug	Sept	Oct	Nov
Jan	·113	·117	·120	·127	·127	·133	·141	·152	·156	·159	·156	·161	·165	·168	·173
Feb	·109	·112	·115	·123	·122	·129	·136	·147	·151	·154	·151	·156	·160	·163	·168
Mar	·104	·108	·111	·118	·117	·124	·132	·143	·147	·149	·147	·151	·155	·158	·163
Apr	·096	·099	·102	·109	·109	·116	·123	·134	·138	·140	·138	·142	·147	·149	·154
May	·089	·093	·096	·103	·102	·109	·116	·127	·131	·134	·131	·136	·140	·142	·147
June	·085	·088	·091	·098	·098	·104	·112	·122	·126	·129	·126	·131	·135	·138	·143
July	·085	·088	·091	·098	·098	·104	·112	·122	·126	·129	·126	·131	·135	·138	·143
Aug	·081	·084	·087	·094	·094	·100	·108	·118	·122	·125	·122	·127	·131	·134	·139
Sept	·076	·079	·082	·089	·089	·095	·103	·113	·117	·120	·117	·122	·126	·128	·133
Oct	·074	·078	·081	·088	·087	·094	·101	·112	·116	·118	·116	·120	·124	·127	·132
Nov	·071	·074	·077	·084	·084	·090	·097	·108	·112	·114	·112	·116	·120	·123	·128
Dec	·062	·066	·069	·075	·075	·081	·089	·099	·103	·106	·103	·108	·111	·114	·119
2007	Sept	Oct	Nov	Dec	Jan	Feb	Mar	Apr	May	June	July	Aug	Sept	Oct	Nov
Jan	·068	·071	·074	·081	·081	·087	·095	·105	·109	·112	·109	·114	·118	·120	·125
Feb	·060	·064	·066	·073	·073	·079	·087	·097	·101	·103	·101	·105	·109	·112	·117
Mar	·053	·057	·060	·067	·066	·072	·080	·090	·094	·096	·094	·098	·102	·105	·110
Apr	·048	·052	·055	·061	·061	·067	·074	·085	·089	·091	·089	·093	·097	·099	·104
May	·044	·048	·050	·057	·057	·063	·070	·081	·084	·087	·084	·089	·093	·095	·100
June	·039	·042	·045	·052	·051	·057	·065	·075	·079	·081	·079	·083	·087	·089	·094
July	·045	·048	·051	·058	·057	·064	·071	·081	·085	·087	·085	·089	·093	·096	·100
Aug	·039	·042	·045	·052	·051	·057	·065	·075	·079	·081	·079	·083	·087	·089	·094
Sept	·035	·038	·041	·048	·048	·054	·061	·071	·075	·077	·075	·079	·083	·086	·090
Oct	·031	·034	·037	·044	·043	·049	·056	·067	·070	·073	·070	·075	·079	·081	·086
Nov	·027	·030	·033	·040	·039	·045	·052	·062	·066	·069	·066	·071	·074	·077	·082
Dec	·021	·024	·027	·034	·033	·039	·046	·056	·060	·063	·060	·064	·068	·071	·075
2008	Sept	Oct	Nov	Dec	Jan	Feb	Mar	Apr	May	June	July	Aug	Sept	Oct	Nov
Jan	·026	·030	·032	·039	·039	·045	·052	·062	·066	·068	·066	·070	·074	·076	·081
Feb	·018	·022	·025	·031	·031	·037	·044	·054	·058	·060	·058	·062	·066	·068	·073
Mar	·015	·018	·021	·028	·027	·033	·041	·050	·054	·057	·054	·058	·062	·065	·069
Apr	·006	·009	·012	·019	·018	·024	·031	·041	·045	·047	·045	·049	·053	·055	·060
May	·001	·004	·007	·013	·013	·019	·026	·036	·040	·042	·040	·044	·047	·050	·054
June	·000	·000	·000	·006	·005	·011	·018	·028	·031	·034	·031	·036	·039	·042	·046
July	·000	·000	·000	·007	·006	·012	·019	·029	·033	·035	·033	·037	·041	·043	·048
Aug	·000	·000	·000	·004	·003	·009	·016	·026	·029	·032	·029	·034	·037	·040	·044
Sept	·000	·000	·000	·000	·000	·004	·011	·020	·024	·026	·024	·028	·032	·034	·038
Oct	·000	·000	·000	·001	·001	·007	·014	·023	·027	·029	·027	·031	·035	·037	·042
Nov	·000	·000	·003	·009	·009	·015	·022	·031	·035	·038	·035	·039	·043	·045	·050
Dec	·011	·015	·017	·024	·023	·030	·037	·047	·050	·053	·050	·054	·058	·061	·065
2009	Sept	Oct	Nov	Dec	Jan	Feb	Mar	Apr	May	June	July	Aug	Sept	Oct	Nov
Jan	·025	·028	·031	·038	·037	·043	·050	·060	·064	·067	·064	·069	·072	·075	·079
Feb	·018	·022	·025	·031	·031	·037	·044	·054	·058	·060	·058	·062	·066	·068	·073
Mar	·019	·022	·025	·032	·031	·037	·044	·054	·058	·061	·058	·062	·066	·069	·073
Apr	·018	·021	·024	·031	·030	·036	·043	·053	·057	·060	·057	·061	·065	·068	·072
May	·012	·015	·018	·024	·024	·030	·037	·047	·051	·053	·051	·055	·059	·061	·066
June	·009	·012	·015	·022	·021	·027	·034	·044	·048	·050	·048	·052	·056	·058	·063
July	·009	·012	·015	·022	·021	·027	·034	·044	·048	·050	·048	·052	·056	·058	·063
Aug	·004	·007	·010	·017	·016	·022	·029	·039	·043	·045	·043	·047	·051	·053	·058
Sept	—	·003	·006	·013	·012	·018	·025	·035	·039	·041	·039	·043	·046	·049	·053
Oct	—	—	·003	·009	·009	·015	·022	·031	·035	·038	·035	·039	·043	·045	·050
Nov	—	—	—	·006	·006	·012	·019	·029	·032	·035	·032	·036	·040	·042	·047
Dec	—	—	—	—	Nil	·006	·012	·022	·026	·028	·026	·030	·033	·036	·040

MONTH OF DISPOSAL

	2010	2011												2012	
2006	Dec	Jan	Feb	Mar	Apr	May	June	July	Aug	Sept	Oct	Nov	Dec	Jan	Feb
Jan	·181	·184	·196	·202	·212	·216	·216	·214	·221	·230	·231	·233	·238	·231	·240
Feb	·176	·179	·191	·197	·207	·211	·211	·209	·216	·225	·226	·228	·233	·226	·235
Mar	·171	·174	·186	·192	·202	·206	·206	·204	·211	·220	·221	·223	·228	·221	·230
Apr	·162	·165	·177	·183	·193	·197	·197	·194	·202	·211	·211	·214	·218	·211	·221
May	·155	·158	·170	·176	·186	·190	·190	·187	·194	·203	·204	·206	·211	·204	·213
June	·151	·154	·165	·171	·181	·185	·185	·182	·189	·198	·199	·202	·206	·199	·209
July	·151	·154	·165	·171	·181	·185	·185	·182	·189	·198	·199	·202	·206	·199	·209
Aug	·147	·150	·161	·167	·177	·181	·181	·178	·185	·194	·195	·197	·202	·195	·204
Sept	·141	·144	·156	·162	·171	·175	·175	·173	·180	·189	·189	·192	·196	·189	·199
Oct	·140	·143	·154	·160	·170	·174	·174	·171	·178	·187	·188	·190	·195	·188	·197
Nov	·136	·139	·150	·156	·166	·170	·170	·167	·174	·183	·183	·186	·190	·183	·193
Dec	·127	·130	·141	·147	·156	·160	·160	·158	·165	·174	·174	·177	·181	·174	·184
2007	Dec	Jan	Feb	Mar	Apr	May	June	July	Aug	Sept	Oct	Nov	Dec	Jan	Feb
Jan	·133	·136	·147	·153	·163	·167	·167	·164	·171	·180	·181	·183	·188	·181	·190
Feb	·125	·128	·139	·145	·154	·158	·158	·156	·162	·171	·172	·174	·179	·172	·181
Mar	·117	·120	·132	·137	·147	·151	·151	·148	·155	·164	·164	·167	·171	·164	·174
Apr	·112	·115	·126	·132	·141	·145	·145	·143	·149	·158	·159	·161	·166	·159	·168
May	·108	·111	·122	·128	·137	·141	·141	·138	·145	·154	·154	·157	·161	·154	·163
June	·102	·105	·116	·122	·131	·135	·135	·132	·139	·148	·148	·151	·155	·148	·157
July	·108	·111	·122	·128	·137	·141	·141	·139	·146	·154	·155	·157	·162	·155	·164
Aug	·102	·105	·116	·122	·131	·135	·135	·132	·139	·148	·148	·151	·155	·148	·157
Sept	·098	·101	·112	·118	·127	·131	·131	·128	·135	·144	·144	·147	·151	·144	·153
Oct	·093	·096	·107	·113	·122	·126	·126	·124	·130	·139	·139	·142	·146	·139	·148
Nov	·089	·092	·103	·109	·118	·122	·122	·119	·126	·134	·135	·137	·142	·135	·144
Dec	·083	·086	·097	·102	·111	·115	·115	·113	·119	·128	·128	·131	·135	·128	·138
2008	Dec	Jan	Feb	Mar	Apr	May	June	July	Aug	Sept	Oct	Nov	Dec	Jan	Feb
Jan	·089	·092	·102	·108	·117	·121	·121	·119	·125	·134	·134	·137	·141	·134	·143
Feb	·080	·083	·094	·100	·109	·113	·113	·110	·117	·125	·126	·128	·132	·126	·135
Mar	·077	·080	·091	·096	·105	·109	·109	·107	·113	·122	·122	·124	·129	·122	·131
Apr	·067	·070	·081	·086	·095	·099	·099	·097	·103	·112	·112	·114	·119	·112	·121
May	·062	·065	·075	·081	·090	·093	·093	·091	·098	·106	·106	·109	·113	·106	·115
June	·054	·056	·067	·072	·081	·085	·085	·083	·089	·097	·098	·100	·104	·098	·107
July	·055	·058	·068	·074	·083	·086	·086	·084	·091	·099	·099	·102	·106	·099	·108
Aug	·052	·054	·065	·070	·079	·083	·083	·081	·087	·095	·096	·098	·102	·096	·105
Sept	·046	·049	·059	·065	·073	·077	·077	·075	·081	·089	·090	·092	·096	·090	·098
Oct	·049	·052	·062	·068	·077	·080	·080	·078	·085	·093	·093	·096	·100	·093	·102
Nov	·057	·060	·071	·076	·085	·089	·089	·087	·093	·101	·102	·104	·108	·102	·111
Dec	·073	·076	·086	·092	·101	·105	·105	·102	·109	·117	·118	·120	·124	·118	·127
2009	Dec	Jan	Feb	Mar	Apr	May	June	July	Aug	Sept	Oct	Nov	Dec	Jan	Feb
Jan	·087	·090	·101	·107	·116	·119	·119	·117	·124	·132	·133	·135	·139	·133	·142
Feb	·080	·083	·094	·100	·109	·113	·113	·110	·117	·125	·126	·128	·132	·126	·135
Mar	·081	·084	·095	·100	·109	·113	·113	·111	·117	·126	·126	·129	·133	·126	·135
Apr	·080	·083	·094	·099	·108	·112	·112	·110	·116	·125	·125	·128	·132	·125	·134
May	·073	·076	·087	·093	·102	·105	·105	·103	·109	·118	·118	·121	·125	·118	·127
June	·070	·073	·084	·090	·098	·102	·102	·100	·106	·115	·115	·118	·122	·115	·124
July	·070	·073	·084	·090	·098	·102	·102	·100	·106	·115	·115	·118	·122	·115	·124
Aug	·065	·068	·079	·084	·093	·097	·097	·095	·101	·110	·110	·112	·117	·110	·119
Sept	·061	·064	·074	·080	·089	·092	·092	·090	·097	·105	·105	·108	·112	·105	·114
Oct	·057	·060	·071	·076	·085	·089	·089	·087	·093	·101	·102	·104	·108	·102	·111
Nov	·054	·057	·068	·073	·082	·086	·086	·084	·090	·098	·099	·101	·105	·099	·108
Dec	·048	·050	·061	·067	·075	·079	·079	·077	·083	·091	·092	·094	·098	·092	·100

	2009				2010										
2010	Sept	Oct	Nov	Dec	Jan	Feb	Mar	Apr	May	June	July	Aug	Sept	Oct	Nov
Jan	—	—	—	—	—	·006	·013	·022	·026	·028	·026	·030	·034	·036	·041
Feb	—	—	—	—	—	—	·007	·016	·020	·022	·020	·024	·028	·030	·035
Mar	—	—	—	—	—	—	—	·010	·013	·015	·013	·017	·021	·023	·028
Apr	—	—	—	—	—	—	—	—	·004	·006	·004	·008	·011	·013	·018
May	—	—	—	—	—	—	—	—	—	·002	Nil	·004	·008	·010	·014
June	—	—	—	—	—	—	—	—	—	—	Nil	·002	·005	·008	·012
July	—	—	—	—	—	—	—	—	—	—	—	·004	·008	·010	·014
Aug	—	—	—	—	—	—	—	—	—	—	—	—	·004	·006	·010
Sept	—	—	—	—	—	—	—	—	—	—	—	—	—	·002	·007
Oct	—	—	—	—	—	—	—	—	—	—	—	—	—	—	·004
Nov	—	—	—	—	—	—	—	—	—	—	—	—	—	—	—
Dec	—	—	—	—	—	—	—	—	—	—	—	—	—	—	—
2011	Dec	Jan	Nov	Dec	Jan	Feb	Mar	Apr	May	June	July	Aug	Sept	Oct	Nov
Jan	—	—	—	—	—	—	—	—	—	—	—	—	—	—	—
Feb	—	—	—	—	—	—	—	—	—	—	—	—	—	—	—
Mar	—	—	—	—	—	—	—	—	—	—	—	—	—	—	—
Apr	—	—	—	—	—	—	—	—	—	—	—	—	—	—	—
May	—	—	—	—	—	—	—	—	—	—	—	—	—	—	—
Jun	—	—	—	—	—	—	—	—	—	—	—	—	—	—	—
July	—	—	—	—	—	—	—	—	—	—	—	—	—	—	—
Aug	—	—	—	—	—	—	—	—	—	—	—	—	—	—	—
Sept	—	—	—	—	—	—	—	—	—	—	—	—	—	—	—
Oct	—	—	—	—	—	—	—	—	—	—	—	—	—	—	—
Nov	—	—	—	—	—	—	—	—	—	—	—	—	—	—	—
Dec	—	—	—	—	—	—	—	—	—	—	—	—	—	—	—
2012	Dec	Jan	Nov	Dec	Jan	Feb	Mar	Apr	May	June	July	Aug	Sept	Oct	Nov
Jan	—	—	—	—	—	—	—	—	—	—	—	—	—	—	—
Feb	—	—	—	—	—	—	—	—	—	—	—	—	—	—	—

MONTH OF DISPOSAL

	2010	2011												2012	
2010	Dec	Jan	Feb	Mar	Apr	May	June	July	Aug	Sept	Oct	Nov	Dec	Jan	Feb
Jan	·048	·051	·061	·067	·076	·079	·079	·077	·084	·092	·092	·095	·099	·092	·101
Feb	·042	·045	·055	·061	·069	·073	·073	·071	·077	·085	·086	·088	·092	·086	·094
Mar	·035	·038	·048	·053	·062	·066	·066	·063	·070	·078	·078	·081	·085	·078	·087
Apr	·025	·028	·038	·044	·052	·056	·056	·053	·060	·068	·068	·070	·075	·068	·077
May	·021	·024	·034	·040	·048	·052	·052	·050	·056	·064	·064	·067	·071	·064	·073
June	·019	·022	·032	·037	·046	·050	·050	·047	·054	·062	·062	·064	·068	·062	·071
July	·021	·024	·034	·040	·048	·052	·052	·050	·056	·064	·064	·067	·071	·064	·073
Aug	·017	·020	·030	·036	·044	·048	·048	·045	·052	·060	·060	·062	·066	·060	·069
Sept	·014	·016	·027	·032	·040	·044	·044	·042	·048	·056	·056	·059	·063	·056	·065
Oct	·012	·014	·024	·030	·038	·042	·042	·039	·046	·054	·054	·056	·060	·054	·062
Nov	·007	·010	·020	·025	·034	·037	·037	·035	·041	·049	·049	·052	·056	·049	·058
Dec	—	·003	·013	·018	·026	·030	·030	·028	·034	·042	·042	·044	·048	·042	·050

2011	Dec	Jan	Feb	Mar	Apr	May	June	July	Aug	Sept	Oct	Nov	Dec	Jan	Feb
Jan	—	—	·010	·015	·024	·027	·027	·025	·031	·039	·039	·041	·045	·039	·048
Feb	—	—	—	·005	·013	·017	·017	·015	·021	·029	·029	·031	·035	·029	·037
Mar	—	—	—	—	—	·008	·012	·009	·015	·023	·024	·026	·030	·024	·032
Apr	—	—	—	—	—	·003	·003	·001	·007	·015	·015	·017	·021	·015	·023
May	—	—	—	—	—	—	Nil	Nil	·004	·011	·012	·014	·018	·012	·020
June	—	—	—	—	—	—	—	Nil	·006	·013	·014	·016	·020	·014	·022
July	—	—	—	—	—	—	—	—	·006	·014	·014	·016	·020	·014	·022
Aug	—	—	—	—	—	—	—	—	—	·008	·008	·010	·014	·008	·016
Sept	—	—	—	—	—	—	—	—	—	—	Nil	·003	·006	·000	·008
Oct	—	—	—	—	—	—	—	—	—	—	—	·002	·006	Nil	·008
Nov	—	—	—	—	—	—	—	—	—	—	—	—	·004	Nil	·006
Dec	—	—	—	—	—	—	—	—	—	—	—	—	—	Nil	·002

2012	Dec	Jan	Feb	Mar	Apr	May	June	July	Aug	Sept	Oct	Nov	Dec	Jan	Feb
Jan	—	—	—	—	—	—	—	—	—	—	—	—	—	—	·008
Feb	—	—	—	—	—	—	—	—	—	—	—	—	—	—	—

Retail prices index

	Jan	Feb	Mar	Apr	May	Jun
1982	78·73	78·76	79·44	81·04	81·62	81·85
1983	82·61	82·97	83·12	84·28	84·64	84·84
1984	86·84	87·20	87·48	88·64	88·97	89·20
1985	91·20	91·94	92·80	94·78	95·21	95·41
1986	96·25	96·60	96·73	97·67	97·85	97·79
1987	100·00	100·40	100·60	101·80	101·90	101·90
1988	103·30	103·70	104·10	105·80	106·20	106·60
1989	111·00	111·80	112·30	114·30	115·00	115·40
1990	119·50	120·20	121·40	125·10	126·20	126·70
1991	130·20	130·90	131·40	133·10	133·50	134·10
1992	135·60	136·30	136·70	138·80	139·30	139·30
1993	137·90	138·80	139·30	140·60	141·10	141·00
1994	141·30	142·10	142·50	144·20	144·70	144·70
1995	146·00	146·90	147·50	149·00	149·60	149·80
1996	150·20	150·90	151·50	152·60	152·90	153·00
1997	154·40	155·00	155·40	156·30	156·90	157·50
1998	159·50	160·30	160·80	162·60	163·50	163·40
1999	163·40	163·70	164·10	165·20	165·60	165·60
2000	166·60	167·50	168·40	170·10	170·70	171·10
2001	171·10	172·00	172·20	173·10	174·20	174·40
2002	173·30	173·80	174·50	175·70	176·20	176·20
2003	178·40	179·30	179·90	181·20	181·50	181·30
2004	183·10	183·80	184·60	185·70	186·50	186·80
2005	188·90	189·60	190·50	191·60	192·00	192·20
2006	193·40	194·20	195·00	196·50	197·70	198·50
2007	201·60	203·10	204·40	205·40	206·20	207·30
2008	209·80	211·40	212·10	214·00	215·10	216·80
2009	210·10	211·40	211·30	211·50	212·80	213·40
2010	218·00	219·20	220·70	222·80	223·60	224·10
2011	229·00	231·30	232·50	234.40	235.20	235.20
2012	238·00	239·90				

Retail prices index, cont.

	Jul	Aug	Sep	Oct	Nov	Dec
1982	81·88	81·90	81·85	82·26	82·66	82·51
1983	85·30	85·68	86·06	86·36	86·67	86·89
1984	89·10	89·94	90·11	90·67	90·95	90·87
1985	95·23	95·49	95·44	95·59	95·92	96·05
1986	97·52	97·82	98·30	98·45	99·29	99·62
1987	101·80	102·10	102·40	102·90	103·40	103·30
1988	106·70	107·90	108·40	109·50	110·00	110·30
1989	115·50	115·80	116·60	117·50	118·50	118·80
1990	126·80	128·10	129·30	130·30	130·00	129·90
1991	133·80	134·10	134·60	135·10	135·60	135·70
1992	138·80	138·90	139·40	139·90	139·70	139·20
1993	140·70	141·30	141·90	141·80	141·60	141·90
1994	144·00	144·70	145·00	145·20	145·30	146·00
1995	149·10	149·90	150·60	149·80	149·80	150·70
1996	152·40	153·10	153·80	153·80	153·90	154·40
1997	157·50	158·50	159·30	159·50	159·60	160·00
1998	163·00	163·70	164·40	164·50	164·40	164·40
1999	165·10	165·50	166·20	166·50	166·70	167·30
2000	170·50	170·50	171·70	171·60	172·10	172·20
2001	173·30	174·00	174·60	174·30	173·60	173·40
2002	175·90	176·40	177·60	177·90	178·20	178·50
2003	181·30	181·60	182·50	182·60	182·70	183·50
2004	186·80	187·40	188·10	188·60	189·00	189·90
2005	192·20	192·60	193·10	193·30	193·60	194·10
2006	198·50	199·20	200·10	200·40	201·10	202·70
2007	206·10	207·30	208·00	208·90	209·70	210·90
2008	216·50	217·20	218·40	217·70	216·00	212·90
2009	213·40	214.40	215.30	216.00	216·60	218·00
2010	223.60	224.50	225.30	225.80	226.80	228.40
2011	234.70	236.10	237.90	238.00	238.50	239.40
2012						

Corporation tax

Rates

Financial year	2007	2008	2009	2010	2011	2012
Full rate	30%	28%	28%	28%	26%	**24%**
Small profits rate[2]	20%	21%	21%	21%	20%	**20%**
lower limit[1]	£300,000	£300,000	£300,000	£300,000	£300,000	**£300,000**
upper limit[1]	£1.5m	£1.5m	£1.5m	£1.5m	£1.5m	**£1.5m**
marginal relief fraction	$^1/_{40}$	$^7/_{400}$	$^7/_{400}$	$^7/_{400}$	$^3/_{200}$	**$^1/_{100}$**
effective marginal rate	32.50%	29.75%	29.75%	29.75%	27.5%	**25%**
Tax credit: from 6 April	10%	10%	10%	10%	10%	**10%**

[1]   Reduced proportionally for accounting periods of less than 12 months. The limits are divided by the number of associated companies (including the company in question).

[2]   For ring fenced trades, the small profits rate remains at 19% for financial years 2007 to 2012 and the main rate of corporation tax remains at 30% for those years. The marginal relief ring fenced fraction is 11/400.

[3]   The full rate of corporation tax will be 23% for financial year 2013 and 22% for 2014.

Marginal relief. The small profits rate applies to total taxable profits where augmented profits (see below) do not exceed the lower limit. Where a company's profits exceed the lower limit but do not exceed the upper limit, the charge to corporation tax on the company's taxable total profits is reduced by an amount calculated in accordance with a statutory formula—

$$F \times (U - A) \times \frac{N}{A}$$

where—
   F is the marginal relief fraction;
   U is the upper limit;
   N is the amount of the taxable total profits;
   A is the amount of the augmented profits—its taxable total profits plus franked investment income (other than from UK companies in the same group or owned by a consortium of which the recipient is a member).

Reliefs

Corporate Venturing Scheme

(FA 2000 s 63, Schs 15, 16; FA 2001 s 64, Sch 16; FA 2004 s 95, Sch 20; FA 2006 s 91, Sch 14)

In relation to shares issued between 1 April 2000 and 31 March 2010, an investing company can obtain 20% CT relief on amounts subscribed for ordinary shares in small higher-risk unquoted trading companies which are held for at least three years. The investor must not own or be entitled to acquire more than 30% of the ordinary shares in the investee company. At least 20% must be owned by independent individuals. Chargeable gains on share disposals can be deferred by reinvestment in another shareholding. Allowable losses (net of 20% relief) can be set against income if not deducted from chargeable gains.

Research and development

(CTA 2009 ss 1039–1142; FA 2000 ss 68, 69, Schs 19–21; FA 2002 s 53, Sch 12; FA 2003 s 168, Sch 31; FA 2007 s 50; FA 2011 s 43)

An 'SME' incurring R&D expenditure (of at least £10,000 for accounting periods ending before 1 April 2012, though this minimum expenditure requirement is now removed) in a 12-month accounting period can obtain relief for 225% (applying from 1 April 2012) of that expenditure (200% for expenditure incurred between 1 April 2011 and 1 April 2012; 175% for expenditure incurred between 1 August 2008 and 1 April 2011; 150% for expenditure incurred before 1 August 2008). Large companies incurring R&D expenditure (of at least £10,000 for accounting periods ending before 1 April 2012) can obtain relief for 130% of that expenditure (125% for expenditure incurred before 1 April 2008). SMEs not yet in profit or which have not yet started to trade can claim relief upfront as a cash payment (R&D tax credit).

An 'SME' is a company with less than 500 employees (250 before 1 August 2008) and either annual turnover of €100m or less (€50m before 1 August 2008; €40m for accounting periods ending before 1 January 2005) or annual balance sheet total of €86m or less (€43m before 1 August 2008; €27m for accounting periods ending before 1 January 2005). Large companies incurring R&D expenditure (of at least £10,000 for accounting periods ending before 1 April 2012) can generally deduct 125% of the expenditure for SMEs.

Large companies can claim a similar relief to that for SMEs above, including tax credits, for expenditure incurred on certain vaccines research. The relief was previously also available to SMEs but is withdrawn for them from April 2012.

Real Estate Investment Trusts (REITs)

(CTA 2010 ss 518–609; FA 2006 ss 103–145, Schs 16, 17)

From 1 January 2007, qualifying rental income from and gains on disposals of investment properties by UK companies within the REIT scheme will be exempt from corporation tax.

Gifts of pre-eminent objects

Companies which gift pre-eminent objects to the nation will receive a reduction in their UK tax liability of 20% of the value of the object they are donating. Applies from a date to be appointed.

Patent box

The patent box will allow companies to elect to apply a 10% corporation tax rate to a proportion of profits attributable to qualifying patents, whether paid separately as royalties or embedded in the sales price of products, and to certain other qualifying intellectual property rights such as regulatory data protection (also called "data exclusivity"), supplementary protection certificates and plant variety rights from 1 April 2013. In the first year the proportion of profits qualifying for the 10% rate will be 60% and this will increase annually to 100% from April 2017.

Environmental taxes and other levies

Aggregates levy

(FA 2001 ss 16–49, Schs 4–10; SI 2004/1959; FA 2010 s 16)

Levy on commercial exploitation of aggregates including rock, gravel or sand together with any other substance incorporated or naturally occurring with it. Applies to all aggregate (not recycled) extracted in the UK or territorial waters unless exempt. It does not apply to quarried or mined products such as clay, shale, slate, metal and metal ores, gemstones, semi-precious gemstones and industrial minerals. It was charged at 20% of the full rate for aggregate processed in Northern Ireland until 30 November 2010. From 1 December 2010 operators in Northern Ireland will have to pay the full aggregate levy.

From 1 April 2013	£2.10 per tonne
1 April 2009 to 31 March 2013	**£2.00 per tonne**
1 April 2008 to 31 March 2009	£1.95 per tonne
1 April 2002 to 31 March 2008	£1.60 per tonne

Air passenger duty

(FA 1994 s 30;FA 2009 s 17, Sch 5; FA 2010, s 14)

APD will be extended to smaller aircraft and business jets (reducing the de minimis weight limit from 10 tonnes to 5.7 tonnes) from 1 April 2013 and passengers on 'luxury' business jets (20 tonnes or more and fewer than 19 seats) will pay APD at twice the standard rate. From 1 November 2011 the band A rates apply to all direct long haul flights departing from Northern Ireland.

Band and distance of capital city of destination country from UK in miles	Reduced rate (lowest class of travel)			Standard rate (all classes other than lowest class)		
	1.11.09– 31.10.10	1.11.10– 31.3.12	**On and after 1.4.12**	1.11.09– 31.10.10	1.11.10– 31.3.12	**On and after 1.4.12**
Band A[1] (0–2,000)	£11	£12	**£13**	£22	£24	**£26**
Band B (2,001–4,000)	£45	£60	**£65**	£90	£120	**£130**
Band C (4,001–6,000)	£50	£75	**£81**	£100	£150	**£162**
Band D (over 6,000)	£55	£85	**£92**	£110	£170	**£184**

[1] Applies to all direct long haul flights from Northern Ireland from 1 November 2011.
[2] From 2013 the reduced rate in bands B, C, and D will increase by £2 and the standard rate in those bands will increase by £4. Band A unchanged.

From 1 February to 31 October 2009	Standard class	Reduced class
Specified European destinations	£20	£10
All other destinations	£80	£40

The following specifies which countries come into which bands.

Band A territories — 0–2,000 miles from London

Albania	Guernsey	Norway (including Svalbard)
Algeria	Hungary	Poland
Andorra	Iceland	Portugal (including Madeira)
Austria	Republic of Ireland	Romania
Azores	Isle of Man	Russian Federation (west of the Urals)
Belarus	Italy (including Sicily and Sardinia)	San Marino
Belgium	Jersey	Serbia
Bosnia and Herzegovina	Republic of Kosovo	Slovak Republic
Bulgaria	Latvia	Slovenia
Croatia	Libya	Spain (including the Balearic Islands and the Canary Islands)
Cyprus	Liechtenstein	Sweden
Czech Republic	Lithuania	Switzerland
Denmark (including the Faroe Islands)	Luxembourg	Tunisia
Estonia	former Yugoslav Republic of Macedonia	Turkey
Finland	Malta	Ukraine
France (including Corsica)	Moldova	Western Sahara[1]
Germany	Monaco	

Gibraltar	Montenegro
Greece	Morocco
Greenland	Netherlands

[1] HMRC Notice 550 Appendix 1 (updated September 2010) does not include Western Sahara.

Band B territories — 2,001–4,000 miles from London

Afghanistan	Gambia	Pakistan
Armenia	Georgia	Qatar
Azerbaijan	Ghana	Russian Federation (east of the Urals)
Bahrain	Guinea	Saint Pierre and Miquelon
Benin	Guinea-Bissau	Sao Tome and Principe
Bermuda	Iran	Saudi Arabia
Burkina Faso	Iraq	Senegal
Cameroon	Israel and the Occupied Palestinian Territories	Sierra Leone
Canada	Ivory Coast	Sudan
Cape Verde	Jordan	Syria
Central African Republic	Kazakhstan	Tajikistan
Chad	Kuwait	Togo
Democratic Republic of Congo	Kyrgyzstan	Turkmenistan
Republic of Congo	Lebanon	Uganda
Djibouti	Liberia	United Arab Emirates
Egypt	Mali	United States of America
Equatorial Guinea	Mauritania	Uzbekistan
Eritrea	Niger	Yemen
Ethiopia	Nigeria	
Gabon	Oman	

Band C territories — 4,001–6,000 miles from London

Angola	Grenada	Nepal
Anguilla	Guadelope	Netherlands Antilles
Antigua and Barbuda	Guatemala	Nicaragua
Aruba	Guyana	Panama
Ascension Island	Haiti	Puerto Rico
Bahamas	Honduras	Reunion
Bangladesh	Hong Kong SAR	Rwanda
Barbados	India	Saint Barthelemy
Belize	Jamaica	Saint Christopher and Nevis (St Kitts and Nevis)
Bhutan	Japan	Saint Helena
Botswana	Kenya	Saint Lucia
Brazil	North Korea	Saint Martin
British Indian Ocean Territory	South Korea	Saint Vincent and the Grenadines
British Virgin Islands	Laos	Seychelles
Burma	Lesotho	Somalia
Burundi	Macao SAR	South Africa
Cayman Islands	Madagascar	Sri Lanka
China	Malawi	Suriname
Columbia	Maldives	Swaziland
Comoros	Martinique	Tanzania
Costa Rica	Mauritius	Thailand
Cuba	Mayotte	Trinidad and Tobago
Dominica	Mexico	Turks and Caicos Islands
Dominican Republic	Mongolia	Venezuela
Ecuador	Montserrat	Vietnam
El Salvador	Mozambique	Virgin Islands
French Guiana	Namibia	Zambia
		Zimbabwe

Band D — journey ends in any other place.

Climate change levy

(FA 2000 s 30, Sch 6; FA 2006 ss 171, 172; FA 2007 s 13; FA 2008 s 19; FA 2010 ss 17, 18; FA 2011 ss 23, 78)

Levy on supply for industrial or commercial purposes of energy, from 1.4.01, in the form of electricity, gas, petroleum and hydrocarbon gas supplied in a liquid state, coal and lignite, coke and semi-coke of coal or lignite and petroleum coke.

Taxable commodity supplied	Rate[1]				
	1.4.08–31.3.09	1.4.09–31.3.11	1.4.11–31.3.12	**1.4.12–31.3.13**	From 1 April 2013
Electricity	0.456p per kWh	0.47p per kWh	0.485p per kWh	**0.509p per kWh**	0.524p
Gas supplied by a gas utility or any gas supplied in a gaseous state that is of a kind supplied by a gas utility	0.159p per kWh	0.164p per kWh	0.169p per kWh	**0.177p per kWh**	0.182p
Gas supplied as above in Northern Ireland	Exempt	Exempt	0.059p per kWh	**0.062p per kWh**	0.064p until 31.10.13 then main rate applies
Any petroleum gas, or other gaseous hydrocarbon supplied in a liquid state	1.018p per kg	1.05p per kg	1.083p per kg	**1.137p per kg**	1.172p
Any other taxable commodity	1.242p per kg	1.281p per kg	1.321p per kg	**1.387p per kg**	1.429p

[1] Rate at which payable if supply is not a reduced-rate supply. The levy is charged at 35% (20% for supplies treated as taking place before 1 April 2011) of the full rate for energy-intensive users. This is reduced to 20% from 1 April 2012 for supplies of taxable commodities used in recycling of steel and aluminium (previously exempt) and to 10% from 1 April 2013 for electricity supplies. It was charged at half the full rate for horticultural producers until 31.3.06. Horticultural businesses which sign climate change agreements can pay the same 35% of full rate outlined above in exchange for meeting specific energy efficiency targets. A carbon price support rate will be introduced from 1 April 2013 for supplies of fossil fuels used to generate electricity.

Fuel duty

(FA 2010 ss 12, 13)

A Rural Fuel Duty relief scheme for retailers of road fuel on the Inner and Outer Hebrides, the Northern Isles, the Islands of the Clyde and the Isles of Scilly was introduced on 1 January 2012. Retailers of road fuel within these areas will be eligible to register with HMRC to claim back five pence per litre relief on unleaded petrol and diesel for retail sale within the eligible areas. The retailers will have 60 days following registration for the scheme to reduce the cost of every litre of road fuel sold by the equivalent amount of the relief claimed. (HMRC Brief 40/11)

	Petrol/diesel	Biodiesel or bioethonal	LPG used as road fuel	Natural gas used as road fuel	Red diesel	Fuel oil
from 1 August 2012	60.97p per litre	60.97p per litre	37.34p per kg	29.07p per kg	11.72p per litre	11.26p per litre
from 6pm 23 March 2011 to 31 July 2012	**57.95p per litre**	**57.95p per litre**	**31.61p per kg**	**24.70p per kg**	**11.14p per litre**	**10.70p per litre**
from 1 January 2011 to 6pm 23 March 2011	58.95p per litre	58.95p per litre	33.04p per kg	26.15p per kg	11.33p per litre	10.88p per litre
from 1 October 2010 to 31 December 2010	58.19p per litre	58.19p per litre	31.95p per kg	25.05p per kg	11.18p per litre	10.74p per litre
from 1 April 2010 to 30 September 2010	57.19p per litre	57.19p per litre	30.53p per kg	23.60p per kg	10.99p per litre	10.55p per litre
from 1 September 2009 to 31 March 2010	56.19p per litre	36.19p per litre	27.67p per kg	22.16p per kg	10.80p per litre	10.37p per litre
from 1 April 2009 to 31 August 2009	54.19p per litre	34.19p per litre	24.82p per kg	19.26p per kg	10.42p per litre	10.00p per litre

from 1 December 2008 to 31 March 2009	52.35p per litre	32.35 per litre	20.77p per kg	16.60p per kg	10.07p per litre	9.66p per litre
from 1 October 2007 to 30 November 2008	50.35 per litre	30.35 per litre	16.49p per kg	13.70p per kg	9.69p per litre	9.29p per litre

Insurance premium tax

(FA 1994 ss 48–74, Schs 6A, 7, 7A; F(No 2)A 2010 s 4)

IPT is a tax on premiums received under insurance contracts other than those which are specifically exempt.

	Standard rate	Higher rate[1]
From 4.1.11	**6.0%**	**20.0%**
1.7.99–3.1.11	5.0%	17.5%
1.4.97–30.6.99	4.0%	17.5%
1.10.94–31.3.97	2.5%	–

[1] The higher rate applies to sales of motor cars, light vans and motorcycles, electrical or mechanical domestic appliances, and travel insurance.

Landfill tax

(FA 1996 ss 39–71, 197, Sch 5; SI 1996/1527; SI 1996/1528, FA 2011 s 25)

Tax on disposal of waste imposed on operators of landfill sites calculated by reference to the weight and type of waste deposited. Exemption applies to mining and quarrying waste, dredging waste, pet cemeteries, waste from reclamation of contaminated land, disposals of NATO waste, inert waste used to fill working and old quarries and (before 1 September 2009) inert waste used to restore landfill sites. The contaminated land exemption was abolished with effect from 30 November 2008 although some exemption certificates will remain valid until 31 March 2012. Legislation introduced in Finance Bill 2012 brings landfill tax legislation in Scotland into line with the rest of the UK and will have retrospective effect back to 21 March 2000.

Period	Active waste per tonne	Inert waste per tonne[2]	Maximum credit[1]
From 1 April 2013	£72	£2.50	5.5%
1.4.12–31.3.13	**£64**	**£2.50**	**5.5%**
1.4.11–31.3.12	£56	£2.50	5.5%
1.4.10–31.3.11	£48	£2.50	5.5%
1.4.09–31.3.10	£40	£2.50	6%
1.4.08–31.3.09	£32	£2.50	6%
1.4.07–31.3.08	£24	£2	6.6%
1.4.06–31.3.07	£21	£2	6.7%
1.4.05–31.3.06	£18	£2	6.0%
1.4.04–31.3.05	£15	£2	6.8%
1.4.03–31.3.04	£14	£2	6.5%
1.4.02–31.3.03	£13	£2	20.0%
1.4.01–31.3.02	£12	£2	20.0%

[1] Tax credits are available to operators who make donations to environmental trusts of 90% of the donation to the maximum percentage above of the tax payable in a 12-month period.

[2] For details of waste materials liable at the lower rate see SI 2011/1017.

Vehicle excise duty

(FA 2009 ss 13, 14; FA 2010 s 11; FA 2011, s 21)

Vehicle tax, or 'road tax' is charged according to CO_2 emissions, as follows:

Standard rates

Band	CO_2(g/km)	2010–11	2011–12	2012–13
A	Up to 100	£0	£0	£0
B	101–110	£20	£20	£20
C	111–120	£30	£30	£30
D	121–130	£90	£95	£100
E	131–140	£110	£115	£120
F	141–150	£125	£130	£135
G	151–165	£155	£165	£170
H	166–175	£180	£190	£195
I	176–185	£200	£210	£215
J	186–200	£235	£245	£250
K	201–225	£245	£260	£270
L	226–255	£425	£445	£460
M	Over 255	£435	£460	£475

There is an alternative fuel discount of £10 for all cars from 2010–11 onwards. From 1 April 2010, a different rate of tax applies in the year of purchase of a new vehicle. In later years, the standard rate applies.

First-year rates

Band	CO_2(g/km)	2010–11 first-year rate	2011–12 first-year rate	2012–13 first-year rate
A	Up to 100	£0	£0	£0
B	101–110	£0	£0	£0
C	111–120	£0	£0	£0
D	121–130	£0	£0	£0
E	131–140	£110	£115	£120
F	141–150	£125	£130	£135
G	151–165	£155	£165	£170
H	166–175	£250	£265	£275
I	176–185	£300	£315	£325
J	186–200	£425	£445	£460
K	201–225	£550	£580	£600
L	226–255	£750	£790	£815
M	Over 255	£950	£1,000	£1,030

Certain heavy goods vehicle rates were increased from 1 April 2011 to comply with the mandatory EU minimum tax rate. Otherwise rates are frozen at 2008–09 level.

Light goods vehicle rates

Tax class	2010–11	2011–12	2012–13
Light goods vehicle[1]	£200	£210	£215
Euro 4 & 5 LGV	£125	£130	£135

[1] Registered on or after 1 March 2001.

Motorcycle rates

VED band	2010–11	2011–12	2012–13
Up to 150 cc	£15	£16	£16
151–400 cc	£33	£35	£36
401–600 cc	£50	£53	£55
Over 600 cc	£70	£74	£76

Bank levy

(FA 2011 Sch 19 para 6)

From 1 January 2011 a bank levy will be charged based on the total chargeable equity and liabilities reported in the relevant balance sheets of affected banks, banking and building society groups at the end of the chargeable period. It will be payable through the existing corporation tax self assessment system. It will not be charged on the first £20 billion of chargeable liabilities.

	1.1.11 – 28.2.11	1.3.11 – 30.4.11	1.5.11 – 31.12.11	1.1.12–31.12.12	From 1.1.13
Short-term chargeable liabilities	0.05%	0.1%	0.075%	0.088%	0.105%
Long-term chargeable equity and liabilities	0.025%	0.05%	0.0375%	0.044%	0.0525%

Income tax

Starting, basic and higher rates

Band of taxable income	Band	Rate	Tax	Cumulative tax
£	£	%	£	£
2012–13				
0–34,370	34,370	20	6,874	6,874
34,371–150,000	115,630	40	46,252	53,126
Over 150,000	–	50	–	–
2011–12				
0–35,000	35,000	20	7,000	7,000
35,001–150,000	115,000	40	46,000	53,000
Over 150,000	–	50	–	–
2010–11				
0–37,400	37,400	20	7,480	7,480
37,401–150,000	112,600	40	45,040	52,520
Over 150,000	–	50	–	–
2009–10				
0–37,400	37,400	20	7,480	7,480
Over 37,400	–	40		
2008–09				
0–34,800	34,800	20	6,960.00	6,960.00
Over £34,800	–	40	–	–
2007–08				
0–2,230	2,230	10	223.00	223.00
2,231–34,600	32,370	22	7,121.40	7,344.40
over 34,600	–	40		

2013–14 rates For 2013–14 the basic rate limit will be £32,245, the additional rate of tax will be 45% and the dividend additional rate will be 37.5%.

Child benefit income tax charge From 7 January 2013 taxpayers with adjusted net income between £50,000 and £60,000 will be subject to an income tax charge of 1% of the amount of child benefit for every £100 of income that exceeds £50,000. For taxpayers with income above £60,000, the amount of the charge will equal the amount of child benefit received.

Taxation of savings: For 2007–08 and earlier years, savings income is chargeable at the rates of 10% (if within the starting rate band), 20% and/or 40% (TA 1988 s 1A; FA 2000 s 32). From 2008–09 onwards the starting rate band is abolished. A new starting rate for savings band for individuals is introduced. For 2008–09 the band is £2,320, for 2009–10 and 2010–11 it is £2,440, for 2011–12 it is £2,560, and for 2012–13 it is £2,710. Where an individual's non-savings income is less than the starting rate limit for savings, the savings income is taxable at the 10% starting rate for savings up to the limit. Where non-savings income exceeds the limit, the starting rate for savings does not apply. Savings income includes interest from banks and building societies, interest distributions from authorised unit trusts, interest on gilts and other securities including corporate bonds, purchased life annuities and discounts. Where income does not exceed the basic rate limit, there will be no further tax to pay on savings income from which the 20% tax rate has been deducted, and any tax over-deducted is repayable. Higher rate taxpayers are liable to pay tax at 40% on that part of their savings income falling above the higher rate limit. From 2010–11 additional rate taxpayers are liable to pay tax at 50% on that part of their savings income falling above the additional rate limit. Savings income is generally treated as the second top slice of income behind dividends. Non-taxpayers may apply to have interest paid without deduction of tax where their total income is expected to be covered by personal allowances. Taxpayers who are entitled to a refund of tax deducted from interest can claim the refund using form R40. For HMRC advice regarding repayments see: www.hmrc.gov.uk/incometax/refund-reclaim.htm.

Taxation of dividends: UK and foreign dividends (except those foreign dividends taxed under the remittance basis) form the top slice of taxable income. Where income does not exceed the basic rate limit the rate is 10% (applied to the dividend grossed-up by a tax credit of 1/9) so that the liability is met by the tax credit. Higher rate taxpayers are liable to pay tax at 32.5% on that part of their dividend income falling above the higher rate limit. From 2010–11 additional rate taxpayers are liable to pay tax at 42.5% on that part of their dividend income falling above the additional rate limit. See ITA 2007 s 13. A non-payable tax credit of one-ninth of the dividend was extended to individuals in receipt of dividends from non-UK resident companies where they had a holding of less than 10% and the company is not an offshore fund, by ITTOIA 2005 s 397A on or after 6 April 2008. The tax credit is extended to taxpayers with a holding of 10% or more and to distributions from offshore funds with effect on or after 22 April 2009.

Construction industry sub-contractors rate of deduction at source from 6 April 2007 (SI 2007/46)

Registered sub-contractors	20%	Unregistered sub-contractors	30%

Taxation of trusts

	Trust rate	Dividend trust rate
2010–11 onwards	**50%**	**42.5%**
2004–05 to 2009–10	40%	32.5%
1999–2000 to 2003–04	34%	25%

2013–14 rates For 2013–14 the trust rate will be 45% and the dividend trust rate will be 37.5%.
From 2005–06 onwards: The first £1,000 for 2006–07 onwards and £500 for 2005–06 of income arising to a trust chargeable at the trust rate or the dividend trust rate is instead chargeable at the basic, savings or dividend rate.
Vulnerable beneficiaries: From 2004–05 onwards, trustees can be taxed (on election) on trust income as if it were income of the vulnerable beneficiary taking into account the beneficiary's personal allowances, starting and basic rate bands (FA 2005 ss 23–45).

Table of income tax reliefs

	2012–13	2011–12
	£	£
Personal allowance[5](age under 65)	8,105	7,475
Total income limit	100,000	100,000
Not beneficial if individual's		
total income exceeds	116,210	114,950
Age allowance[1]		
Total income limit	25,400	24,000
Personal allowance age 65–74	10,500	9,940
Not beneficial if individual's		
total income exceeds	30,190	28,930
Personal allowance age 75 and over	10,660	10,090
Not beneficial if individual's		
total income exceeds	30,510	29,230
Married couple's allowance[2,4]		
Elder partner 65 before 6.4.2000		
Basic allowance	2,960	2,800
Age allowance[3,4]		
Total income limit	25,400	24,000
Neither partner aged 75 or over	N/A	N/A
Not beneficial if relevant partner[3]		
under 65 and his total income exceeds	N/A	N/A
65–74 and his total income exceeds	N/A	N/A
Either partner aged 75 and over and born before 6 April 1935	7,705	7,295
Not beneficial if relevant partner[3]		
under 65 and his total income exceeds	34,890	32,990
65–74 and his total income exceeds	39,680	37,920
75 or over and his total income exceeds	40,000	38,220
Blind person's allowance[6]	2,100	1,980

[1] The higher age allowances are available if the claimant's adjusted net income does not exceed the statutory income limit.
Where the adjusted net income exceeds the statutory limit, the maximum allowance is reduced by one-half of the excess until it is reduced to the ordinary personal allowance. For 2013–14 for persons born after 5 April 1938 but before 6 April 1948 the maximum allowance will be £10,500, and for those born before 6 April 1938 the maximum allowance will be £10,660. The allowances will be frozen at these levels from 2013–14.

[2] The universal married couple's allowance was withdrawn for 2000–01 onwards but continues to be available to any married couple or, from 2005–06, civil partnership where at least one spouse or partner was born before 6 April 1935.
The relief is given as a reduction in income tax liability restricted to the lower of 10% of the amount of the allowance or the claimant's total income tax liability.

[3] The higher age allowances are available if the claimant's adjusted net income does not exceed the statutory income limit (subject to relief given as a reduction in tax liability as in note 2 above).
Where the adjusted net income exceeds the statutory limit, the maximum allowance is reduced by one-half of the excess (less any reduction made in the personal age allowance as in note 1 above) but it cannot be reduced to less than the basic couple's allowance.

National insurance contributions – self-employed

		2012–13	2011–12
Class 2	Flat rate per week	£2.65	£2.50
	Small earnings exception	5,595	5,315
Class 4	Band	7,605–42,475	7,225–42,475
	Rate	34,870@ 9%	35,250@ 9%
	Amount payable to upper limit	3,138.30	3,172.50
	Charge on profits above the limit	2%	2%

Table of income tax reliefs (cont.)

2010–11	2009–10	2008–09	2007–08	2006–07
£	£	£	£	£
6,475	6,475	6,035	5,225	5,035
100,000	N/A	N/A	N/A	N/A
112,950	N/A	N/A	N/A	N/A
22,900	22,900	21,800	20,900	20,100
9,490	9,490	9,030	7,550	7,280
28,930	28,930	27,790	25,550	24,590
9,640	9,640	9,180	7,690	7,420
29,230	29,230	28,090	25,830	24,870
2,670	2,670	2,540	2,440	2,350
22,900	22,900	21,800	20,900	20,100
N/A	N/A	6,535	6,285	6,065
N/A	N/A	29,790	28,590	27,530
N/A	N/A	35,780	33,240	32,020
6,965	6,965	6,625	6,365	6,135
31,490	31,490	29,790	28,750	27,670
37,520	37,520	35,960	33,400	32,160
37,820	37,820	36,260	33,680	32,440
1,890	1,890	1,800	1,730	1,660

[4] For marriages entered into before 5 December 2005, married couple's allowance is given to the husband (subject to right of transfer to the wife), the amount of the allowance being determined by the level of the husband's income. For marriages and civil partnerships entered into on or after that date, the allowance is given to whichever of the two partners has the higher total income for the tax year in question, the amount of the allowance being determined by the level of that partner's income (subject to the right to transfer half or all of the basic allowance or excess allowances to the partner). Couples married before 5 December 2005 may make a joint election to be brought within the above rules for couples marrying on or after that date. The election must be made before the start of the first tax year for which it is to have effect. It will continue to have effect for all subsequent tax years and is irrevocable.

[5] From 2010–11, the basic personal allowance for income tax is gradually reduced to nil for individuals with adjusted net incomes in excess of £100,000. The reduction is £1 for every £2 of income over the limit. For 2013–14 the basic personal allowance will be £9,205 for individuals born after 5 April 1948.

[6] The allowance is available for persons who are registered blind but not for persons registered partially-sighted.

National insurance contributions – self-employed (cont.)

£2.40	£2.40	£2.30	£2.20	£2.10
5,075	5,075	4,825	4,635	4,465
5,715–43,875	5,715–43,875	5,435–40,040	5,225–34,840	5,035–33,540
38,160@ 8%	38,160@8%	34,605@8%	29,615@8%	28,505@8%
3,052.80	3,052.80	2,768.40	2,369.20	2,280.40
1%	1%	1%	1%	1%

Cars, vans and related benefits

Cars

From 6 April 2002: The income tax charge is based on a percentage of the car's price graduated according to the level of the car's carbon dioxide measured in grams per kilometre (g/km) and rounded down to the nearest 5g/km. (ITEPA 2003 ss 114–148, 169.)

| CO$_2$ emissions figure not exceeding[1] | | | | | % of list price | |
2005–06–2007–08	2008–09–2009–10	2010–11	2011–12	2012–13	Petrol	Diesel[1]
N/A	N/A	75[1]	75[1]	75[1]	5%	8%
N/A	120[1]	120[1]	120[1]	99[1]	10%	13%
N/A	N/A	N/A	N/A	100	11%	14%
N/A	N/A	N/A	N/A	105	12%	15%
N/A	N/A	N/A	N/A	110	13%	16%
N/A	N/A	N/A	N/A	115	14%	17%
140	135	130	125	120	15%	18%
145	140	135	130	125	16%	19%
150	145	140	135	130	17%	20%
155	150	145	140	135	18%	21%
160	155	150	145	140	19%	22%
165	160	155	150	145	20%	23%
170	165	160	155	150	21%	24%
175	170	165	160	155	22%	25%
180	175	170	165	160	23%	26%
185	180	175	170	165	24%	27%
190	185	180	175	170	25%	28%
195	190	185	180	175	26%	29%
200	195	190	185	180	27%	30%
205	200	195	190	185	28%	31%
210	205	200	195	190	29%	32%
215	210	205	200	195	30%	33%
220	215	210	205	200	31%	34%
225	220	215	210	205	32%	35%
230	225	220	215	210	33%	35%
235	230	225	220	215	34%	35%
240	235	230	225	220	35%	35%

[1] Where a car's CO$_2$ figure is not a multiple of 5, it is rounded down to the nearest 5. For 2008–09 to 2011–12, however, a car's emissions figure must be exactly 120g/km or less to qualify for the 10%/13% rate, from 2010–11 it must be exactly 75g/km or less to qualify for the 5%/8% rate, and for 2012–13 it must be exactly 99g/km or less to qualify for the 10%/13% rate.

For 2008–09 to 2010–11: For cars registered on or after 1.1.98 which are constructed to be capable of being propelled by bioethanol or E85 fuel, the percentage chargeable was reduced by 2%.

For 2010–11 to 2014–15:
No benefit applies to cars which are incapable of producing carbon dioxide when driven.

For 2013–14: The relevant threshold which sets the 11%/14% rate will be reduced to 95g/km. Therefore, the 10%/13% rate will apply to cars with CO$_2$ emissions of 76g/km to 94g/km

Cars registered after 28 February 2001

For cars registered on or after 1.3.01, the definitive CO$_2$ emissions figure is recorded on the vehicle registration document. For cars first registered between 1.1.98 and 28.2.01, the Vehicle Certification Agency supply relevant information on their website at carfueldata.direct.gov.uk/ and in their free, twice-yearly edition of the 'New Car Fuel Consumption & Emission Figures' booklet.

Cars registered on or after 1 January 1998 with no CO$_2$ emission figures

Cylinder capacity of car[3]	Appropriate percentage[1,2]
1,400cc or less	15%
Over 1,400cc up to 2,000cc	25%
Over 2,000cc	35%
Before 6 April 2010: Electrically propelled vehicle	15%
From 6 April 2010 to 5 April 2015: Cars incapable of producing CO$_2$ when driven	0%

[1] **Diesel cars:** A 3% supplement applies to diesel cars up to a maximum of 35%. The supplement does not apply before 5.4.06 to diesel cars meeting the Euro IV emissions standards. For 2006–07 to 2010–11 it does not apply to such cars registered before 1 January 2006.

[2] **Discounts:** Special discounts applied to cars, with or without CO_2 emission figures, registered on or after 1.1.98: 6% for electrically propelled vehicles (before 2010–11 only), 3% for hybrid electric vehicles (before 2011–12 only, 2% before 2006–07) and 2% for gas or bi-fuel cars with CO_2 emission figures for gas (before 2011–12 only, 1% before 2006–07).

[3] **No cylinder capacity:** For a car with no cylinder capacity 35% applies.

Cars registered before 1.1.98 with no CO_2 emission figures: Tax is charged on 15% of the list price for engines to 1,400cc, 22% for engines of 1,401 to 2,000cc and 32% for engines above 2,000cc. Cars without a cylinder capacity are taxed on 32% of the list price.

Automatic cars for disabled drivers: CO_2 figure reduced to equivalent for manual car (ITEPA 2003 s 138).

Car unavailable for part of year: Value of the benefit is reduced proportionately (ITEPA 2003 s 143).

National Insurance: Also used to calculate the national insurance contributions payable by employers on the benefit of cars they provide for the private use of their employees, see p 105.

The cash equivalent is reduced proportionately where the car is not available for the whole tax year. The amount (as so reduced) is reduced by any payments made by the employee for private use.

List price of car:
(1) Includes qualifying accessories, excluding accessories provided after car made available if its list price was less than £100. Accessories designed for use only by disabled people also excluded. From 6 April 2011 accessories do not include certain security enhancements provided to meet the threat to an employee's personal physical security arising from the nature of the employment. Where a car is manufactured so as to be capable of running on road fuel gas, its price is proportionately reduced by so much of that price as is reasonably attributable to it being manufactured in that way. Where a new car is converted to run on road fuel gas, the equipment is not regarded as an accessory. With effect from 6 April 2009 disabled drivers of automatic cars who hold a disabled person's badge can use the list price of an equivalent manual car.
(2) Reduced by capital contributions made by employee up to £5,000.
(3) Classic cars (aged 15 years or more and with a market value of £15,000 or more at end of tax year): substitute market value at end of tax year if higher than adjusted list price. Reduction for capital contributions (and for earlier years the £80,000 cap) applies.
(4) For 2010–11 and earlier years the list price as adjusted was capped at £80,000.

(ITEPA 2003 ss 120–132)

Vans and fuel for vans

(ITEPA 2003 ss 114–119, 154–164, 168, 169A, 170)

	Van's age at end of tax year	
	Under 4 years	4 years or more
2007–08 to 2012–13		
Vehicle weight up to 3,500kg	**£3,000**	**£3,000**
1993–94 to 2006–07		
Vehicle weight up to 3,500kg	£500	£350

From 6 April 2005: no charge applies to employees who have to take their van home and private use is restricted other than for ordinary commuting (insignificant use is disregarded).
From 6 April 2007: an additional **fuel charge of £550** (£500 before 2010–11) also applies for unrestricted private use.
For 2010–11 to 2014–15: No benefit applies to vans which are incapable of producing carbon dioxide when driven.

Related benefits

Parking facilities: No taxable benefit for work place provision of car parking spaces, or parking for bicycles or motorcycles or, from 6 April 2005, vans (ITEPA 2003 s 237).

Cycles and cyclist's safety equipment: No taxable benefit in respect of the provision to employees of bicycles or cycling safety equipment for travel to and from work (ITEPA 2003 s 244) nor, from 6 April 2005, for subsequent transfer to the employee at market value (ITEPA 2003 s 206).

On-call emergency vehicles: From 6 April 2004 onwards no tax or NIC charge where emergency service workers have private use of their emergency vehicle when on call (ITEPA 2003 s 248A).

Bus services: From 6 April 2002 onwards no taxable benefit in respect of the provision of works buses with a seating capacity of nine or more provided to employees (or their children) to travel to and from work (ITEPA 2003 s 242).

Car and motorcycle hire: restricted allowances

(ITTOIA 2005 ss 48–50B; CTA 2009 ss 56–58B)

Before April 2009, if a car with a retail price when new of more than £12,000 is acquired under a rental lease the maximum allowable deduction in computing trading profits is restricted to:

$$\frac{£12,000 + P}{2P} \times R$$

P = retail price of car when new. R = annual rental.

From April 2009, the disallowance is a flat rate of 15%. This applies only to cars with CO_2 emissions exceeding 160g/km.

Capital allowances see p 35.

Car fuel: company cars

(ITEPA 2003 ss 149–153)

For 2003–04 onwards, the same percentage figures on p 74 used to calculate the car benefit charge for the company car, which are directly linked to the car's CO_2 emissions, are used to calculate the benefit charge for fuel provided for private motoring. The relevant percentage figure is multiplied by £14,400 for 2003–04 to 2007–08, by £16,900 for 2008–09 and 2009–10, by £18,000 for 2010–11, by £18,800 for 2011–12 and by £20,200 for 2012–13.

CO_2 emissions grams per kilometre	Petrol	Diesel
2012–13	£	£
75	1,010	1,616
99	2,020	2,626
100	2,222	2,828
105	2,424	3,030
110	2,626	3,232
115	2,828	3,434
120	3,030	3,636
125	3,232	3,838
130	3,434	4,040
135	3,636	4,242
140	3,838	4,444
145	4,040	4,646
150	4,242	4,848
155	4,444	5,050
160	4,646	5,252
165	4,848	5,454
170	5,050	5,656
175	5,252	5,858
180	5,454	6,060
185	5,656	6,262
190	5,858	6,464
195	6,060	6,666
200	6,262	6,868
205	6,464	7,070
210	6,666	7,070
215	6,868	7,070
220	7,070	7,070

CO_2 emissions grams per kilometre	Petrol	Diesel
2011–12	£	£
75	940	1,504
120	1,880	2,444
125	2,820	3,384
130	3,008	3,572
135	3,196	3,760
140	3,384	3,948
145	3,572	4,136
150	3,760	4,324
155	3,948	4,512
160	4,136	4,700
165	4,324	4,888
170	4,512	5,076
175	4,700	5,264
180	4,888	5,452
185	5,076	5,640
190	5,264	5,828
195	5,452	6,016
200	5,640	6,204
205	5,828	6,392
210	6,016	6,580
215	6,204	6,580
220	6,392	6,580
225	6,580	6,580

CO_2 emissions grams per kilometre	Petrol	Diesel
2010–11	£	£
75	900	1,440
120	1,800	2,340
130	2,700	3,240
135	2,880	3,420
140	3,060	3,600
145	3,240	3,780
150	3,420	3,960
155	3,600	4,140
160	3,780	4,320
165	3,960	4,500
170	4,140	4,680
175	4,320	4,860
180	4,500	5,040
185	4,680	5,220
190	4,860	5,400
195	5,040	5,580
200	5,220	5,760
205	5,400	5,940
210	5,580	6,120
215	5,760	6,300
220	5,940	6,300
225	6,120	6,300
230	6,300	6,300

CO_2 emissions grams per kilometre	Petrol	Diesel
2008–09– 2009–2010	£	£
120	1,690	2,197
135	2,535	3,042
140	2,704	3,211
145	2,873	3,380
150	3,042	3,549
155	3,211	3,718
160	3,380	3,887
165	3,549	4,056
170	3,718	4,225
175	3,887	4,394
180	4,056	4,563
185	4,225	4,732
190	4,394	4,901
195	4,563	5,070
200	4,732	5,239
205	4,901	5,408
210	5,070	5,577
215	5,239	5,746
220	5,408	5,915
225	5,577	5,915
230	5,746	5,915
235	5,915	5,915

CO_2 emissions grams per kilometre			Petrol	Diesel
2003–04	2004–05	2005–06– 2007–08	£	£
155	145	140	2,160	2,592
160	150	145	2,304	2,736
165	155	150	2,448	2,880
170	160	155	2,592	3,024
175	165	160	2,736	3,168
180	170	165	2,880	3,312
185	175	170	3,024	3,456
190	180	175	3,168	3,600
195	185	180	3,312	3,744
200	190	185	3,456	3,888
205	195	190	3,600	4,032
210	200	195	3,744	4,176
215	205	200	3,888	4,320
220	210	205	4,032	4,464
225	215	210	4,176	4,608
230	220	215	4,320	4,752
235	225	220	4,464	4,896
240	230	225	4,608	5,040
245	235	230	4,752	5,040
250	240	235	4,896	5,040
255	245	240	5,040	5,040

The benefit is reduced to nil if the employee is required to, and does, make good all fuel provided for private use. There is no taxable benefit where the employer only provides fuel for business travel. The charge is proportionately reduced where the employee stops receiving free fuel part way through the tax year, but where free fuel is subsequently provided in the same tax year, the full year's charge is payable. The benefit is proportionately reduced where a car is not available or is incapable of being used for part of a year (being at least 30 days).

Mileage allowances

Advisory fuel rates for company cars

Engine size	Cost per mile		
	Petrol	Diesel	LPG
from 1 March 2012			
1,400cc or less	**15p**	**–**	**10p**
1,600cc or less	**–**	**13p**	**–**
1,401–2,000cc	**18p**	**–**	**12p**
1,601–2,000cc	**–**	**15p**	**–**
Over 2,000cc	**26p**	**19p**	**18p**
1 December 2011–29 February 2012			
1,400cc or less	15p	–	10p
1,600cc or less	–	12p	–
1,401–2,000cc	18p	–	12p
1,601–2,000cc	–	15p	–
Over 2,000cc	26p	18p	18p
1 September 2011–30 November 2011			
1,400cc or less	15p	–	11p
1,600cc or less	–	12p	–
1,401–2,000cc	18p	–	12p
1,601–2,000cc	–	15p	–
Over 2,000cc	26p	18p	18p
1 June 2011–31 August 2011			
1,400cc or less	15p	–	11p
1,600cc or less	–	12p	–
1,401–2,000cc	18p	–	13p
1,601–2,000cc	–	15p	–
Over 2,000cc	26p	18p	18p
1 March 2011–31 May 2011			
1,400cc or less	14p	13p	10p
1,401–2,000cc	16p	13p	12p
Over 2,000cc	23p	16p	17p
1 December 2010–28 February 2011			
1,400cc or less	13p	12p	9p
1,401–2,000cc	15p	12p	10p
Over 2,000cc	21p	15p	15p
1 June 2010–30 November 2010			
1,400cc or less	12p	11p	8p
1,401–2,000cc	15p	11p	10p
Over 2,000cc	21p	16p	14p
1 December 2009–31 May 2010			
1,400cc or less	11p	11p	7p
1,401–2,000cc	14p	11p	8p
Over 2,000cc	20p	14p	12p
1 July 2009–30 November 2009			
1,400cc or less	10p	10p	7p
1,401–2,000cc	12p	10p	8p
Over 2,000cc	18p	13p	12p

Engine size	Cost per mile		
	Petrol	Diesel	LPG
1 January 2009–30 June 2009			
1,400cc or less	10p	11p	7p
1,401–2,000cc	12p	11p	9p
Over 2,000cc	17p	14p	12p
1 July 2008–31 December 2008			
1,400cc or less	12p	13p	7p
1,401–2,000cc	15p	13p	9p
Over 2,000cc	21p	17p	13p
1 January 2008–30 June 2008			
1,400cc or less	11p	11p	7p
1,401–2,000cc	13p	11p	8p
Over 2,000cc	19p	14p	11p
1 August 2007–31 December 2007			
1,400cc or less	10p	10p	6p
1,401–2,000cc	13p	10p	8p
Over 2,000cc	18p	13p	10p
1 February 2007–31 July 2007			
1,400cc or less	9p	9p	6p
1,401–2,000cc	11p	9p	7p
Over 2,000cc	16p	12p	10p

1   Advisory fuel rates can be used to negotiate dispensations for mileage payments from 28 January 2002 where:
    (a)   employers reimburse employees for business travel in their company cars; or
    (b)   employers require employees to repay the cost of fuel used for private travel.
    (In the case of (b) the figures may be used for reimbursements of private travel from 6 April 2001.)
2   Payments at or below these rates are tax and NIC free. The table figures will be accepted for VAT purposes.
3   Other rates may be used if the employer can demonstrate that they are justified.
4   Rates are currently reviewed by HMRC quarterly.
5   The 1 July 2008 rates can be used from 1 June 2008 if the employer wishes.

Authorised mileage rates

	Rate per business mile	
Cars	*First 10,000 miles*	*Over 10,000 miles*
2011–12 onwards[1]	**45p**	**25p**
2002–03 to 2010–11[1]	40p	25p
Car passengers		
Allowance for each fellow passenger carried		
2002–03 onwards[1]		**5p**[2]
Cycles and motorcycles	Cycles	Motorcycles
2002–03 onwards[1]	**20p**	**24p**

1   Where the employer pays less than the authorised rate the employee can claim tax relief for the difference (ITEPA ss 229–232, 235, 236).

Charities

Gift Aid scheme

Under the Gift Aid scheme an individual donor can claim higher rate relief (and, if applicable, additional rate relief from 2010–11) on the grossed up amount of a monetary donation against income tax and capital gains tax. The charity claims basic rate relief on the grossed up amount of the donation. Donors must make a declaration that they are UK taxpayers to allow the charity to reclaim the repayment, although it is proposed to amend this requirement from April 2013 for charities that receive donations of £10 or less, subject to certain requirements and to be capped at £5,000 per year per charity. One declaration can cover a series of donations to the same charity and the declaration can be made by writing, by electronic means or orally, although an oral declaration is not effective until a written confirmation is sent to the donor. New model written declaration forms were issued by HMRC on 24 February 2012, and only forms based on the new wording will be accepted from 1 January 2013. A declaration can be backdated for up to six years prior to the declaration for donations made after 5 April 2000. The basic rate tax deemed to have been deducted by the donor at source is clawed back if the donor's tax liability is insufficient to match it. Following the reduction of the basic rate to 20% for 2008–09 onwards, a transitional relief supplement of 2% of grossed up qualifying donations was payable to charities for 2008–09 to 2010–11. Donors may elect in their self-assessment tax returns for donations made after 5 April 2003 to be treated as made in the preceding tax year for higher rate (and if applicable, additional rate) relief purposes.

From April 2004, taxpayers could nominate a charity to receive all or part of any tax repayment due to them. The nomination was made on the taxpayer's self-assessment tax return for 2003–04 and later years, with an indication of whether Gift Aid should apply to the donation. However, this scheme has been withdrawn for repayments due on tax returns for 2011–12 onwards, and for repayments made for earlier years on or after 6 April 2012.

From 6 April 2002, the scheme applies also to gifts to Community Amateur Sports Clubs.

Relief for payments falling due after 5 April 2000 under charitable covenants is given under the Gift Aid scheme. (ITA 2007 ss 413–430)

Gifts in kind

Relief is available for gifts by traders to charities, community amateur sports clubs or educational establishments of goods produced or sold or of plant or machinery used for the purposes of the trade (CAA 2001 s 63(2)–(4); ITTOIA 2005 ss 107–109; CTA 2009 ss 105–107; CTA 2010 ss 658–671).

Gifts of land, shares and securities etc

Relief is available where a person disposes of listed shares and securities, unit trust units, AIM shares, etc or of freehold or leasehold interests in land to a charity by way of a gift or sale at an undervalue. The amount deductible from total income is the market value of the shares etc on the date of disposal plus incidental disposal costs less any consideration or value of benefits received by the donor or a connected person. This is in addition to any capital gains tax relief (ITA 2007 ss 431–446).

Payroll giving

Under the payroll giving scheme, employees authorise their employer to deduct charitable donations from their pay and receive tax relief on their donation at their top rate of tax. From 6 April 2004 to 31 December 2006, the first £10 donated by each employee every month was matched for a period of six months. (FA 2000 s 38; ITEPA 2003 ss 713–715; SI 1986/2211 as amended.)

Inheritance tax relief see p 102. **Capital gains tax** see p 43. **Gifts of pre-eminent objects** see p 93.

Employment benefits

The following benefits on pp 83 to 86 cover some common benefits not detailed separately elsewhere. References to 'lower-paid' employees are to those whose annual remuneration plus benefits is less than £8,500.

Accommodation, supplies, etc used in employment duties

(ITEPA 2003 s 316)

The provision of accommodation, supplies or services used by employees in performance of employment duties is not taxable provided:
- (a)   if the benefit is provided on premises occupied by the employer, any private use by the employee (or the employee's family or household) is not significant; or
- (b)   in any other case, the sole purpose of providing the benefit is to enable the employee to perform those duties, any private use is not significant and the benefit is not an excluded benefit (eg the provision of a motor vehicle, boat or aircraft).

Assets given to employees

(ITEPA 2003 ss 203, 204)

If new, tax is chargeable on the cost to the employer (market value in the case of a 'lower-paid' employee). If used, tax is chargeable on the greater of:
- (a)   market value at the time of transfer; and
- (b)   where the asset is first applied for the provision of a benefit after 5 April 1980 and a person has been chargeable to tax on its use, market value when first so applied less amounts charged to tax for use up to and including the year of transfer.

Buses to shops

(SI 2002/205)

The provision of buses for journeys of ten miles or less from the workplace to shops etc on a working day is not taxable.

Cheap loans

(ITEPA 2003 ss 174–190)

A taxable benefit arises on employer-related loans to directors or employees earning £8,500 or more a year, on the difference between the interest paid and interest payable at the 'official rate' below. There is no tax charge where:

(a)   all the employer-related loans (or all loans not qualifying for tax relief) do not exceed £5,000;

(b)   all the interest payable is or would be eligible for tax relief; and

(c)   the loans are ordinary commercial loans.

The provisions can apply to alternative finance arrangements entered into after 21 March 2006.

The 'official rate' is:

From 6 April 2010	4.00%
From 1 March 2009 to 5 April 2010	4.75%
From 6 April 2007 to 28 February 2009	6.25%
From 6 January 2002 to 5 April 2007	5.00%

The average rate for the tax year is:

2011–12	4.00%
2010–11	4.00%
2009–10	4.75%
2008–09	6.10%
2007–08	6.25%

From 2000–01 the official rate is set in advance for the whole of the following tax year, subject to review if the typical mortgage rates were to fall sharply during a tax year.

Childcare provision

(ITEPA 2003 ss 318–318D; SI 2006/882)

From 2005–06, no liability arises:

(a)   where the premises (which are not wholly or mainly used as a private dwelling) are made available by the employer or, where the scheme is provided under arrangements with other persons, by one or more of those persons; or

(b)   where (a) does not apply, on the first £55 per week of registered or approved childcare, or where the employee joins the scheme after 5 April 2011, the first £55 (basic rate taxpayers), £28 per week (higher rate taxpayers), £22 per week (additional rate taxpayers) of registered or approved childcare. £50 per week for 2005–06.

Before 2005–06, broadly similar provisions to (a) applied.

Christmas parties and annual functions

(ITEPA 2003 s 264; SI 2003/1361)

Not taxable if cost does not exceed £150 per head per tax year and open to staff generally. Otherwise, fully taxable. Expenditure may be split between more than one function. (Not taxable on 'lower-paid' employees.)

Credit tokens

(ITEPA 2003 ss 90–96A, 363)

Where money goods or services are provided to employees through credit tokens, the cost to the employer, less any employee contribution, is taxable on the employee, except if they were used to buy certain non-taxable benefits.

Cyclists' breakfasts

(SI 2002/205)

Before 6 April 2013 breakfast provided for employees arriving at the workplace by bicycle in recognition of having cycled to work is not taxable. No limit on number of such breakfasts per year. This exemption is removed from 2013–14 onwards.

Disabled employees

(ITEPA 2003 ss 246, 247; SI 2002/1596)

The provision of or payment for transport for disabled employees for ordinary commuting is tax free. From 9 July 2002, this also applies to the provision of equipment, services or facilities to disabled employees to help them carry out their duties of employment.

Emergency service vehicles

(ITEPA 2003 s 248A)

From 2004–05, there is no tax charge on any benefit arising from use of an emergency vehicle by an employee of an emergency service where private use is prohibited.

Employees' liability insurance

(ITEPA 2003 s 346)

This is non-taxable.

Eye tests and corrective appliances

(ITEPA 2003 s 320A; FA 2006 s 62)

From 2006–07, no liability arises where the provision of tests or special corrective appliances are required under health and safety legislation and are available as required to employees generally.

Homeworkers

(ITEPA 2003 s 316A)

From 2003–04, employer contributions to additional household costs not taxable where employee works at home. Supporting evidence required if contributions exceed £4 per week (£208 per year). Before 6 April 2012 the limit was £3 per week (£156 per year) and before 6 April 2008 the limit was £2 per week (£104 per year).

Incidental overnight expenses

(ITEPA 2003 ss 240, 241)

Not taxable where employee stays away from home on business and payment from employer does not exceed:
  (a)   £5 per night in the UK; or
  (b)   £10 per night overseas.

Living accommodation

(ITEPA 2003 ss 97–113)

A taxable benefit (the '*basic charge*') arises on the annual rental value (or actual rent if greater) less any sums made good by the employee. There is an *additional charge* (if the basic charge is not calculated on the full open market rental value) where the cost of accommodation (including costs of any capital improvements less amounts made good by the employee) exceeds £75,000. The additional charge is the excess cost over £75,000 multiplied by the official rate for cheap loans (see above) in force at the start of the tax year less any rent paid by the employee in excess of the basic charge.

For leases of ten years or less entered into on or after 22 April 2009, a lease premium paid is to be treated as if it were rent and spread over the period of the lease accordingly.

The charges are apportioned in the case of multiple occupation or if the property is provided for only part of the year or part is used exclusively for business purposes.

Exemption: No taxable benefit arises where living accommodation is provided:
  (a)   for the proper performance of duties;
  (b)   by reason that it is customary to do so; or
  (c)   by reason of special threat to the employee's security.

The above exemptions apply to a full-time working director whose interest in the company does not exceed 5%, otherwise only exemption (c) applies to directors.

Living expenses

(ITEPA 2003 ss 313–315)

A taxable charge arises on the cost to the employer of the employee's living expenses. For the provision of assets such as furniture, see 'Use of employer's assets' below.

Where the exemption for living accommodation above applies, the tax charge relating to living expenses (including the provision of furniture and items normal for domestic occupation) is restricted to 10% of the employee's net earnings from the related employment less any sums made good by the employee.

Expenditure on alteration and structural repairs which are normally the landlord's responsibility do not give rise to a taxable benefit.

Long service awards

(ITEPA 2003 s 323; SI 2003/1361)

Not taxable provided the employee has at least 20 years' service and cost to the employer does not exceed £50 (£20 where made before 13 June 2003) for each year of service. No similar award may be made within ten years of such an award.

Meals

(ITEPA 2003 s 317; FA 2010 s 60)

Subsidised or free meals provided for staff generally at the workplace are not taxable. For 2011–12 onwards, however, this relief does not apply if the provision of meals is made under salary sacrifice or flexible remuneration arrangements.

Medical check-ups and insurance

(ITEPA 2003 ss 320B, 325; HMRC Employment Income Manual EIM21765)

Check-ups:

2009–10 onwards: One screening and one check-up each year not taxable.

2007–08 and 2008–09: By concession, HMRC continued the previous concessionary practice not to collect tax and NICs which might arise from the previous regulations.

2006–07 and earlier years: Routine health checks and medical screenings for employee (or members of the family or household) are not taxable.

Insurance: Premiums paid on behalf of employees (other than 'lower-paid' employees) are taxable unless for treatment outside the UK whilst the employee is performing duties abroad.

Personal expenses

(ITEPA 2003 ss 70–72, 336–341)

Unless covered by specific exemptions, payments to an employee by reason of his employment in respect of expenses or allowances are taxable. Deduction is allowed for expenses the employee is obliged to incur which are:

(a) qualifying travelling expenses (broadly those necessarily incurred other than for ordinary commuting or private travel); or

(b) other amounts incurred wholly, exclusively and necessarily in the performance of employment duties.

Relocation expenses

(ITEPA 2003 ss 271–289)

Qualifying removal expenses and benefits up to £8,000 per move in connection with job-related residential moves are not taxable. Included are expenses of disposal, acquisition, abortive acquisition, transport of belongings, travelling and subsistence, bridging loans and duplicate expenses (replacement domestic items).

Scholarships

(ITEPA 2003 ss 211–215)

An employee is taxable on the cost of any scholarship from a trust fund which does not satisfy a 25% distribution test or which is paid because of the employee's employment.

Third party gifts

(ITEPA 2003 ss 270, 324; SI 2003/1361)

Gifts during the tax year of goods and non-cash vouchers up to £250 (£150 for 2002–03) not taxable where provided by a party unconnected with the employer and not for services provided in connection with employment.

Use of employer's assets

(ITEPA 2003 ss 203–206, 242, 244, 319, 320; FA 2005 s 17; FA 2006 ss 60, 61, HMRC Brief 02/2012)

Tax is chargeable on the annual rental value of land and, for other assets, at 20% of the market value when they are first lent or the rental charge to the employer if higher. No taxable benefit arises on:

(a) the loan of a mobile phone for private use. From 6 April 2006 this is restricted to one mobile phone per employee and no longer extends to the employee's family or household but phones first loaned before 6 April 2006 are not affected by the change. HMRC's view from January 2012 is that exemption applies to smartphones with retrospective effect;

(b) the use of works buses (see p 83);

(c) bicycles and cycle safety equipment (see p 83);

(d) to 5 April 2006, the loan of computer equipment for private use, provided use is not restricted to directors or senior staff and value of benefit does not exceed £2,500 (computers made available for private use before 6 April 2006 are not affected by the change).

From 6 April 2005, no benefit arises on the subsequent purchase by an employee at market value of computer or cycling equipment previously on loan.

Vouchers

(ITEPA 2003 ss 73–89, 95, 96, 268–270, 362)

Vouchers are taxable as follows.

(a)	Cash vouchers	On amount for which voucher can be exchanged.
(b)	Non-cash vouchers	On cost to employer less any contribution from employee (except where used to obtain certain non-taxable benefits).
(c)	Luncheon vouchers	Before 6 April 2013 on excess over 15p per working day[1].
(d)	Transport vouchers	On cost to employer less any contribution from employee.

[1]   The 15p exemption on luncheon vouchers is repealed from 2013–14 onwards.

Employment income

PAYE and national insurance thresholds

	2007–08	2008–09	2009–10	2010–11	2011–12	2012–13
	£	£	£	£	£	£
Weekly (NI only from 2008/09)	100	105	110	110	136/139	144/146
Weekly PAYE		116	125	125	144	156
Monthly (NI only from 2008/09)	435	453	476	476	589/602	624/634
Monthly PAYE		503	540	540	623	675

The 2008–09 PAYE figures apply from 7 September 2008.

For full list of national insurance rates see p 105.

PAYE settlement agreements

(SI 2003/2682 Part 6)

These are voluntary agreements between the employer and HMRC under which the employer agrees to meet the tax payable on certain expenses and benefits in kind that are given to his employees. Once an agreement has been signed for a tax year, there is no need to:

- enter the items covered on form P9D or P11D;
- operate PAYE on them, or
- calculate a liability for included items which are liable for Class 1 or Class1A NICs.

The employer pays Class 1B NICs on the items included in PAYE settlement agreements and on the total amount of tax payable. To be effective for a tax year, an agreement must be signed before 6 July following the end of the year and tax must be paid by 19 October following (or 22 October where paid electronically). They are most suited for payments and benefits provided on an irregular basis, or where benefits are for a group of employees and apportionment is difficult.

Personal service companies

(ITEPA 2003 ss 48–61)

These provisions affect 2000–01 and subsequent years. They are commonly known under the name 'IR35' and apply where personal services are provided to a client through an intermediary – normally the worker's personal service company. The effect of the legislation is to treat the worker as an employee of the client for working out the 'deemed employment payment'. The computation involves taking into account all payments and benefits, including those paid direct to the worker for a tax year paid other than by the intermediary for his services. Certain, restricted, allowable expenses, are deducted from 'earnings'. Finally, any payments or benefits received by the worker from the intermediary are deducted. Tax (under PAYE) and NIC is calculated and the amounts due are payable by the worker and his company.

Managed service companies

(ITEPA 2003 ss 61A-61J)

Where an individual provides his services through a managed service company (as defined) all payments made to him by the company on or after 6 April 2007 are deemed to be employment income and PAYE and NIC have to be applied.

National minimum wage

(Hourly rate)

Age of worker	apprentice rate[3]	Under 18[1]	18–20[2]	21 or more
From 1.10.2012	£2.65	£3.68	£4.98	£6.19
1.10.11–30.9.12	£2.60	£3.68	£4.98	£6.08
1.10.10–30.9.11	£2.50	£3.64	£4.92	£5.93
1.10.09–30.9.10	n/a	£3.57	£4.83	£5.80
1.10.08–30.9.09	n/a	£3.53	£4.77	£5.73
1.10.07–30.9.08	n/a	£3.40	£4.60	£5.52
1.10.06–30.9.07	n/a	£3.30	£4.45	£5.35
1.10.05–30.9.06	n/a	£3.00	£4.25	£5.05
1.10.04–30.9.05	n/a	£3.00	£4.10	£4.85

[1] Applies to all workers under 18 who are no longer of compulsory school age.
[2] Applies to workers aged 18–21 before 1 October 2010. Also applies to workers aged 21 or more, starting a new job with a new employer, doing accredited training.

From 1 October 2010 the apprentice rate applies to apprentices aged under 19 and other apprentices in their first year of apprenticeship.

Basis of assessment

(ITEPA 2003 ss 14–41E)

	Services performed			
Persons domiciled in UK	*Wholly in UK*	*Partly in UK*	*Partly abroad*	*Wholly abroad*
Non-resident	All	That part	None	None
Resident but not ordinarily resident	All	That part	Remittances	Remittances
Resident and ordinarily resident	All	All[1]	All[1]	All[1]
Persons domiciled outside the UK				
UK employer	As for person domiciled in the UK			
Foreign employer				
Non-resident	All UK earnings			
Resident but not ordinarily resident	All UK earnings and remittances for duties performed outside UK			
Resident and ordinarily resident	All UK earnings and remittances for duties performed outside UK			

[1] Exemption for seafarers if at least half of qualifying period of over 364 days worked abroad (including 183 consecutive days). Deduction extended in April 2011 with retrospective effect to seafarers who are resident for tax purposes in a European Economic Area or European Union State, other than the United Kingdom. (ITEPA 2003 ss 378–385, HMRC Brief 10/2012).

[2] A statutory residence test will be introduced from 6 April 2013 and ordinary residence will be abolished from that date.

Termination payments

(ITEPA 2003 ss 401–416)

The following lump sum payments are exempt from tax:

(a) Payments in connection with the cessation of employment on the death, injury or disability of the employee.
(b) Payments under tax-exempt pension schemes by way of compensation for loss of employment (or of earnings due to ill-health) or which can properly be regarded as a benefit earned by past service.
(c) Certain payments of terminal grants to members of the armed forces.
(d) Certain benefits under superannuation schemes for civil servants in Commonwealth overseas territories.
(e) Payments in respect of foreign service where the period of foreign service comprises:
   (i) 75% of the whole period of service; or
   (ii) the whole of the last 10 years of service; or
   (iii) where the period of service exceeded 20 years, one-half of that period, including any 10 of the last 20 years.
   Otherwise, a proportion of the payment is exempt, as follows:

$$\frac{\text{length of foreign service}}{\text{length of total service}} \times \text{amount otherwise chargeable}$$

(f) The first £30,000 of genuine ex gratia payments (where there is no 'arrangement' by the employer to make the payment).
(g) Statutory redundancy payments (included in computing £30,000 limit in (f) above).

Fixed rate expenses

For most classes of industry fixed rate allowances for the upkeep of tools and special clothing have been agreed between HMRC and the trade unions concerned. Alternatively, the individual employee may claim as a deduction his or her actual expenses (ITEPA 2003 s 367). (HMRC Employment Income Manual EIM32712.)

Industry	Occupation		Deduction from 2004–05 to 2007–08	Deduction from 2008–09
Agriculture	All workers[1]		70	100
Airlines	See note 5 below			
Aluminium	(a)	Continual casting operators, process operators, de-dimplers, driers, drill punchers, dross unloaders, firemen[2], furnace operators and their helpers, leaders, mouldmen, pourers, remelt department labourers, roll flatteners	130	140
	(b)	Cable hands, case makers, labourers, mates, truck drivers and measurers, storekeepers	60	80
	(c)	Apprentices	45	60
	(d)	All other workers[1]	100	120
Banks and building societies	Uniformed doormen and messengers (£40 before 2004–05)		45	60
Brass and copper	Braziers, coppersmiths, finishers, fitters, moulders, turners and all other workers		100	120
Building	(a)	Joiners and carpenters	105	140
	(b)	Cement works, roofing felt and asphalt labourers	55	80
	(c)	Labourers and navvies (£40 before 2004–05)	45	60
	(d)	All other workers	85	120
Building materials	(a)	Stone masons	85	120
	(b)	Tilemakers and labourers (£40 before 2004–05)	45	60
	(c)	All other workers	55	80
Clothing	(a)	Lacemakers, hosiery bleachers, dyers, scourers and knitters, knitwear bleachers and dyers	45	60
	(b)	All other workers	45	60
Constructional engineering[3]	(a)	Blacksmiths and their strikers, burners, caulkers, chippers, drillers, erectors, fitters, holders up, markers off, platers, riggers, riveters, rivet heaters, scaffolders, sheeters, template workers, turners, welders	115	140
	(b)	Banksmen, labourers, shop-helpers, slewers, straighteners	60	80
	(c)	Apprentices and storekeepers	45	60
	(d)	All other workers	75	100
Electrical and electricity supply	(a)	Those workers incurring laundry costs only	45	60
	(b)	All other workers	90	120
Engineering (trades ancillary to)	(a)	Pattern makers	120	140
	(b)	Labourers, supervisory and unskilled workers	60	80
	(c)	Apprentices and storekeepers	45	60
	(d)	Motor mechanics in garage repair shops	100	120
	(e)	All other workers	100	120
Fire service	Uniformed firefighters and fire officers		60	80
Food	All workers		45	60
Forestry	All workers		70	100
Glass	All workers		60	80
Healthcare staff in the NHS, private hospitals and nursing homes	(a)	Ambulance staff on active service	110	140
	(b)	Nurses and midwives, chiropodists, dental nurses, occupational, speech and other therapists, phlebotomists and radiographers	70	100
	(c)	Plaster room orderlies, hospital porters, ward clerks, sterile supply workers, hospital domestics, hospital catering staff	60	100
	(d)	Laboratory staff, pharmacists, pharmacy assistants	45	60
	(e)	Uniformed ancillary staff: maintenance workers, grounds staff, drivers, parking attendants and security guards, receptionists and other uniformed staff	45	60
Heating	(a)	Pipe fitters and plumbers	100	120
	(b)	Coverers, laggers, domestic glaziers, heating engineers and their mates	90	120
	(c)	All gas workers, all other workers	70	100
Iron mining	(a)	Fillers, miners and underground workers	100	120
	(b)	All other workers	75	100
Iron and steel	(a)	Day labourers, general labourers, stockmen, time keepers, warehouse staff and weighmen	60	80
	(b)	Apprentices	45	60
	(c)	All other workers	120	140

Industry	Occupation		Deduction from 2004–05 to 2007–08	Deduction from 2008–09
Leather	(a)	Curriers (wet workers), fellmongering workers, tanning operatives (wet)	55	80
	(b)	All other workers (£40 before 2004–05)	45	60
Particular engineering[4]	(a)	Pattern makers	120	140
	(b)	Chainmakers, cleaners, galvanisers, tinners and wire drawers in the wire drawing industry, tool-makers in the lock making industry	100	120
	(c)	Apprentices and storekeepers	45	60
	(d)	All other workers	60	80
Police force	Uniformed police officers (ranks up to and including Chief Inspector) (£110 for 2007–08 only) Community Support officers and other police service employees — see note 6 below		55	140
Precious metals	All workers		70	100
Printing	(a)	Letterpress section — electrical engineers (rotary presses), electro-typers, ink and roller makers, machine minders (rotary), maintenance engineers (rotary presses) and stereotypers	105	140
	(b)	Bench hands (periodical and bookbinding section), compositors (letterpress section), readers (letterpress section), telecommunications and electronic section wire room operators, warehousemen (paper box making section)	45	60
	(c)	All other workers	70	100
Prisons	Uniformed prison officers		55	80
Public service	(i)	Dock and inland waterways		
		(a) Dockers, dredger drivers, hopper steerers	55	80
		(b) All other workers (£40 before 2004–05)	45	60
	(ii)	Public transport		
		(a) Garage hands (including cleaners)	55	80
		(b) Conductors and drivers (£40 before 2004–05)	45	60
Quarrying	All workers		70	100
Railways	(See the appropriate category for craftsmen, eg engineers, vehicles etc.) All other workers		70	100
Seamen	Carpenters			
	(a)	Passenger liners	165	165
	(b)	Cargo vessels, tankers, coasters and ferries	130	140
Shipyards	(a)	Blacksmiths and their strikers, boilermakers, burners, carpenters, caulkers, drillers, furnacemen (platers), holders up, fitters, platers, plumbers, riveters, sheet iron workers, shipwrights, tubers, welders	115	140
	(b)	Labourers	60	80
	(c)	Apprentices and storekeepers	45	60
	(d)	All other workers	75	100
Textiles and textile printing	(a)	Carders, carding engineers, overlookers and technicians in spinning mills	85	120
	(b)	All other workers	60	80
Vehicles	(a)	Builders, railway vehicle repairers, and railway wagon lifters	105	140
	(b)	Railway vehicle painters and letterers, builders' and repairers' assistants	60	80
	(c)	All other workers	45	60
Wood & furniture	(a)	Carpenters, cabinet makers, joiners, wood carvers and woodcutting machinists	115	140
	(b)	Artificial limb makers (other than in wood), organ builders and packing case makers	90	120
	(c)	Coopers not providing own tools, labourers, polishers and upholsterers	45	60
	(d)	All other workers	75	100

[1] 'All workers' and 'all other workers' refer only to manual workers who have to bear the cost of upkeep of tools and special clothing. They do not extend to other employees such as office staff.

[2] 'Firemen' means persons engaged to light and maintain furnaces.

[3] 'Constructional engineering' means engineering undertaken on a construction site, including buildings, shipyards, bridges, roads and other similar operations.

[4] 'Particular engineering' means engineering undertaken on a commercial basis in a factory or workshop for the purposes of producing components such as wire, springs, nails and locks.

[5] With effect from 2006–07 a basic flat rate expenses allowance of £850 applies to all uniformed commercial pilots, co-pilots and other flight deck crew working in the UK (but not stewards/stewardesses). A further £100 allowance is allowed for the cost of travel to certain regular specified activities.

[6] From 2008–09 the allowance for police officers applies to community support officers. Other police service employees who must clean their own uniform can claim a deduction of £60 (£45 from 1998–99 to 2007–08).

Investment reliefs

Community investment tax credit

(ITA 2007 ss 333–382; CTA 2010 ss 218–269)

Investments made after 16 April 2002 by an individual or company in an accredited community development finance institution (CDFI) are eligible for tax relief up to 25%. The investment may be a loan or a subscription for shares or securities. Tax relief may be claimed for the tax year in which the investment is made and each of the four subsequent years. Relief for each year is the smaller of 5% of the invested amount, or the amount which reduces the investor's income tax liability for the year to nil.

Enterprise investment scheme

(ITA 2007 ss 156–257)

The EIS applies to investments in qualifying unquoted companies trading in the UK. Eligible shares must be held for at least three years from the issue date or commencement of trade if later (five years from the issue date for shares issued before 6 April 2000). The following reliefs apply subject to this and other conditions.

Relief on investment

Maximum investment:	**From 2012–13**	**£1,000,000**
	2008–09 to 2011–12	£500,000
	2006–07 to 2007–08	£400,000
	2004–05 to 2005–06	£200,000
	1998–99 to 2003–04	£150,000
Minimum investment:	**From 2012–13**	**No minimum**
	1993–94 to 2011–12	£500
Maximum carry-back to preceding year	**From 2009–10**	**No restriction (subject to annual maximum)**
(Up to ½ amount invested between 6 April and 5 October)	2006–07 to 2008–09	£50,000
	1998–99 to 2005–06	£25,000
Rate of relief	**From 2011–12**	**30%**[1]
	1993–94 to 2010–11	20%[1]

[1] Given as a deduction against income tax liability.

Other reliefs (TCGA 1992 ss 150A–150C, Sch 5B)
- (a) A gain on a disposal of shares on which EIS relief has been given and not withdrawn is exempt from capital gains tax.
- (b) Deferral relief is available for gains on assets where the disposal proceeds are reinvested in eligible shares in a qualifying company one year before or three years after the disposal.
- (c) A loss on a disposal of shares on which EIS relief has been given may be relieved against income tax or capital gains tax.

Seed enterprise investment scheme

(ITA 2007 ss 257A–257HG)

Between 6 April 2012 and 5 April 2017 SEIS applies to investments in companies with fewer than 25 employees and assets up to £200,000 carrying on or preparing to carry on new business. The following reliefs apply subject to this and other conditions.

Relief on investment

Maximum investment:	**From 2012–13**	**£100,000**
Maximum carry-back to preceding year	**From 2013–14**	**No restriction (subject to annual maximum)**[2]
Rate of relief	**From 2012–13**	**50%**[1]

[1] Given as a deduction against income tax liability.
[2] Carry back cannot therefore apply until 2013–14.

Other reliefs (TCGA 1992 ss 150E, 150G, Sch 5BB)
- (a) A gain on a disposal of shares on which SEIS relief has been given and not withdrawn is exempt from capital gains tax.
- (b) Reinvestment relief is available for gains on assets where the disposal proceeds are reinvested in SEIS in 2012–13 only (see p 43).

Venture capital trusts

(ITA 2007 ss 258–332)

An individual who subscribes for ordinary shares in a VCT obtains income tax reliefs at the rates in the table below subject to conditions. The shares must be held for at least five years (three years for shares issued before 6 April 2006 and five years for shares issued before 6 April 2000).

Relief on investment

Maximum annual investment:	From 2004–05	£200,000
	1995–96 to 2003–04	£100,000
Rate of relief:	From 2006–07	30%
	2004–05 to 2005–06	40%
	1995–96 to 2003–04	20%

Other reliefs

(a) Dividends on shares within investment limit exempt from income tax (unless the investor's main purpose is tax avoidance – from 9 March 1999) (ITTOIA 2005 s 709).
(b) Capital gains reliefs (see p 44).

Urban Regeneration Companies

Relief is available from 1 April 2003 for expenditure incurred by businesses in making contributions to designated Urban Regeneration Companies (ITTOIA 2005 ss 82, 86; CTA 2009 ss 82, 86).

Individual savings accounts ('ISAs')

(TA 1988 s 333; ITTOIA 2005 ss 694–701; SI 1998/1870; SI 2001/908)

Savers can subscribe to an ISA up to the following limits per tax year.

Overall annual subscription limit	1999–2000 to 2007–08	£7,000	2008–09 to 2009–10*	£7,200	2010–11	£10,200	2011–12	£10,680	2012–13	£11,280
Cash limit	1999–2000 to 2007–08	£3,000	2008–09 to 2009–10*	£3,600	2010–11	£5,100	2011–12	£5,340	2012–13	£5,640
Life insurance limit	1999–2000 to 2004–05	£1,000	2008–09 to 2009–10*	N/A	2010–11	N/A	2011–12	N/A	2012–13	N/A

Before 2008–09 a limit of £4,000 (£3,000 before 2005–06) also applied to stocks and shares held in a mini-ISA. The subscription limit applies to each spouse or civil partner. Shares acquired under an approved share incentive plan, profit sharing scheme or SAYE option scheme may be transferred to a stocks and shares component of an ISA within 90 days without tax consequences. From 2008-09 PEPs are transferred into ISA accounts. For 2012–13 onwards the subscription limits are to be increased each year in line with the consumer prices index.

*For taxpayers aged 50 or over in 2009–10 the limits for 2010–11 apply for 2009–10 also, with effect from 6 October 2009.

Reliefs

(a) Investments under the scheme are free from income tax and capital gains tax. When an investment is transferred to an investor he is deemed to have made a disposal and reacquisition at market value and any notional gain is exempt from capital gains tax.
(b) 10% tax credit paid until 5 April 2004 on dividends from UK equities.
(c) Withdrawals may be made at any time without loss of tax relief.

Junior individual savings accounts (Junior ISAs)

(ITTOIA 2005 s 695A; SI 2011/1780)

A Junior ISA scheme was introduced from November 2011, available to all UK resident children under 18 who do not have a Child Trust Fund account. Children will be able to have one cash and one stocks and shares Junior ISA at any time, with an overall annual contribution limit of £3,600.

Personal equity plans ('PEPs')

(Subscriptions made **before 6 April 1999**: TA 1988 s 333; SI 1989/469; SI 1998/1869)

From 2008–09, all PEP accounts are transferred to ISA accounts.

Before 6 April 1999, subscriptions to PEPs could be made up to a maximum per year of £6,000 to a general plan and £3,000 to a single company plan. Dividend income is tax free and a 10% tax credit was payable until 5 April 2004 on dividends from UK equities. Interest on cash held is paid gross and is tax free if reinvested.

PEPs held at 5 April 1999 can continue to be held with the same tax advantages as an ISA (see above) and without affecting the amount that can be subscribed to an ISA.

National Savings Bank interest

(ITTOIA 2005 s 691; FA 2011 Sch 26)

Before 19 July 2011 the first £70 of any interest received from a National Savings Ordinary Account was tax free. It is not possible to open a new Ordinary Account after 28 January 2004.

Miscellaneous reliefs

Foster carers and shared lives carers (Qualifying care)

(ITTOIA 2005 ss 803–828)

Generally, local authority payments to foster carers are not taxable to the extent they do no more than meet the actual costs of caring. In other cases, for 2003–04 onwards (and for shared lives carers from 6 April 2010):

- where gross receipts do not exceed the 'individual limit' and shared lives care is not being provided to more than three people, the carer is treated as having a nil profit and nil loss for the tax year concerned;
- where gross receipts exceed the 'individual limit' and shared lives care is not being provided to more than three people, the carer can choose to either be taxed on the excess or compute profit or loss using the normal business rules.

The 'individual limit' is made up of a fixed amount of £10,000 per residence for a full tax year plus an amount per adult or child for each week or part week that the individual provides qualifying care. The weekly amounts are £200 for a child under 11 years and £250 for a child of 11 or over and an adult.

For 2010–11 only, shared lives carers could choose to apply the simplified arrangements for adult placement carers.

Gift of pre-eminent objects

Individuals who gift pre-eminent objects to the nation will receive a reduction in their UK tax liability of 30% of the value of the object they are donating. The tax reduction can be against income or capital gains tax and can be spread forward across a period of up to five years starting with the tax year in which the object is offered. Applies from a date to be appointed.

Landlord's energy-saving allowance

(ITTOIA 2005 ss 312–314; CTA 2009 ss 251–253; SI 2007/831; SI 2007/3278; SI 2008/1520)

From 6 April 2004 to 5 April 2015 individual landlords who let residential property and pay income tax may claim a deduction from the property business profits for expenditure in the dwelling-houses let to install:

- loft insulation or cavity wall insulation; or
- (from 7 April 2005) solid wall insulation; or
- (from 6 April 2006) draught-proofing and insulation for hot water systems; or
- (from 6 April 2007) floor insulation.

Expenditure is restricted to £1,500 per building until 5 April 2007 and to £1,500 per dwelling-house from 6 April 2007.

The relief is extended to corporate landlords of residential property for expenditure on or after 8 July 2008.

Life assurance premium relief

(TA 1988 s 266, Sch 14 para 7)

For premiums due and payable before 6 April 2015, or payable before that date and actually paid before 6 July 2015, relief for premiums paid on qualifying life assurance policies for contracts made before 14 March 1984 is available by deduction of 12.5% from admissible premiums.

Maintenance payments

(ITTOIA 2005 ss 727, 729; ITA 2007 ss 453–456)

Where either party to the marriage was born before 6 April 1935 tax relief may be claimed by the payer in respect of the lower of:

- the amount of the payments in the year concerned and
- the minimum amount of the married couple's allowance for the year concerned (see p 74).

The relief is restricted to 10% of the relevant amount. The payment must be made to the divorced or separated spouse. It is made gross and is not taxable in the hands of the recipient.

Rent-a-room relief

(ITTOIA 2005 ss 784–802)

Gross annual receipts from letting furnished accommodation in the only or main home are exempt from tax up to a maximum of £4,250 (provided no other taxable income is derived from a trade, letting or arrangement from which the rent-a-room receipts are derived).

If the gross receipts exceed £4,250, the taxpayer can pay tax on the net receipts after deduction of expenses. Alternatively, the taxpayer can elect to pay tax on the amount by which the gross receipts exceed £4,250, without relief for the actual expenses.

An individual's maximum is halved to £2,125 if during the 'relevant period' for the year (normally the tax year) some other person received income from letting accommodation in that property.

An election can be made to disapply the relief for a particular tax year (for example, if the individual would otherwise make an allowable loss).

Pension provision from 6 April 2006

(FA 2004 ss 149–284, Schs 28–36)

From 6 April 2006, a new pension scheme tax regime fully replaced pre-existing rules for occupational pension schemes, personal (and stakeholder) pension schemes and retirement annuity schemes.

Tax relief on contributions

Individual contributions: Contributions to registered schemes are not limited by reference to a fraction of earnings and there is no earnings cap. There is no provision for the carry-back or carry-forward of contributions to tax years other than the year of payment.

An individual may make unlimited contributions and tax relief is available on contributions up to the higher of:
*   the full amount of relevant earnings; or
*   £3,600 provided the scheme operates tax relief at source.

Employer contributions: Employer contributions to registered schemes are deductible for tax purposes, with statutory provision for spreading abnormally large contributions over a period of up to four years. The contributions are not treated as taxable income of the employee.

Special annual allowance charge: A special annual allowance charge applied for 2009–10 and 2010–11 for individuals with income of £130,000 or over. Tax relief above basic rate is recovered from pension savings above an individual's special annual allowance by the application of the special annual allowance charge. An individual's special annual allowance is the higher of their regular pension savings and £20,000 (or in certain circumstances, where contributions have been less regular than quarterly, £30,000).

Annual allowance

Each individual has an annual allowance as set out in the table below. If the annual increase in an individual's rights under all registered schemes exceeds the annual allowance, the excess is chargeable at the individual's marginal rate (40% for 2010–11 and earlier years). The individual is liable for the tax, unless, for 2011–12 onwards, he makes an election for the scheme to pay the charge if it exceeds £2000. In such cases a consequential adjustment is made to the individual's entitlement to benefits.

Annual allowance	2007–08	2008–09	2009–10	2010–11	2011–12	2012–13
	£225,000	£235,000	£245,000	£255,000	£50,000[1]	**£50,000[1]**

[1] From 2011–12 unused allowance can be carried forward three years. For these purposes the annual allowance for 2008–09 to 2010–11 is assumed to be £50,000.

Taxable benefits

'Tax-free' lump sum: The maximum 'tax-free' lump sum that can be paid to a member under a registered scheme is broadly the lower of:
*   25% of the value of the pension rights; and
*   25% of the member's lifetime allowance.

Lifetime allowance: Each individual has a lifetime allowance for contributions as set out in the table below. The excess over the lifetime allowance of the benefits crystallising (usually when a pension begins to be paid) is taxable at the following rates:
*   55% if taken as a lump sum;
*   25% in other cases.

Any tax due may be deducted from the individual's benefits.

Lifetime allowance	2007–08	2008–09	2009–10	2010–11	2011–12	2012–13
	£1,600,000	£1,650,000	£1,750,000	£1,800,000	£1,800,000	**£1,500,000**

Transitional. There are transitional provisions for the protection of lump sum and other pension rights accrued before 6 April 2006. A new form of protection is also available to protect pension rights from 6 April 2012 when the lifetime allowance is decreased.

Age restrictions

Minimum pension age: The minimum pension age is 55 (50 before 6 April 2010). A pension cannot be paid before the minimum age except on grounds of ill health. Those with existing contractual rights to draw a pension earlier will have those rights protected and there is special protection for members of pre-6 April 2006 approved schemes with early retirement ages. A reduced lifetime allowance will apply in the case of early retirement before minimum pension age except in the case of certain professions such as the police and the armed forces (to be prescribed by regulations).

Maximum benefit age: Before 2011–12 benefits must be taken by the age of 77 at the latest (age 75 before 22 June 2010). A member of a money purchase scheme may take a pension from the age of 77 (previously 75) by way of income withdrawal (known as an 'alternatively secured pension') instead of taking a scheme pension or purchasing a lifetime annuity. The maximum alternatively secured pension is 70% of a comparable annuity. These requirements are withdrawn for 2011–12 onwards.

Share schemes

Share incentive plans ('SIPs')

(TCGA 1992 ss 236A, 238A, Schs 7C, 7D Pt 1; ITEPA 2003 ss 488–515, Sch 2; FA 2003 s 139, Sch 21) Applications for approval of Share Incentive Plans could be made from 28 July 2000.

Free share plan

2000–01 onwards	*annual maximum*	£3,000

Partnership share plan

2000–01 to 2002–03	*monthly maximum*	£125 or 10% of monthly salary if lower
2003–04 onwards	*annual maximum*	£1,500 or 10% of annual salary if lower

Matching shares

2000–01 onwards	*Maximum number of shares given by employer to employee for each partnership share bought*	2

Shares are free of tax and NICs if held in the plan for five years. Dividends up to £1,500 per employee per tax year are tax free if reinvested in shares. Shares withdrawn from the plan at any time are exempt from capital gains tax and are treated as acquired by the employee at their market value at that time.

If shares are withdrawn within between three and five years (with exceptions such as on death, disability, normal retirement or redundancy), liability to income tax and NICs arises on the lower of their value on entering and on leaving the plan. If shares are withdrawn within three years (with similar exceptions), liability is on their value on leaving the plan.

Enterprise management incentives

(TCGA 1992 s 238A, Sch 7D Pt 4; ITEPA 2003 ss 527–541, Sch 5)

Certain independent trading companies with gross assets not exceeding £30 million may grant share options then worth up to £250,000 (from a date set out in a statutory instrument, subject to state aid approval — previously £120,000, and £100,000 for options granted before 6 April 2008) to an eligible employee. The total value of shares in respect of which unexercised qualifying options exist must not exceed £3 million. An additional restriction, limiting the scheme to companies with fewer than 250 full-time equivalent employees, applies to options granted on or after 21 July 2008.

Where the conditions of the scheme are complied with:

(a) There is no charge to tax or NICs when the option is granted provided the option to acquire the shares is not at less than their market values at that date, and there is no charge on exercise providing the option is exercised within ten years.

(b) Capital gains tax will be payable when the shares are sold, though the Government intends to legislate in Finance Bill 2013 so that gains made on shares acquired through exercising EMI options on or after 6 April 2012 will be eligible for capital gains tax entrepreneurs' relief.

Approved save as you earn (SAYE) share option schemes

(TCGA 1992 s 238A, Sch 7D Pt 2; ITEPA 2003 ss 516–519, Sch 3; FA 2003 s 139, Sch 21)

The scheme is linked to an approved savings scheme, on which bonuses are exempt from tax, to provide funds for the acquisition of shares when the option is exercised at the end of a three or five-year contract. A five-year contract may offer the option of repayment on the seventh anniversary.

Monthly contributions to SAYE scheme

Minimum	£5–£10[1]
Maximum	£250

[1] The company may choose a minimum savings contribution between £5 and £10.

See the Treasury website (www.hm-treasury.gov.uk) for the bonus rates.

Where the conditions of the scheme are complied with, no income tax charge arises on the employee in respect of:

(a) the grant of an option to acquire shares at a discount of up to 20% of the share price at time of the grant;

(b) the exercise of the option (options must not be exercised before the bonus date subject to cessation of employment due to injury, disability, redundancy, retirement or death); or

(c) any increase in the value of the shares.

Capital gains tax is chargeable on disposal of the shares: the CGT base cost is the consideration given by the employee for both the shares and the option.

Company share option plans ('CSOPs')

(TCGA 1992 s 238A, Sch 7D Pt 3; ITEPA 2003 ss 521–526, Sch 4; FA 2003 s 139, Sch 21)

Limit on value of shares under option held by employee at any one time

From 29 April 1996	£30,000

Scheme shares must be fully paid up, not redeemable and not subject to special restrictions. Only full-time directors or qualifying employees may participate in the scheme.

Where the conditions of the scheme are complied with, no tax charge arises on the employee in respect of:

(a) the grant of an option to acquire shares[1];

(b) the exercise of the option[2]; or

(c) any increase in the value of the shares.

Capital gains tax is chargeable on disposal of the shares: the CGT base cost is the consideration given by the employee for both the shares and the option.

[1] At the time the option is granted the price at which shares can be acquired must not be less than the market value of shares of the same class at that time.

[2] The option must be exercised between three and ten years after the grant (or may be exercised less than three years after the grant where the individual ceases to be an employee due to injury, disablement, redundancy or retirement). For options granted before 9 April 2003, the options must be exercised between three and ten years after the grant (without exception) and not less than three years after a previous exempt exercise of another option under the same or another approved company share option scheme.

Tax credits

From 6 April 2003, child tax credit and working tax credit replaced children's tax credit, working families' tax credit and disabled person's tax credit in addition to the child-related elements of certain social security benefits. Administered and paid by HMRC, they are non-taxable. Claims must be made after the commencement of the tax year and can be backdated for a maximum of one month (three months before 6 April 2012). Claims must be renewed by 31 July.

Child tax credit and working tax credit

	2012–13 Annual amount	2011–12 Annual amount
Child tax credit	£	£
Family element[1]	545	545
Child element (for each child or young person)	2,690	2,555
Addition for disabled child or young person	2,950	2,800
Enhancement for severe disabled child or young person	1,190	1,130
Working tax credit	£	£
Basic element	1,920	1,920
Lone parent and couple element	1,950	1,950
30-hour element	790	790
Disability element	2,790	2,650
Severe disability element	1,190	1,130
50+ element – 16–29 hours worked[2]	NIL	1,365

	2012–13 Annual amount	2011–12 Annual amount
50+ element – 30 or more hours worked[2]	NIL	2,030
Childcare element – up to 70% (80% for 2006–07 to 2010–11) of eligible costs	Weekly	Weekly
– maximum eligible cost for one child	175	175
– maximum eligible cost for two or more children	300	300

[1] Only one family element per family. Before 2011–12, baby element payable in addition in the first year of the child's life.

[2] Where an individual qualifies for the 50+ (30+ hours) payment, they cannot also qualify for the 50+ (16–29 hours) payment. The 50+ element is withdrawn from 6 April 2012.

Income thresholds and withdrawal rates	2012–13	2011–12
First income threshold for those entitled to CTC and WTC	£6,420	£6,420
First withdrawal rate	41%	41%
Second income threshold	N/A	£40,000
Second withdrawal rate	N/A	41%
First threshold for those entitled to CTC only	£15,860	£15,860
Income rise disregarded	£10,000	£10,000
Income fall disregard	£2,500	N/A

Calculation of award. Tax credits are awarded on an annual basis. They are initially based on the income of the claimant or joint claimants for the preceding tax year and then adjusted based on actual income in the tax year in which the credit is claimed. Income broadly includes all taxable income excluding the first £300 of income from pensions, savings, property or foreign assets. If actual income is greater than the previous year's income by less than £10,000 (£25,000 before 2011–12), the award is not adjusted. If actual income is less than the previous year's income or if it is greater than the previous year's income by £10,000 or more (£25,000 from 2006–07 to 2010–11), the award is adjusted to reflect actual income. Where circumstances change during a tax year and different rates apply, the award is recalculated on a proportional, daily basis. Such changes must be notified to HMRC within one month if tax credit entitlement will be reduced as a result. Before April 2007, this time limit was three months. An income fall disregard of £2,500 is introduced from 6 April 2012. This means that from 2012–13, where previous year's income exceeds the current year's income by not more than £2,500, the previous year's income will be used, but where the previous year's income exceeds the current year's income by more than £2,500, the current year's income plus £2,500 will be used.

Eligibility. CTC is payable to UK resident single parents and couples responsible for a child or young person. WTC is payable to UK residents who are at least 16 years old and who work at least 16 hours a week (or in the case of a couple, one of whom works at least 16 hours a week and, from 6 April 2012, who jointly work at least 24 hours a week). Additionally, the claimant (or one of them if a couple) must either:

- be at least 25 years old and work at least 30 hours a week; or
- have a dependent child or children; or
- before 6 April 2012, be over 50 and qualify for the 50+ element; or
- have a mental or physical disability which puts them at a disadvantage in getting a job and have previously been in receipt of some form of disability benefit; or
- from 6 April 2011, be over 60 and work at least 16 hours a week, regardless of whether they have dependent children.

Renewal claim. Claims for tax credit must be renewed by 31 July.

Inheritance tax

Rates of tax

(IHTA 1984 s 7, Schs 1, 1A; HMRC Inheritance Tax Manual IHTM14544)

From 15 March 1988 onwards

	Rate
Cumulative gross transfer rate:	
for gross transfers on death over the cumulative chargeable transfer limit	40%
reduced rate for estates leaving 10% or more to charity for deaths on or after 6 April 2012	36%[1]
for gross lifetime transfers over the cumulative chargeable transfer limit	20%
Grossing-up net transfer rate for each £1 over the chargeable transfer limit:	
for net transfers on death not bearing own tax	$^2/_3$
for net lifetime transfers	$^1/_4$

[1] For deaths occurring on or after 6 April 2012 a reduced rate of 36% is introduced where at least 10% of the net estate is left to charity.

Cumulative chargeable transfer limits

Period	Limit	Period	Limit
	£		£
2012–13	**325,000[1]**		
2011–12	325,000	1999–2000	231,000
2010–11	325,000	1998–99	223,000
2009–10	325,000	1997–98	215,000
2008–09	312,000	1996–97	200,000
2007–08	300,000	1995–96	154,000
2006–07	285,000	10.3.92–5.4.95	150,000
2005–06	275,000	6.4.91–9.3.92	140,000
2004–05	263,000	1990–91	128,000
2003–04	255,000	1989–90	118,000
2002–03	250,000	15.3.88–5.4.89	110,000
2001–02	242,000	17.3.87–14.3.88	90,000
2000–01	234,000	18.3.86–16.3.87	71,000

Capital transfer tax nil rate bands

Period	Limit	Period	Limit
	£		£
6.4.85–17.3.86	67,000	26.3.80–8.3.82	50,000
13.3.84–5.4.85	64,000	27.10.77–25.3.80	25,000
15.3.83–12.3.84	60,000	13.3.75–26.10.77	15,000
9.3.82–14.3.83	55,000		

Estate duty nil rate bands (England, Scotland and Wales)

Period	Limit	Period	Limit
	£		£
22.3.72–12.3.75	15,000	9.4.62–3.4.63	4,000
31.3.71–21.3.72	12,500	30.7.54–8.4.62	3,000
16.4.69–30.3.71	10,000	10.4.46–29.7.54	2,000
4.4.63–15.4.69	5,000	16.8.14–9.4.46	100

[1] Any nil-rate band which is unused on a person's death can be transferred to their surviving spouse or civil partner for the purposes of the charge to tax on the death of the survivor on or after 9 October 2007.

Delivery of accounts: due dates

(IHTA 1984 s 216)

Type of transfer	Due date
Chargeable lifetime transfers	Later of: (*a*) 12 months after the end of the month in which the transfer took place; and (*b*) three months after the date on which the person delivering the account became liable
PETs which become chargeable	12 months after the end of the month in which the transferor died
Gifts with reservation chargeable on death	12 months after the end of the month in which the death occurred
Transfers on death	Later of: (*a*) 12 months after the end of the month in which the death occurred; and (*b*) three months after the date on which the personal representatives first act or the person liable first has reason to believe that he is liable to deliver an account
National heritage property	Six months after the end of the month in which the chargeable event occurred

Delivery of accounts: excepted transfers and estates

(SI 2002/1733; SI 2004/2543; SI 2008/606)

Date of transfer or death	6 April 2000–5 April 2002	6 April 2002–5 April 2003	6 April 2003–31 Aug 2006	From 1 Sept 2006
Excepted transfers:	*Value below*	*Value below*	*Value below*	*Value below*
Total chargeable transfers since 6 April	£10,000	£10,000	£10,000	£10,000
Total chargeable transfers during last ten years	£40,000	£40,000	£40,000	£40,000
Excepted estates:				
Total gross value[1]	£210,000	£220,000	(see (*a*) below)	(see (*a*) below)
Total gross value of property outside UK	£50,000	£75,000	£75,000	£100,000
Aggregate value of 'specified transfers'[2]	£75,000	£100,000	£100,000	£150,000
Settled property passing on death	–	£100,000	£100,000	£150,000

For chargeable transfers after 5 April 2007, no account need be delivered where:
(i) the transfer is of cash or quoted shares or securities and the value of the transfer and other chargeable transfers made in the preceding seven years does not exceed the IHT threshold; or
(ii) the value of the transfer and other chargeable transfers made in the preceding seven years does not exceed 80% of the IHT threshold and the value of the transfer does not exceed the net amount of the threshold available to the transferor at the time of the transfer.

For footnotes see the list below.

Excepted estates

For deaths occurring after 5 April 2004, no account need be delivered where the deceased died domiciled in the UK provided either conditions (a) or (b) below are met, and both conditions (c) and (d) below are met.

- (a) the aggregate of the gross value of the estate, and of any 'specified transfers'[2] or 'specified exempt transfers'[3] does not exceed the appropriate IHT threshold[4];
- (b) the aggregate of the gross value of the estate, and of any 'specified transfers'[2] or 'specified exempt transfers'[3] does not exceed £1,000,000; for deaths after 28 February 2011 at least part of the estate passes to the person's spouse, civil partner or to a charity; and after deducting from that aggregate figure any exempt spouse, civil partner and charity transfers and total estate liabilities, it does not exceed the appropriate IHT threshold[4];
- (c) the gross value of settled property or foreign assets do not exceed the limits in the above table; and
- (d) there were no chargeable lifetime transfers in the seven years before death other than specified transfers not exceeding the limits in the above table[5].

For deaths occurring after 31 August 2006 and before 6 April 2011, an estate will not be an excepted estate if the provisions for alternatively secured pension funds in IHTA 1984 ss 151A–151C (now repealed) apply by reason of the individual's death.

For deaths after 5 April 2002 and before 6 April 2004, no account need be delivered where the deceased died domiciled in the UK provided that:

- (i) the aggregate of the gross value of the estate, and of any 'specified transfers' does not exceed the limits in the above table; and
- (ii) the gross value of settled property or foreign assets do not exceed the limits in the above table; and
- (iii) there were no chargeable lifetime transfers in the seven years before death other than specified transfers not exceeding the limits in the above table.

Where the deceased was never domiciled in the UK, no account need be delivered for deaths after 5 April 2002 provided that:

- the value of the estate in the UK is wholly attributable to cash and quoted shares and securities not exceeding £150,000 (£100,000 before 1 September 2006); and
- for deaths occurring after 31 August 2006, the provisions for alternatively secured pension funds in IHTA 1984 ss 151A–151C do not apply by reason of the individual's death.

1   See table above — This limit applies to the aggregate gross value of the estate and of 'specified transfers' and 'specified exempt transfers'. For deaths after 28 February 2011 transfers treated as normal expenditure out of income made within 7 years before death and totalling more than £3,000 in any tax year will be treated as chargeable transfers for these purposes.

2   'Specified transfers' are chargeable transfers of cash, quoted shares and securities and, after 6 April 2002, interests in or over land and, after 5 April 2004, personal chattels or corporeal moveable property. For deaths after 28 February 2011 transfers treated as normal expenditure out of income made within 7 years before death and totalling more than £3,000 in any tax year will be treated as chargeable transfers for these purposes.

3   'Specified exempt transfers' are transfers in the seven years before death between spouses or civil partners, gifts to charity, political parties or housing associations, transfers to maintenance funds for historical buildings, etc or to employee trusts.

4   For deaths after 5 April 2010 the IHT threshold for these purposes is increased by 100% where—
- (a) the deceased is a surviving spouse or civil partner;
- (b) a claim has been made for the transfer of the unused nil-rate band of their deceased spouse or civil partner;
- (c) all of the first deceased spouse's or civil partner's nil-rate band was unused; and
- (d) the first deceased met certain other criteria similar to those listed above for excepted estates.

5   For deaths after 28 February 2011 transfers treated as normal expenditure out of income made within 7 years before death and totalling more than £3,000 in any tax year will be treated as chargeable transfers for these purposes.

Excepted settlements

No account need be delivered of property comprised in an excepted settlement (i.e. one with no qualifying interest in possession) where a chargeable event occurs after 5 April 2007 and cash not exceeding £1,000 is the only property comprised in the settlement. Other conditions to be fulfilled are that, the settlor has not provided further property, the trustees are UK resident throughout the settlement's existence and there are no related settlements.

Reliefs

The following is a summary of the main reliefs and exemptions under the Inheritance Tax Act 1984 (Parts II and V). The legislation should be referred to for conditions and exceptions.

Agricultural property

Transfer with vacant possession (or right to obtain it within 12 months); transfer on or after 1 September 1995, of land let (or treated as let) on or after that date.   100% of agricultural value

Any other case.   50% of agricultural value

Note: The 100% relief is extended in limited circumstances by Concession F17.

Annual gifts	£3,000

Business property

Unincorporated business.	100%		
Unquoted shares (including shares in AIM or USM companies) (held for 2 years or more).[1]	100%	Controlling holding in fully quoted companies.	50%
Unquoted securities which alone, or together with other such securities and unquoted shares, give the transferor control of the company (held for 2 years or more).[1]	100%	Land, buildings, machinery or plant used in business of company or partnership.	50%
Settled property used in life tenant's business.	100%		

[1] Tax charges arising and transfers occurring after 5 April 1996. 10 March 1992–5 April 1996 minority holding of shares or securities of up to 25% in unquoted or USM company qualified for 50% relief; larger holdings qualified for 100% relief.

Charities, gifts to	Exempt

From 1 April 2002, Community Amateur Sports Clubs are treated as charities.

Marriage gifts

Made by:	parent	£5,000
	remoter ancestor	£2,500
	party to marriage	£2,500
	other person	£1,000

National purposes

Property given or bequeathed to bodies listed in IHTA 1984 Sch 3.	Exempt
Political parties, gifts to	Exempt

Potentially exempt transfers

Exempt if made 7 or more years before the date of death. Except for gifts with reservation etc, they include:
- (a)   transfers by individuals to other individuals or certain trusts for the disabled;
- (b)   transfers after 21 March 2006 by individuals to a bereaved minor's trust on the coming to an end of an immediate post-death interest;
- (c)   transfers before 22 March 2006 by individuals to accumulation and maintenance trusts;
- (d)   transfers by individuals into interest in possession trusts in which, for transfers after 21 March 2006, the beneficiary has a disabled person's interest; and
- (e)   certain transfers on the termination or disposal of an individual's beneficial interest in possession in settled property (in restricted circumstances following FA 2006).

Quick succession relief

Estate increased by chargeable transfer followed by death within 5 years.

Death within 1st year.	100%
Each additional year: decreased by	20%

Small gifts to same person £250

Spouses/civil partners with separate domicile (one not being in the UK)

Total exemption. £55,000

Tapering relief

The value of the estate on death is taxed as the top slice of cumulative transfers in the 7 years before death. Transfers on or within 7 years of death are taxed on their value at the date of the gift on the death rate scale, but using the scale in force at the date of death, subject to the following taper:

Years between gift and death	Percentage of full charge at death rates
0–3	100
3–4	80
4–5	60
5–6	40
6–7	20

Penalties see p 14.

104

National insurance contributions

From 6 April 2012

Class 1 contributions[1]

Earnings limits and threshold	Weekly £	Monthly £	Yearly £
Lower earnings limit	107	464	5,564
Secondary threshold[3]	144	624	7,488
Primary threshold[3]	146	634	7,605
Upper earnings limit	817	3,540	42,475
Upper accruals point	770	3,337	40,040

		Not contracted out	Contracted out *Salary-related schemes[5]*
Employees' contributions			
Weekly earnings:	Over £146.01–770	12%	10.6%
	£770.01–£817	12%	12%
	Over £817	2%	2%
	– rebate £107–£146		1.4%[2, 5]
Employers' contributions[4]			
Weekly earnings:	£144.01–£770	13.8%	10.4%
	£770–817	13.8%	13.8%
	Over £817	13.8%	13.8%
	– rebate £107–£144		3.4%[2, 5]
Women at reduced rate			
Employees' contributions			
Weekly earnings:	£146.01–£817	5.85%	
	Over £817	2%	
Employers' contributions	Normal employers' contributions apply as above		

Class 1A and Class 1B contributions	13.8%

[1] Employees' rates are nil for children under 16 and those over state pensionable age but employers' contributions are still payable. Employees' NICs are not payable on earnings up to the primary threshold, employers' NICs are not payable on earnings up to the secondary threshold.

[2] The rebate is given on earnings between the lower earnings limit and the primary threshold for employees, and between the lower earnings limit and the secondary threshold for employers. The rebate for employees is given to employers to the extent that insufficient contributions have been paid by the employee for offset.

[3] From 6 April 2011 the primary threshold applies for employees' contributions and the secondary threshold applies for employers' contributions.

[4] An employer NIC 'holiday' applies to new businesses started in certain regions between 22 June 2010 and 5 September 2013. Between 6 September 2010 and 5 September 2013 the businesses may qualify for a deduction of up to £5,000 of their employer Class 1 contributions for each of the first ten employees hired in the first year of business.

[5] For 2012 to 2017 the rebates for defined benefit schemes (salary-related schemes) are reduced to 3.4% for employers and 1.4% for employees. Contracting out on a defined contribution basis (money purchase schemes) is abolished from 6 April 2012. Contracting out via a personal pension plan is also not possible from 6 April 2012.

From 6 April 2011–5 April 2012

Class 1 contributions[1]				
Earnings limits and threshold		Weekly £	Monthly £	Yearly £
Lower earnings limit		102	442	5,304
Secondary threshold[3]		136	589	7,072
Primary threshold[3]		139	602	7,225
Upper earnings limit		817	3,540	42,475
Upper accruals point		770	3,337	40,040

		Not contracted out	Contracted out	
Employees' contributions				
Weekly earnings:	Over £139.01–770	12%	10.4%	
	£770.01–£817	12%	12%	
	Over £817	2%	2%	
	– rebate £102–£139		1.6%[2, 5]	

		Not contracted out	Salary-related schemes	Money purchase schemes
Employers' contributions[4]				
Weekly earnings:	£136.01–£770	13.8%	10.1%	12.4%
	£770–£817	13.8%	13.8%	13.8%
	Over £817	13.8%	13.8%	13.8%
	– rebate £102–£136		3.7%[2]	1.4%[2]

Women at reduced rate			
Employees' contributions			
Weekly earnings:	£139.01–£817	5.85%	
	Over £817	2%	
Employers' contributions	Normal employers' contributions apply as above		

Class 1A and Class 1B contributions	13.8%

[1] Employees' rates are nil for children under 16 and those over state pensionable age but employers' contributions are still payable. Employees' NICs are not payable on earnings up to the primary threshold, employers' NICs are not payable on earnings up to the secondary threshold.

[2] The rebate is given on earnings between the lower earnings limit and the primary threshold for employees, and between the lower earnings limit and the secondary threshold for employers. The rebate for employees is given to employers to the extent that insufficient contributions have been paid by the employee for offset.

[3] From 6 April 2011 the primary threshold applies for employees' contributions and the secondary threshold applies for employers' contributions.

[4] An employer NIC 'holiday' applies to new businesses started in certain regions between 22 June 2010 and 5 September 2013. Between 6 September 2010 and 5 September 2013 the businesses may qualify for a deduction of up to £5,000 of their employer Class 1 contributions for each of the first ten employees hired in the first year of business.

From 6 April 2010–5 April 2011

Class 1 contributions[1]				
Earnings limits and threshold		Weekly £	Monthly £	Yearly £
Lower earnings limit		97	421	5,044
Earnings threshold		110	476	5,715
Upper earnings limit		844	3,656	43,875
Upper accruals point		770	3,337	40,040
Not contracted out		Employees' contributions		Employers' contributions
Weekly earnings:	£110.01–£844	11%		12.8%
	Over £844	1%		12.8%
Contracted out			Salary-related schemes	Money purchase schemes
Weekly earnings:	£110.01–£770	9.4%	9.1%	11.4%
	£770–£844	11%	12.8%	12.8%
	Over £844	1%	12.8%	12.8%
	– rebate £97–£110	1.6%[2]	3.7%	1.4%
Women at reduced rate				
Weekly earnings:	£110.01–£844	4.85%	*as above*	
	Over £844	1%	*as above*	
Class 1A and Class 1B contributions				12.8%

[1] Employees' rates are nil for children under 16 and those over state pensionable age but employers' contributions are still payable. NICs are not payable on earnings up to the earnings threshold.

[2] The rebate is given on earnings between the lower earnings limit and the earnings threshold. The rebate for employees is given to employers to the extent that insufficient contributions have been paid by the employee for offset.

6 April 2009–5 April 2010

Class 1 contributions[1]				
Earnings limits and threshold		Weekly £	Monthly £	Yearly £
Lower earnings limit		95	412	4,940
Earnings threshold		110	476	5,715
Upper earnings limit		844	3,656	43,875
Upper accruals point		770	3,337	40,040
Not contracted out		Employees' contributions		Employers' contributions
Weekly earnings:	£110.01–£844	11%		12.8%
	Over £844	1%		12.8%
Contracted out			Salary-related schemes	Money purchase schemes
Weekly earnings:	£110.01–£770	9.4%	9.1%	11.4%
	£770–£844	11%	12.8%	12.8%
	Over £844	1%	12.8%	12.8%
	– rebate £95–£110	1.6%[2]	3.7%	1.4%
Women at reduced rate				
Weekly earnings:	£110.01–£844	4.85%	*as above*	
	Over £844	1%	*as above*	
Class 1A and Class 1B contributions				12.8%

[1] Employees' rates are nil for children under 16, men over 65 and women over 60 but employers' contributions are still payable. NICs are not payable on earnings up to the earnings threshold.

[2] The rebate is given on earnings between the lower earnings limit and the earnings threshold. The rebate for employees is given to employers to the extent that insufficient contributions have been paid by the employee for offset.

6 April 2008–5 April 2009

Class 1 contributions[1]				
Earnings limits and threshold		Weekly £	Monthly £	Yearly £
Lower earnings limit		90	390	4,680
Earnings threshold		105	453	5,435
Upper earnings limit		770	3,337	40,040
Not contracted out		**Employees' contributions**		**Employers' contributions**
Weekly earnings:	£105.01–£770	11%		12.8%
	Over £770	1%		12.8%
Contracted out			*Salary-related schemes*	*Money purchase schemes*
Weekly earnings:	£105.01–£770	9.4%	9.1%	11.4%
	Over £770	1%	12.8%	12.8%
	– rebate £90–£105	1.6%[2]	3.7%	1.4%
Women at reduced rate				
Weekly earnings:	£105.01–£770	4.85%	as above	
	Over £770	1%	as above	
Class 1A and Class 1B contributions				12.8%

[1] Employees' rates are nil for children under 16, men over 65 and women over 60 but employers' contributions are still payable. NICs are not payable on earnings up to the earnings threshold.
[2] The rebate is given on earnings between the lower earnings limit and the earnings threshold. The rebate for employees is given to employers to the extent that insufficient contributions have been paid by the employee for offset.

6 April 2007–5 April 2008

Class 1 contributions[1]				
Earnings limits and threshold		Weekly £	Monthly £	Yearly £
Lower earnings limit		87	377	4,524
Earnings threshold		100	435	5,225
Upper earnings limit		670	2,904	34,840
Not contracted out		**Employees' contributions**		**Employers' contributions**
Weekly earnings:	£100.01–£670	11%		12.8%
	Over £670	1%		12.8%
Contracted out			*Salary-related schemes*	*Money purchase schemes*
Weekly earnings:	£100.01–£670	9.4%	9.1%	11.4%
	Over £670	1%	12.8%	12.8%
	– rebate £87–£100	1.6%[2]	3.7%	1.4%
Women at reduced rate				
Weekly earnings:	£100.01–£670	4.85%	as above	
	Over £670	1%	as above	
Class 1A and Class 1B contributions				12.8%

[1] Employees' rates are nil for children under 16, men over 65 and women over 60 but employers' contributions are still payable. NICs are not payable on earnings up to the earnings threshold.
[2] The rebate is given on earnings between the lower earnings limit and the earnings threshold. The rebate for employees is given to employers to the extent that insufficient contributions have been paid by the employee for offset.

Class 2, 3 and 4 contributions

	2012–13	2011–12	2010–11
Class 2 (self-employed)			
Flat rate—per week	£2.65	£2.50	£2.40
Share fishermen—per week	£3.30	£3.15	£3.05
Volunteer development workers—per week	£5.35	£5.10	£4.85
Small earning exception—per year	£5,595	£5,315	£5,075
Class 3 (voluntary contributions)			
Flat rate—per week	£13.25	£12.60	£12.05
Class 4 (self-employed)[1]			
Lower annual profits limit	£7,605	£7,225	£5,715
Upper annual profits limit	£42,475	£42,475	£43,875
Rate between lower and upper limits	9%	9%	8%
Rate on profits above upper limit	2%	2%	1%
Maximum contributions			
Class 1 or Class 1/Class 2[2]	£4,267.56	£4,312.08	£4,279.22
– plus rate on earnings above upper limit	2%	2%	1%
Class 4 limiting amount[3]	£3,278.75	£3,305.00	£3,180.00
– plus rate on profits above upper limit	2%	2%	1%

[1] Not payable if pensionable age is reached by the beginning of the tax year.
[2] Where an earner has more than one employment (including self-employment), liability for Class 1 or Class 1 and Class 2 contributions cannot exceed a maximum amount equal to 53 employees' Class 1 contributions at the maximum standard rate, plus, from 2003–04 onwards, 2% (1% before 2011–12) on earnings over the individual's upper earnings limit (which varies depending on individual circumstances).
[3] Where Class 4 contributions are payable in addition to Class 1 and/or Class 2 contributions, liability for Class 4 contributions cannot exceed such an amount as, when added to the Class 1/Class 2 contributions payable (after applying the maximum if appropriate), equals the limiting amount. The limiting amount is the maximum Class 4 contributions payable (including, from 2003–04 onwards, 2% (1% before 2011–12) on earnings over the upper profit limit) plus 53 Class 2 contributions. If a contributor expects to exceed this amount he may apply for deferment of Class 4 contributions for the year in question. Deferment has no effect on the 2% (1% before 2011–12) payable on earnings over the upper profit limit, which is still payable.

	2009–10	2008–09	2007–08
Class 2 (self-employed)			
Flat rate—per week	£2.40	£2.30	£2.20
Share fishermen—per week	£3.05	£2.95	£2.85
Volunteer development workers—per week	£4.75	£4.50	£4.35
Small earning exception—per year	£5,075	£4,825	£4,635
Class 3 (voluntary contributions)			
Flat rate—per week	£12.05	£8.10	£7.80
Class 4 (self-employed)[1]			
Lower annual profits limit	£5,715	£5,435	£5,225
Upper annual profits limit	£43,875	£40,040	£34,840
Rate between lower and upper limits	8%	8%	8%
Rate on profits above upper limit	1%	1%	1%
Maximum contributions			
Class 1 or Class 1/Class 2[2]	£4,279.22	£3,876.95	£3,323.10
– plus rate on earnings above upper limit	1%	1%	1%
Class 4 limiting amount[3]	£3,180.00	£2,890.30	£2,485.80
– plus rate on profits above upper limit	1%	1%	1%

[1] Not payable if pensionable age is reached by the beginning of the tax year.
[2] Where an earner has more than one employment (including self-employment), liability for Class 1 or Class 1 and Class 2 contributions cannot exceed a maximum amount equal to 53 employees' Class 1 contributions at the maximum standard rate, plus, from 2003–04 onwards, 1% on earnings over the individual's upper earnings limit (which varies depending on individual circumstances).
[3] Where Class 4 contributions are payable in addition to Class 1 and/or Class 2 contributions, liability for Class 4 contributions cannot exceed such an amount as, when added to the Class 1/Class 2 contributions payable (after applying the maximum if appropriate), equals the limiting amount. The limiting amount is the maximum Class 4 contributions payable (including, from 2003–04 onwards, 1% on earnings over the upper profit limit) plus 53 Class 2 contributions. If a contributor expects to exceed this amount he may apply for deferment of Class 4 contributions for the year in question. Deferment has no effect on the 1% payable on earnings over the upper profit limit, which is still payable.

Employers' contributions: benefits in kind

Class 1A national insurance contributions are payable by employers on most taxable benefits in kind, excluding benefits:

(1)	which are covered by a dispensation;
(2)	included in a PAYE settlement agreement;
(3)	provided to employees not earning more than £8,500 pa (including benefits in kind and expenses payments);
(4)	otherwise not required to be included on a P11D;
(5)	on which Class 1 national insurance contributions were due.

Class 1B contributions are payable by employers by reference to the value of any items included in a PAYE settlement agreement (PSA) which would otherwise be earnings for Class 1 or Class 1A, including the amount of tax paid. Income tax and Class 1B contributions on a PSA are payable by 19 October after the end of the tax year to which the PSA relates (or 22 October if paid electronically).

Common benefits subject to Class 1 and Class 1A NICs (CWG5 2012)

Benefit		NICs Class	PAYE or P11D
Assets transferred to employees but not readily convertible assets		1A	P11D
Assets placed at employee's disposal for mixed business and private use		1A	P11D
Car fuel supplied for private motoring in company car		1A	P11D
Car/van fuel supplied for private motoring in privately owned car	– supplied using company credit card, garage account, agency card or employer's own fuel pump	1A	P11D
	– any other circumstances	1	P11D
Cars available for private use		1A	P11D
Car parking facilities other than at or near place of work or as part of business travel		1A	P11D
Car parking fees paid for or reimbursed to employee other than at or near place of work or as part of business travel		1	P11D
Childcare where employer contracts with provider and either the value exceeds the permitted maximum or the qualifying conditions are not met		1A	P11D
Childcare where employee reimbursed or additional salary provided to meet cost		1	PAYE
Christmas boxes	– cash	1	PAYE
	– goods	1A	P11D
Clothing and uniforms			
– cash payment to employee for clothing that can be worn at any time		1	PAYE or P11D[1]
– clothing provided by employer that can be worn at any time		1A	P11D
Council tax, unless employee provided with living accommodation which is not a benefit		1	P11D
Credit and charge cards – personal expenses not reimbursed		1	P11D
Entertaining — staff expenses/ allowances	– employer contract with provider	1A	P11D
	– employee contract with provider	1	PAYE or P11D[1]
Expenses not covered by dispensation — any profit element in payment		1	P11D[4]
Food, groceries, farm produce	– employer contract with provider	1A	P11D
	– employee contract with provider	1	PAYE or P11D[1]
Goods transferred to employee	– employer contract with provider	1A	P11D
	– employee contract with provider	1	PAYE or P11D[1]
Holidays	– employer contract with provider	1A	P11D
	– employee contract with provider, or holiday vouchers	1	PAYE or P11D[1]
Income tax paid but not deducted from employee, or paid on notional payments not borne by employee within 90 days of receipt of each notional payment		1	P11D
Insurance premiums for pensions etc on employee's death or retirement, employee contract with provider		1	PAYE or P11D[1]
Living accommodation (beneficial)		1A	P11D
Loans	– non-qualifying	1A	P11D
	– written off	1	P11D

Benefit		NICs Class	PAYE or P11D
Meals vouchers other than 15p a day of value		1	P11D
Meals provided other than at canteen or at business premises open to all staff on a reasonable scale where all employees may obtain free or subsidised meal		1A	P11D
Medical, dental insurance or treatment provided in the UK by employer	– employer contract with provider	1A	P11D
	– employee contract with provider	1	PAYE or P11D[1]
Mobile phone[5] — cost of private calls, employee contract with provider		1	PAYE or P11D[1]
Personal bills		1	PAYE or P11D[1]
Readily convertible assets[2]		1	PAYE
Relocation payments	– qualifying over £8,000	1A	P11D
	– non-qualifying benefits or qualifying expenses paid after relevant day	1A	P11D
	– non-qualifying expenses	1	P11D
Round sum allowances (not identified as business expense)		1	P11D
Scholarships awarded to students because of parent's employment or payment of school fees	– employer contract with provider	1A	P11D
	– employee contract with provider	1	PAYE or P11D[1]
Social functions unless ITEPA 2003 s 264 satisfied		1A	P11D
Sporting or recreational facilities unless ITEPA 2003 s 261 satisfied		1A	P11D
Subscriptions, professional and fees not allowable as tax deduction	– employer contract with provider	1A	P11D
	– employee contract with provider	1	PAYE or P11D[1]
Telephones	– employer contract with provider, unless private use is insignificant or employee reimburses cost of all private calls	1A	P11D
	– employee contract with provider, unless used exclusively for business. If mixed use, not applicable to business calls if supported by evidence	1	PAYE or P11D[1]
Training payments	– employer contract with provider, unless work-related or encouraged by employer	1A	P11D
	– employee contract with provider, unless work-related or encouraged by employer	1	PAYE or P11D[1]
Vans available for commuting and other private use		1A[3]	P11D
Van fuel provided for use in van available for commuting and other private use		1A[3]	P11D
Vouchers (other than exceptions for childcare, meals, etc)		1	P11D

[1] Payments by employer to provider should be entered on P11D. Reimbursements to the employee are subject to PAYE.

[2] See detailed information in HMRC booklet CWG2(2012) para 34.

[3] No Class 1A due if van is available mainly for employee's business travel and commuting and other private use is insignificant.

[4] Specific and distinct business expenses within the payments should be recorded in appropriate section of P11D.

[5] No limit to number of mobile phones which employer can contract to provide NIC free solely for business with insignificant private use. Only one mobile per employee NIC free for private use where employer contracts.

Overseas

Average rates of exchange

Average for year ending	31.03.10	31.12.10	31.03.11	31.12.11	31.03.12
Abu Dhabi (Dirham)	5.8497	5.6727	5.7021	5.8887	5.8691
Afghanistan (Afghani)	not listed	69.192	68.543	69.079	69.855
Albania (Lek)	not listed	160.437	162.221	161.709	162.360
Algeria (Dinar)	115.670	114.005	114.760	117.054	117.306
Angola (Readj Kwanza)	not listed	141.857	143.686	150.194	150.405
Antigua (EC$)	4.3023	4.1700	4.1917	4.3288	4.3144
Argentina (Peso)	6.0580	6.0481	6.1478	6.6113	6.7074
Armenia (Dram)	not listed	574.115	569.704	595.023	602.532
Aruba (Florin)	not listed	2.7646	2.7790	2.8699	2.8603
Australia (A$)	1.8829	1.6872	1.6526	1.5532	1.5274
Austria (Euro)	1.1298	1.1664	1.1779	1.1517	1.1582
Azerbaijan (New Manat)	not listed	1.2405	1.2439	1.2666	1.2579
Bahamas ($ pegged to US$)	1.5962	1.5457	1.5535	1.6038	1.5958
Bahrain (Dinar)	0.6005	0.5823	0.5853	0.6243	0.6231
Bangladesh (Taka)	110.103	107.448	108.732	118.157	122.098
Barbados (BD$)	3.1853	3.0889	3.1049	3.2065	3.1958
Belarus (Rouble)	not listed	4,601.43	4,667.52	8,126.32	10,098.71
Belgium (Euro)	1.1298	1.1664	1.1779	1.1517	1.1582
Belize (Dollar)	not listed	3.0117	3.0273	3.1651	3.1536
Benin (CFA Franc)	739.927	763.824	771.029	755.749	758.896
Bermuda ($ pegged to US$)	1.5692	1.5457	1.5535	1.6038	1.5958
Bhutan (Ngultrum)	not listed	70.7247	70.8063	74.5576	76.2045
Bolivia (Boliviano)	11.1804	10.8403	10.8805	11.1260	11.0614
Bosnia-Herzegovina (Marka)	not listed	2.2775	2.2990	2.2534	2.2628
Botswana (Pula)	10.8900	10.5076	10.5025	10.9159	11.1162
Brazil (Real)	2.9799	2.7217	2.6850	2.6776	2.7055
Brunei ($)	2.2677	2.1075	2.0707	2.0139	1.9994
Bulgaria (Lev)	2.2063	2.2775	2.2990	2.2534	2.2628
Burkina Faso (CFA Franc)	739.927	763.824	771.029	755.749	758.896
Burundi (Franc)	1,959.83	1,900.76	1,912.32	2,015.16	2,065.46
Cambodia (Riel)	not listed	6,449.20	6,411.57	6,475.58	6,475.17
Cameroon Republic (CFA Franc)	739.927	763.824	771.029	755.749	758.896
Canada (Can$)	1.7398	1.5943	1.5808	1.5844	1.5824
Cape Verde Islands (Escudo)	not listed	125.334	127.476	124.082	125.241
Cayman Islands (CI$)	1.3067	1.2665	1.2730	16.269	16.876
Central African (CFA Franc)	739.927	763.824	771.029	755.749	758.896
Chad (CFA Franc)	739.927	763.824	771.029	755.749	758.896
Chile (Peso)	854.751	788.608	778.013	771.550	771.868
China (Renminbi Yuan)	10.8798	10.4587	10.4195	10.3745	10.2339
Colombia (Peso)	3,183.33	2,932.07	2,919.66	2,959.41	2,918.79
Comoros (Franc)	not listed	572.868	578.272	566.813	569.174
Congo Brazzaville (CFA Franc)	739.927	763.824	771.029	755.749	758.896
Congo Dem Rep (Zaire) (Congolese Franc)	1,354.89	1,398.04	1,408.81	1,458.64	1,452.24
Costa Rica (Colon)	906.539	812.659	797.682	810.964	810.612
Cote d'Ivoire (CFA Franc)	739.927	763.824	771.029	755.749	758.896
Croatia (Kuna)	not listed	8.4828	8.5942	8.5609	8.6416
Cuba (Peso)	1.5935	1.5445	1.5525	1.6033	1.5979

113

Average for year ending	31.03.10	31.12.10	31.03.11	31.12.11	31.03.12
Cyprus (Euro from 1.1.08)	1.1298	1.1664	1.1779	1.1517	1.1582
Czech Republic (Koruna)	29.3613	29.4579	29.3266	28.3142	28.6081
Denmark (Krone)	8.4083	8.6860	8.7744	8.5762	8.6238
Djibouti (Franc)	not listed	269.667	272.593	280.387	279.289
Dominica (EC$)	4.3023	4.1700	4.1917	4.3288	4.3144
Dominican Republic (Peso)	not listed	55.6198	57.3989	60.8161	61.1402
Dubai (Dirham)	5.8497	5.6727	5.7021	5.8887	5.8691
Ecuador (US$)	1.5962	1.5457	1.5535	1.6038	1.5958
Egypt (£)	8.8012	8.6950	8.8874	9.5196	9.5564
El Salvador (Colon)	13.9391	13.5101	13.5802	14.0245	13.9777
Equatorial Guinea (CFA Franc)	739.927	763.824	771.029	755.749	758.896
Eritrea (Nakfa)	not listed	23.1667	23.2870	24.0489	23.9685
Estonia (Euro from 1.1.11)				1.8004	1.1582
Ethiopia (Birr)	19.7973	22.2520	23.7448	27.1943	27.3735
European Union (Euro)	1.1298	1.1664	1.1779	1.1517	1.1582
Fiji Islands (F$)	3.1723	2.9662	2.9422	2.8741	2.8385
Finland (Euro)	1.1298	1.1664	1.1779	1.1517	1.1582
France (Euro)	1.1298	1.1664	1.1779	1.1517	1.1582
French Cty/Africa (CFA franc)	739.927	763.824	771.029	755.749	758.896
French Polynesia (CFP franc)	134.515	138.859	140.179	137.471	138.059
Gabon (CFA franc)	739.927	763.824	771.029	755.749	758.896
Gambia (Dalasi)	42.4940	42.8581	43.6735	45.4873	46.1451
Georgia (Lari)	not listed	46.8977	46.9793	47.0579	47.1474
Germany (Euro)	1.1298	1.1664	1.1779	1.1517	1.1582
Ghana (Cedi)	2.3068	2.2108	2.2561	2.4716	2.5342
Greece (Euro)	1.1298	1.1664	1.1779	1.1517	1.1582
Grenada/Wind. Isles (EC$)	4.3023	4.1700	4.1917	4.3288	4.3144
Guatemala (Quetzal)	not listed	12.4608	12.3875	12.4988	12.4276
Guinea Bissau (CFA Franc)	739.927	763.824	771.029	755.749	758.896
Guinea Republic (Franc)	not listed	8,621.47	9,528.78	11,127.68	11,045.72
Guyana (G$)	322.95	313.613	315.166	325.051	323.392
Haiti (Gourde)	not listed	61.4083	61.8747	64.5992	64.5382
Honduras (Lempira)	30.1084	29.1825	29.3339	30.2872	30.2414
Hong Kong (HK$)	12.3810	12.0140	12.0853	12.4843	12.4121
Hungary (Forint)	308.141	320.901	324.947	321.141	328.864
Iceland (Krona)	200.920	188.909	185.726	185.767	187.988
India (Rupee)	75.5588	70.7247	70.8063	74.5576	76.2045
Indonesia (Rupiah)	15,601.10	14,035.67	13,976.90	14,037.29	14,013.84
Iran (Rial)	15,770.00	15,547.67	15,803.40	16,977.89	17,459.89
Iraq (Dinar)	1,838.48	1,798.33	1,812.31	1,872.54	1,863.11
Ireland (Euro)	1.1298	1.1664	1.1779	1.1517	1.1582
Israel (Shekel)	6.1280	5.7775	5.7496	5.7247	5.7699
Italy (Euro)	1.1298	1.1664	1.1779	1.1517	1.1582
Jamaica (J$)	141.387	134.234	133.470	137.120	137.063
Japan (Yen)	148.193	136.105	133.405	128.004	126.099
Jordan (Dinar)	1.1278	1.0936	1.0993	1.1359	1.1323
Kazakhstan (Tenge)	not listed	227.608	228.322	235.107	234.888
Kenya (Shilling)	121.942	122.237	124.987	142.141	142.959
Korea North (Won)	not listed	6.4556	5.9760	6.1196	2.0773
Korea South (Won)	1,924.48	1,789.25	1,789.59	1,774.79	1,769.75
Kuwait (Dinar)	0.4582	0.4433	0.4425	0.4433	0.4410
Kyrgyz Republic (Som)	not listed	46.8977	46.9793	47.0579	47.1474
Laos (New Kip)	13,502.70	12,730.20	12,629.81	12,823.65	12,758.14
Latvia (Lat)	0.7975	0.8252	0.8319	0.8140	0.8158

Average for year ending	31.03.10	31.12.10	31.03.11	31.12.11	31.03.12
Lebanon (£)	2,391.71	2,318.38	2,330.14	2,413.90	2,407.45
Lesotho (Loti)	not listed	11.3297	11.1799	11.5600	11.8049
Liberia ($ pegged to US$)	1.5962	1.5457	1.5535	1.6038	1.5958
Libya (Dinar)	1.9751	1.9501	1.9555	1.9466	1.9392
Lithuania (Litas)	3.8949	4.0207	4.0586	3.9782	3.9947
Luxembourg (Euro)	1.1298	1.1664	1.1779	1.1517	1.1582
Macao (Pataca)	not listed	12.3571	12.4303	12.8549	12.8021
Macedonia (Denar)	not listed	71.6306	72.3545	70.8774	71.1307
Madagascar (Malagasy Ariary)	not listed	3,239.96	3,235.71	3,246.63	3,282.52
Malawi (Kwacha)	229.365	232.259	234.096	250.397	255.309
Malaysia (Ringgit)	5.5113	4.9881	4.8847	4.8993	4.8819
Maldive Islands (Rufiyaa)	not listed	19.7691	19.8716	23.0937	24.0370
Mali Republic (CFA Franc)	739.927	763.824	771.029	755.749	758.896
Malta (Euro from 1.1.08)	1.1298	1.1664	1.1779	1.1517	1.1582
Mauritania (Ouguiya)	not listed	426.049	435.961	451.256	452.906
Mauritius (Rupee)	49.6959	47.4706	47.4584	46.0469	45.6847
Mexico (Peso)	20.8849	19.5447	19.3675	19.8679	20.1604
Moldova (Leu)	not listed	19.1203	19.0176	18.8119	18.6449
Mongolia (Tugrik)	not listed	2,099.57	2,036.42	2,021.84	2,054.57
Montserrat (EC$)	4.3023	4.1700	4.1917	4.3288	4.3144
Morocco (Dirham)	12.7327	12.9957	13.1101	12.7406	12.7649
Mozambique (Metical)	not listed	53.0503	53.4337	46.6306	44.6301
Myanmar (Burma) (Kyat)	10.2089	9.8999	9.9513	10.2769	10.2425
Nepal (Rupee)	120.696	112.992	113.132	119.028	121.368
Netherlands (Euro)	1.1298	1.1664	1.1779	1.1517	1.1582
N'nd Antilles (Guilder)	2.8523	not listed	not listed	not listed	not listed
New Caledonia (CFP Franc)	134.515	138.859	140.179	137.471	138.059
New Zealand (NZ$)	2.3637	2.1476	2.1253	2.0295	1.9819
Nicaragua (Gold Cordoba)	32.8596	32.9591	33.5288	35.9042	36.2063
Niger Republic (CFA Franc)	739.927	763.824	771.029	755.749	758.896
Nigeria (Naira)	239.591	233.242	235.513	249.169	250.633
Norway (Krone)	9.6327	9.3441	9.3501	8.9773	8.9649
Oman (Rial Omani)	0.6132	0.5927	0.5959	0.6173	0.6152
Pakistan (Rupee)	132.082	131.523	132.552	138.292	139.666
Panama (Balboa)	not listed	1.5445	1.5525	1.6033	1.5979
Papua New Guinea (Kina)	4.2584	4.1785	4.1689	3.7924	3.5751
Paraguay (Guarani)	7,779.04	7,356.67	7,336.74	6,744.83	6,668.88
Peru (New Sol)	4.6586	4.3644	4.3585	4.4165	4.3665
Philippines (Peso)	75.1918	69.7964	69.2370	69.4108	68.7961
Poland (Zloty)	4.7177	4.6601	4.6847	4.7312	4.8349
Portugal (Euro)	1.1298	1.1664	1.1779	1.1517	1.1582
Qatar (Riyal)	5.7982	5.6218	5.6514	5.8379	5.8186
Romania (Leu)	4.7312	4.9026	4.9798	4.8875	4.9379
Russia (Rouble-Market)	48.6544	46.8977	46.9793	47.0579	47.1474
Rwanda (R Franc)	908.223	900.073	914.593	961.775	961.237
Saotome & Principe (Dobra)	not listed	27,844.14	28,529.41	28,235.14	28,351.28
Saudi Arabia (Riyal)	5.9728	5.7997	5.8298	6.0147	5.9846
Senegal (CFA Franc)	739.927	763.824	771.029	755.479	758.896
Serbia (Dinar)	not listed	119.804	122.469	117.515	118.896
Seychelles (Rupee)	19.6567	18.6821	19.0717	19.8320	20.3733
Sierra Leone (Leone)	5,723.55	6,134.07	6,301.38	6,965.58	6,990.35
Singapore (S$)	2.2719	2.1104	2.0721	2.0153	2.0009
Slovakia Euro from 1.1.09	1.1298	1.1664	1.1779	1.1517	1.1582
Slovenia (Euro)	1.1298	1.1664	1.779	1.1517	1.1582

Average for year ending	31.03.10	31.12.10	31.03.11	31.12.11	31.03.12
Solomon Islands (SI$)	12.7244	12.1739	12.1766	12.1145	11.8226
Somali Republic (Shilling)	2,236.85	2,337.21	2,385.47	2,510.12	2,511.69
South Africa (Rand)	12.4676	11.3267	11.1774	11.5787	11.8522
Spain (Euro)	1.1298	1.1664	1.1779	1.1517	1.1582
Sri Lanka (Rupee)	183.205	174.698	174.212	177.075	178.794
St Christopher & Nevis (EC$)	4.3023	4.1700	4.1917	4.3288	4.3144
St Lucia (EC$)	4.3023	4.1700	4.1917	4.3288	4.3144
St Vincent (EC$)	4.3023	4.1700	4.1917	4.3288	4.3144
Sudan (£)	3.7308	3.5934	3.6865	4.2308	4.2857
Surinam (Dollar)	4.3741	4.2396	4.3989	5.2053	5.2731
Swaziland (Lilangeli)	12.3156	11.3297	11.1799	11.5600	11.8049
Sweden (Krona)	11.7215	11.1487	10.9374	10.3955	10.4489
Switzerland (Franc)	1.6961	1.6134	1.5769	1.4214	1.4073
Syria (Pound)	73.1795	71.4883	72.2270	76.8639	80.3194
Taiwan (New T$)	51.7867	48.7931	47.9891	47.0816	47.0278
Tajikistan (Somoni)	not listed	46.8977	46.9793	47.0578	47.1474
Tanzania (Shilling)	2,118.02	2,220.88	2,290.21	2,535.73	2,565.88
Thailand (Baht)	53.7107	49.1001	48.3929	48.8202	48.7955
Togo Republic (CFA Franc)	739.927	763.824	771.029	755.749	758.896
Tonga Islands (Pa'Anga)	3.1071	1.6872	1.6526	1.5532	1.5274
Trinidad and Tobago (TT$)	10.0652	9.8047	9.8754	10.2618	10.2329
Tunisia (Dinar)	2.1345	2.2082	2.2402	2.2536	2.2764
Turkey (Lira)	2.4160	2.3259	2.3646	2.6779	2.7522
Turkmenistan (New Manat)	not listed	40.7772	30.3560	4.5608	4.5436
Uganda (New Shilling)	3,237.06	3,353.60	3,504.67	4,042.47	4,055.64
Ukraine (Hryvnia)	not listed	12.2721	12.3143	12.7979	12.7843
United Arab Emirates (Dirham)	5.8497	5.6727	5.7021	5.8887	5.8691
Uruguay (Peso Uruguayo)	34.3153	30.8988	31.0534	30.8226	30.6354
USA (US$)	1.5962	1.5457	1.5535	1.6038	1.5958
Uzbekistan (Sum)	not listed	2,446.84	2,507.69	2,741.07	2,792.52
Vanuatu (Vatu)	not listed	154.136	153.126	149.979	148.545
Venezuela (Bolivar Fuerte) 1.4.09 to 10.1.10	3.4498				
From 11.1.10 (petro-dollar rate)	6.6804	6.4983	6.6673	6.8855	6.8624
Vietnam (Dong)	28,974.50	29,549.79	30,237.45	33,063.93	33,256.91
Wallis & Futuna Islands (CFP Franc)	134.515	138.859	140.179	137.471	138.059
Western Samoa (Tala)	not listed	3.8430	3.8095	3.7202	3.6667
Yemen (Rial)	329.603	338.922	340.988	345.071	345.455
Zambia (Kwacha)	7,741.14	7,400.46	7,497.68	7,779.14	7,907.84
Zimbabwe (Dollar)	not listed	582.838	587.473	606.220	604.136

Rates of exchange on year-end dates

	31.03.10	31.12.10	31.03.11	31.12.11	31.03.12
Australia (A$)	1.6527	1.5274	1.55	1.5159	1.5423
Canada (Can$)	1.5390	1.5557	1.5593	1.5825	1.5969
Denmark (Krone)	8.3459	8.697	8.4221	8.8978	8.9259
European Union (Euro)	1.1211	1.1671	1.1296	1.1972	1.1998
Hong Kong (HK$)	11.7783	12.1708	12.4681	12.0701	12.405
Japan (Yen)	141.739	126.982	132.853	119.572	131.487
Norway (Krone)	9.0038	9.1003	8.8671	9.2748	9.1137
South Africa (Rand)	11.1401	10.358	10.8351	12.5469	12.262
Sweden (Krona)	10.9171	10.5256	10.1121	10.6539	10.6016
Switzerland (Franc)	1.5967	1.4593	1.4665	1.4532	1.4442
USA (US$)	1.5169	1.5657	1.603	1.5541	1.5978

Note: The material on p 113–117 is reproduced from information provided by HMRC and is Crown copyright.

Double taxation agreements (including protocols and regulations)

Agreements in force covering taxes on income and capital gains

Country	SI/SR & O	Country	SI/SR & O
Antigua & Barbuda	**1947/2865**		1996/3166
	1968/1096	France	**2009/226**
Argentina	**1997/1777**	Gambia	**1980/1963**
Armenia[1]	**2011/2722**	Georgia	**2004/3325**
Austria	**1970/1947**		2010/2972
	1979/117	Germany	1967/25
	1994/768		1971/874
	2010/2688		**2010/2975**[5]
Australia	**2003/3199**	Ghana	**1993/1800**
Azerbaijan	**1995/762**	Greece	**1954/142**
Bangladesh	**1980/708**	Grenada	**1949/361**
Barbados	**1970/952**		1968/1867
	1973/2096	Guernsey	**1952/1215**
Belarus[1]	**1986/224**		1994/3209
Belgium	**1987/2053**		2009/3011
	2010/2979	Guyana	**1992/3207**
Belize	**1947/2866**	Hong Kong	**2010/2974**
	1968/573	Hungary	**2011/2726**[6]
	1973/2097	Iceland	**1991/2879**
Bolivia	**1995/2707**	India	**1993/1801**
Bosnia Herzegovina[2]	**1981/1815**	Indonesia	**1994/769**
Botswana	**2006/1925**	Irish Republic	**1976/2151**
British Virgin Islands	**2009/3013**		1976/2152
Brunei	**1950/1977**		1995/764
	1968/306		1998/3151
	1973/2098	Isle of Man	**1955/1205**
Bulgaria	**1987/2054**		1991/2880
Canada	**1980/709**		1994/3208
	1980/1528		2009/228
	1980/1996	Israel	**1963/616**
	1985/1996		1971/391
	2003/2619	Italy	**1990/2590**
Cayman Islands	**2010/2973**	Ivory Coast	**1987/169**
Chile	**2003/3200**	Jamaica	**1973/1329**
China[4]	**1984/1826**	Japan	**2006/1924**
	1996/3164	Jersey	**1952/1216**
Croatia[2]	**1981/1815**		1994/3210
Cyprus	**1975/425**		2009/3012
	1980/1529	Jordan	**2001/3924**
Czech Republic[3]	**1991/2876**	Kazakhstan	**1994/3211**
Denmark	**1980/1960**		1998/2567
	1991/2877	Kenya	**1977/1299**
	1996/3165	Kiribati (and Tuvalu)	**1950/750**
Egypt	**1980/1091**		1968/309
Estonia	**1994/3207**		1974/1271
Falkland Islands	**1997/2985**	Korea (South)	**1996/3168**
Faroes	**2007/3469**	Kuwait	**1999/2036**
Fiji	**1976/1342**	Kyrgyzstan[1]	
Finland	**1970/153**	Latvia	**1996/3167**
	1973/1327	Lesotho	**1997/2986**
	1980/710	Libya	**2010/243**
	1985/1997	Lithuania[1]	**2001/3925**
	1991/2878		2002/2847

Country	SI/SR & O	Country	SI/SR & O
Luxembourg	**1968/1100**	Romania	**1977/57**
	1980/567	Russian Federation	**1994/3213**
	1984/364	St Kitts and Nevis	**1947/2872**
	2010/237	Saudi Arabia	**2008/1770**
Macedonia[2]	**2007/2127**	Serbia[2]	**1981/1815**
Malawi	**1956/619**	Sierra Leone	**1947/2873**
	1964/1401		1968/1104
	1968/1101	Singapore	**1997/2988**
	1979/302		2010/2685
Malaysia	**1997/2987**	Slovak Republic[3]	**1991/2876**
	2010/2971	Slovenia[2]	**2008/1796**
Malta	**1995/763**	Solomon Islands	**1950/748**
Mauritius	**1981/1121**		1968/574
	1987/467		1974/1270
	2003/2620	South Africa	**2002/3138**
	2011/2442		2011/2441
Mexico	**1994/3212**	Spain	**1976/1919**
	2010/2686		1995/765
Moldova[1]	**2008/1795**	Sri Lanka	**1980/713**
Mongolia	**1996/2598**	Sudan	**1977/1719**
Montenegro[2]	**1981/1815**	Swaziland	**1969/380**
Montserrat	**1947/2869**	Sweden	**1984/366**
	1968/576	Switzerland	**1978/1408**
	2011/1083		1982/714
Morocco	**1991/2881**		1994/3215
Myanmar (Burma)	**1952/751**		2007/3465
Namibia	**1962/2352**		2010/2689
	1962/2788	Taiwan	**2002/3137**
	1967/1489	Tajikistan[1]	**1986/224**
	1967/1490	Thailand	**1981/1546**
Netherlands	**2009/227**	Trinidad and Tobago	**1983/1903**
New Zealand	**1984/365**	Tunisia	**1984/133**
	2004/1274	Turkey	**1988/932**
	2008/1793	Turkmenistan[1]	**1986/224**
Nigeria	**1987/2057**	Tuvalu (and Kiribati)	**1950/750**
Norway	**2000/3247**		1968/309
Oman	**1998/2568**		1974/1271
	2010/2687	Uganda	**1993/1802**
Pakistan	**1987/2058**	Ukraine	**1993/1803**
Papua New Guinea	**1991/2882**	USA	**2002/2848**
Philippines	**1978/184**	Uzbekistan	**1994/770**
Poland	**2006/3323**	Venezuela	**1996/2599**
Portugal	**1969/599**	Vietnam	**1994/3216**
Qatar	**2010/241**	Zambia	**1972/1721**
	2011/1684		1981/1816
		Zimbabwe	**1982/1842**

[1] Following dissolution of the USSR, new agreements are in force with Azerbaijan, Estonia, Kazakhstan, Latvia, Lithuania, Moldova, the Russian Federation, Ukraine and Uzbekistan. *SI 1986 No 224* (former USSR agreement) treated as continuing to apply to Belarus, Tajikistan and Turkmenistan (for Belarus until coming into force of *SI 1995 No 2706*). It was similarly so treated by the UK until 31 March 2002 for Armenia, Georgia, Kyrgyzstan and Lithuania (none of which considered itself bound by that convention) but as ceasing so to apply after that date (but new treaties in force with Armenia, Lithuania and Georgia). (SP 4/01.)

[2] *SI 1981 No 1815* (former Yugoslavia agreement) treated as remaining in force between the UK and, respectively, Bosnia-Herzegovina, Croatia and Serbia and Montenegro. (SP 3/04.) Negotiations for new double taxation convention taking place with Croatia, Serbia and Montenegro (Revenue Press Release, 29 September 2004).

[3] *SI 1991 No 2876* (former Czechoslovakia agreement) treated as remaining in force between the UK and, respectively, Czech Republic and Slovak Republic. (SP 5/93.)

[4] *SI 1984 No 1826* does not apply to the Hong Kong Special Administrative Region.

Treaty replaces 1967/25 with effect from 1 January 2011 or 6 April 2011 depending on type of income. However, where a resident of Germany was, before 30 December 2010, in receipt of a UK pension (including State Pension) or annuity relievable under Article X of prior treaty 1967/25, the individual may elect for the terms of the prior treaty to continue to apply to the pension or annuity.

6 New treaty effective in UK from 1 January 2012 for property income dividends, interest, royalties (and annuities not subject to PAYE), 6 April 2012 for pensions and annuities within PAYE. Prior treaty was 1978/1056.

Tax information exchange agreements in force

Country	SI	Country	SI
Anguilla	2010/2677	Guernsey	2009/3011
Antigua and Barbuda	2011/1075	Isle of Man	2009/228
Aruba	2011/2435	Jersey	2009/3012
Bahamas	2010/2684	Liberia	2011/2434
Belize	2011/1685	Liechtenstein	2010/2678
Bermuda	2008/1789	San Marino	2011/1688
British Virgin Islands	2009/3013	St Christopher and Nevis	2011/1077
Dominica	2011/1686	St Lucia	2011/1076
Gibraltar	2010/2680	St Vincent and Grenadines	2011/1078
Grenada	2011/1687	Turks and Caicos Islands	2010/2679

Tax information exchange agreements signed but not in force

Country

Curaçao, Sint Maarten and
BES Islands (formerly the
Netherlands Antilles)

Tax information exchange agreements in force — EU savings directives

Country	SI	Country	SI
Aruba	2005/1458	Isle of Man	2005/1263
British Virgin Islands	2005/1457	Jersey	2005/1261
Gibraltar	2006/1453	Montserrat	2005/1459
Guernsey	2005/1262	Netherlands Antilles	2005/1460

Agreements in force covering shipping and air transport profits

Country	SI/SR & O	Country	SI/SR & O
Algeria (air)	**1984/362**	Iran (air)	**1960/2419**
Armenia (USSR air)*	**1974/1269**	Kyrgyzstan (USSR air)*	**1974/1269**
Belarus (USSR air)*	**1974/1269**	Lebanon	**1964/278**
Brazil	**1968/572**	Moldova (USSR air)*	**1974/1269**
Cameroon (air)	**1982/1841**	Saudi Arabia (air)	**1994/767**
China (air)	**1981/1119**	Tajikistan (USSR air)*	**1974/1269**
Congo Democratic Republic	**1977/1298**	Turkmenistan (USSR air)*	**1974/1269**
Ethiopia (air)	**1977/1297**		
Georgia (USSR air)*	**1974/1269**		
Hong Kong (air)	**1998/2566**		
(shipping)	**2000/3248**		

* HMRC have confirmed that this Arrangement will be treated in the same way as the Convention covering income and capital gains (SI 1986/224). See note 1 p 119.

Agreements in force covering estates, inheritances and gifts

Country	SI/SR & O	Country	SI/SR & O
France*	**1963/1319**	Pakistan*	**1957/1522**
India*	**1956/998**	South Africa	**1979/576**
Ireland	**1978/1107**	Sweden	**1981/840**
Italy*	**1968/304**		1989/986
Netherlands	**1980/706**	Switzerland	**1994/3214**
	1996/730	USA	**1979/1454**

* Agreements pre-date UK inheritance tax/capital transfer tax.

Overseas income – basis of assessment

	Professions, trades, etc	Pensions	Other income
Non-residents	Exempt	Exempt	Exempt
Residents			
(1) **Foreign domicile**[2]	Remittance	Remittance	Remittance
(2) **UK domicile**			
(a) ordinarily resident	Arising	90%[1] arising	Arising
(b) not ordinarily resident	Remittance	Remittance	Remittance

[1] Pensions paid by the governments of the Federal Republic of Germany or of Austria to victims of Nazi persecution are exempt.

[2] Where from 6 April 2008, an individual not domiciled or not ordinarily resident in the UK who has overseas income (or, for non-domiciles only, gains) in excess of £2,000 claims the remittance basis, he will not qualify for personal allowances or the capital gains tax annual exemption. The claim for remittance basis must be made annually. If the individual is not UK domiciled or ordinarily resident in a year and has been resident in the UK for at least seven out of the last nine tax years and has overseas income or gains in excess of £2,000, there is an additional charge of £30,000. This charge is increased to £50,000 from 6 April 2012 for non-domiciles who have been UK resident for at least twelve tax years in the previous fourteen. (ITA 2007 ss 809A–809Z7)

[3] A statutory residence test will be introduced from 6 April 2013 and ordinary residence will be abolished from that date.

Employment income liability of non-resident employees see p 87.

Tax-free (FOTRA) securities

Interest on all government stock is exempt from tax where the beneficial owner is not ordinarily resident in the UK (FA 1996 s 154; FA 1998 s 161; ITTOIA 2005 ss 713, 714). Except in the case of $3^1/_2$% War Loan 1952 or after, the exemption does not apply where the securities are held for the purposes of a trade or business carried on in the UK.

Social security benefits

Taxable state benefits

	Weekly 9.4.12	Total 2012–13 (52 weeks)	Weekly 11.4.11	Total 2011–12 (52 weeks)
	£	£	£	£
Bereavement benefits[1]				
Standard rate (widow's pension)	105.95	5,509	100.70	5,236
Widowed parent's allowance	105.95	5,509	100.70	5,236
Carer's allowance	58.45	3,039	55.55	2,888
– Adult dependency increase	34.40	1,788	32.70	1,700
Employment and support allowance[6]				
–under 25	56.25	–	53.45	–
–25 or over	71.00	–	67.50	–
Incapacity benefit[6]				
Long-term (after 52 weeks)	99.15	5,155	94.25	4,901
– Adult dependency increase	57.60	2,995	54.75	2,847
– Age increase: higher rate	11.70	608	13.80	717
lower rate	5.90	306	5.60	291
Short term				
– Under pension age: higher rate	88.55	–	84.15	–
– Adult dependency increase	44.85	–	42.65	–
– Over pension age: higher rate	99.15	–	94.25	–
– Adult dependency increase	55.45	–	52.70	–
Industrial death benefit[2]				
Widow's pension: higher rate	107.45	5,587	102.15	5,311
lower rate	32.24	1,676	30.65	1,593
Widower's pension	107.45	5,587	102.15	5,311
Invalidity allowance[3]				
Higher rate	20.25	1,053	19.25	1001
Middle rate	13.00	676	12.40	644
Lower rate	6.50	338	6.20	322
Jobseeker's allowance[4]				
Single: under 25	56.25	–	53.45	–
25 or over	71.00	–	67.50	–
Couple: both under 18	56.25	–	53.45	–
both under 18 higher rate	84.95	–	80.75	–
one under 18, one under 25	56.25	–	53.45	–
one under 18, one 25 or over	71.00	–	67.50	–
both 18 or over	111.45	–	105.95	–
State pension				
Single person (Category A or B)	107.45	5,587	102.15	5,311
Adult dependency increase	61.85	3,216	58.80	3,057
Non-contributory pension				
– single (Category C or D)	64.40	3,348	61.20	3,182
Age addition (over 80) (each)	0.25	13	0.25	13
Statutory adoption pay				
Rate[5]	135.45	–	128.73	–
Earnings threshold	107.00	–	102.00	–
Statutory maternity pay				
Rate[5]	135.45	–	128.73	–
Earnings threshold	107.00	–	102.00	–
Statutory paternity pay				
Rate[5]	135.45	–	128.73	–
Earnings threshold	107.00	–	102.00	–

	Weekly 9.4.12	Total 2012–13 (52 weeks)	Weekly 11.4.11	Total 2011–12 (52 weeks)
	£	£	£	£
Statutory sick pay				
Rate	**85.85**	–	81.60	–
Earnings threshold	**107.00**	–	102.00	–

1   Paid to widows and widowers for up to 52 weeks.
2   For deaths before 11 April 1988 only.
3   When paid with retirement pensions. See note below on non-taxable benefits on p 125.
4   Where the allowance exceeds the amount shown above, the excess is not taxable.
5   The allowance is 90% of average weekly earnings if less than the above amount. In the first six weeks the rate of SMP is 90% of average weekly earnings even if higher than the standard rate.
6   Employment and support allowance replaces incapacity benefits for new claimants on or after 27 October 2008. Only contributory employment and support allowance is taxable. Income related allowance is not taxable.

Non-taxable state benefits

Weekly rates from	9.4.12	11.4.11
	£	£
Attendance allowance		
Higher rate (day and night)	77.45	73.60
Lower rate (day or night)	51.85	49.30
Child benefit[4]		
Eldest child	20.30	20.30
Each subsequent child	13.40	13.40
Child dependency addition		
Paid with state pension; widowed mothers/parents allowance; short-term incapacity benefit - higher rate or over state pension age; long-term incapacity benefit; carer's allowance; severe disablement allowance; industrial death benefit (higher rate);	11.35	11.35
Disability living allowance[3]		
Care component higher rate	77.45	73.60
middle rate	51.85	49.30
lower rate	20.55	19.55
Mobility component higher rate	54.05	51.40
lower rate	20.55	19.55
Guardian's allowance	15.55	14.75
Incapacity benefit (short-term)[1]		
Under pension age – lower rate (first 28 weeks)	74.80	71.10
– Adult dependency increase	44.85	42.65
Over pension age – lower rate (first 28 weeks)	95.15	90.45
– Adult dependency increase	55.45	52.70
Maternity allowance (where SMP not available)		
Standard rate	135.45	128.73
MA threshold	30.00	30.00
– Adult dependency increase[2]	–	–
Severe disablement allowance		
Basic rate	69.00	62.95
Age-related addition higher rate	11.70	13.80
middle rate	5.90	7.10
lower rate	5.90	5.60
– Adult dependency increase	34.60	32.90

[1] Incapacity benefit replaced invalidity allowance from April 1995. The benefits are taxable except those paid in the first 28 weeks of incapacity and those paid to persons already receiving invalidity benefit on 13 April 1995 so long as they remain incapable of work.
[2] Not available for maternity allowance periods beginning after 5 April 2010.
[3] To be replaced by personal independence payments (PIP) in 2013–14.
[4] See note on p 73 regarding the income tax charge arising to certain child benefit claimants from 7 January 2013.

Other non-taxable benefits include:

Bereavement payment (lump sum £2,000)

Child tax credit (see Tax Credits, p 96)

Christmas bonus (with retirement pension)

Cold weather payments

Council tax benefit (income related)

Earnings top-up

Housing benefit (income related)

Income support (income related)

Industrial death benefit

Industrial injuries disablement pension

Jobfinder's grant

Pension credit

Pneumoconiosis, byssinosis and miscellaneous disease benefits

Redundancy payment

Social fund payments

Television licence payment

Vaccine damage (lump sum)

War pensions

Winter fuel payment (£200, plus £100 for those aged over 80, for 2011–12)

Working tax credit (see Tax Credits, p 96)

Stamp taxes

Stamp duty land tax

Stamp duty land tax applies to contracts entered into (or varied) after 10.7.03 and completed after 30.11.03 and to leases granted after that date (FA 2003 ss 55, 56, Sch 5). With effect from 22.7.04, it also applies to the transfer of an interest in land into, or out of, a partnership and to the acquisition of an interest in a partnership where the partnership property includes an interest in land. With effect from 19.7.06, it applies to transfers of partnership interests only where the sole or main activity of the partnership is investing or dealing in interests in land.

Land transactions		Consideration[1]	
Effective date	Residential property[A]	Non-residential or mixed property	Rate[5]
From 22.3.12	**Up to £125,000**	**Up to £150,000**	**Nil**
	£125,001–£250,000	**£150,001–£250,000**	**1%**
	£250,001–£500,000	**£250,001–£500,000**	**3%**
	£500,001–£1,000,000	**£500,001 or more**	**4%**
	£1,000,001–£2,000,000		**5%**
	£2,000,001 or more		**7%**
From 6.4.11–21.3.12	Up to £125,000	Up to £150,000	Nil
	£125,001–£250,000[2]	£150,001–£250,000	1%
	£250,001–£500,000	£250,001–£500,000	3%
	£500,001–£1,000,000	£500,001 or more	4%
	£1,000,001 or more		5%
From 1.1.10–5.4.11	Up to £125,000	Up to £150,000	Nil
	£125,001–£250,000[2]	£150,001–£250,000	1%
	£250,001–£500,000	£250,001–£500,000	3%
	£500,001 or more	£500,001 or more	4%
3.9.08–31.12.09	Up to £175,000	Up to £150,000	Nil
	£175,001–£250,000	£150,001–£250,000	1%
	£250,001–£500,000	£250,001–£500,000	3%
	£500,001 or more	£500,001 or more	4%
23.3.06–2.9.08	Up to £125,000	Up to £150,000	Nil
	£125,001–£250,000	£150,001–£250,000	1%
	£250,001–£500,000	£250,001–£500,000	3%
	£500,001 or more	£500,001 or more	4%
17.3.05–22.3.06	Up to £120,000	Up to £150,000	Nil
	£120,001–£250,000	£150,001–£250,000	1%
	£250,001–£500,000	£250,001–£500,000	3%
	£500,001 or more	£500,001 or more	4%
Lease rentals	On net present value of rent over term of lease (applying a discount rate of 3.5%)[3]		
Effective date	Residential property	Non-residential or mixed property	Rate
From 1.1.10	**Up to £125,000**	**Up to £150,000**	**Nil**
	£125,001 or more	**£150,001 or more**	**1%**
3.9.08–31.12.09	Up to £175,000	Up to £150,000	Nil
	£175,001 or more	£150,001 or more	1%
23.3.06–2.9.08	Up to £125,000	Up to £150,000	Nil
	£125,001 or more	£150,001 or more	1%
17.3.05–22.3.06	Up to £120,000	Up to £150,000	Nil
	£120,001 or more	£150,001 or more	1%
1.12.03–16.3.05	Up to £60,000	Up to £150,000	Nil
	£60,001 or more	£150,001 or more	1%

Premiums
The same tax is payable for a premium granted as for a land transaction. Special rules apply to a premium in respect of non-residential property where the rent exceeds £1,000 a year. For transactions before 12 March 2008, the rules applied to all property where the rent exceeded £600 a year.

[1] Rates apply to the full consideration, not only to that in excess of the previous band.
[2] For residential property, purchases by first-time buyers between 25 March 2010 and 24 March 2012 inclusive attract a nil rate of SDLT for purchase consideration up to £250,000.
[3] Rates apply to the amount of npv in the slice, not the whole value.
[4] With effect from 19 July 2011, where a purchaser (or a connected person) of residential property acquires more than one dwelling from the same vendor (or a connected person) and makes a claim, the rate of SDLT will be calculated based on the mean consideration for each property, subject to a minimum rate of 1%.
[5] From 21 March 2012 a 15% rate applies to certain non-natural persons acquiring a residential property where consideration exceeds £2,000,000.

Exemptions and reliefs

No SDLT (or, where relevant, stamp duty) is chargeable on:

(1)   transfers to charities for use for charitable purposes.

(2)   transfers to bodies established for national purposes.

(3)   gifts inter vivos.

(4)   certain transfers on divorce or dissolution of a civil partnership.

(5)   transfers of property to beneficiaries under a will or an intestacy.

(6)   land transfers within groups of companies.

(7)   land transferred in exchange for shares on company reconstruction and acquisitions.

(8)   certain transfers to or leases granted by registered providers of social housing. The relief is repealed for instruments executed on or after 6 April 2013.

(9)   sale and leaseback and lease and leaseback arrangements involving commercial and residential property.

(10)   certain acquisitions of residential property by house building companies or property traders from personal representatives, or when people move into a new dwelling or a chain of transactions break down, or by employers involving employee relocations.

(11)   transfers on sale of residential property for a consideration of up to £150,000 in disadvantaged parts of the UK. This also applies to leases broadly, on rent where the relevant rental value does not exceed £150,000 and to premiums not exceeding £150,000. This relief is repealed in relation to instruments executed on or after 6 April 2013. No claims can be made after 5 May 2014.

(12)   from 1.10.07 until 30.9.12 for new zero carbon homes (including flats) with a purchase price of up to £500,000, there is no SDLT charged. Where the purchase price is in excess of £500,000, the SDLT liability on the purchase price will be reduced by £15,000.

(13)   from 25.3.10 until 24.3.12 purchases of residential property by first-time buyers for consideration of more than £125,000 but not more than £250,000 (see p 127).

(14)   demutualisation of building societies and insurance companies.

(15)   incorporation of limited liability partnerships.

(16)   transfers of land between public bodies under a statutory reorganisation.

(17)   compulsory purchase of land facilitating redevelopment.

(18)   land transactions in compliance with planning obligations enforceable against the vendor and made within five years of the obligation where the purchaser is one of certain public authorities.

(19)   transfers by a local constituency association in consequence of a reorganisation of parliamentary constituencies.

(20)   purchases or leases of certain diplomatic or consular premises or headquarters premises of certain international organisations.

Relief from SDLT may also apply on:

(a)   right to buy transactions, shared ownership leases and rent to loan transactions.

(b)   alternative property finance schemes.

(c)   exercise of collective rights by leaseholders.

(d)   crofting community right to buy.

(e)   certain arrangements relating to land transactions involving public or educational bodies.

Stamp duty

For contracts entered into (or varied) after 10 July 2003 and completed after 30 November 2003 and for leases granted after that date, stamp duty is abolished for all transfers other than stocks and marketable securities, and interests in partnerships. From 22 July 2004 stamp duty is also abolished for certain partnership transactions involving an interest in land. From those dates, transfers of land are subject to stamp duty land tax (see p 127).

Shares, etc	
Shares put into depository receipts or put into duty free clearance systems	1.5%
Purchase of own shares by company	0.5%
Transfers of stock or marketable securities	0.5%
Takeovers, mergers, demergers, schemes of reconstruction and amalgamation (except where no real change of ownership)	0.5%

(a)   Stamp duty is rounded to the next multiple of £5.

(b)   For instruments executed after 11 March 2008 stamp duty is not chargeable where the amount or value of the consideration is less than £1,000.

Fixed duties

Instruments affecting land transactions	£5

From 13 March 2008 fixed duties are generally abolished other than as above. The £5 rate applies to instruments effected from 1 October 1999.

Stamp Duty Reserve Tax (SDRT)

Agreements to transfer chargeable securities for money or money's worth (eg renounceable letters of allotment)[1]	0.5%
Chargeable securities put into a clearance service[2] or converted into depositary receipts	1.5%
Dealings of units in unit trusts and shares in open-ended investment companies[3]	0.5%
Transfers of foreign currency bearer shares and agreements to transfer sterling or foreign currency convertible or equity-related loan stock issued by UK companies	0.5%

[1] If the transaction is completed by a duly stamped instrument within six years from the date on which the charge is imposed, the SDRT will be cancelled or repaid.

[2] Where the operator of a clearance service elects to collect and account for SDRT on the normal rate of 0.5% on dealing within the system the higher SDRT charge of 1.5% does not apply.

[3] From 6 April 2001 transfers of units in a unit trust and surrenders of shares in open-ended investment trusts are exempt when held within individual pension accounts.

Interest on unpaid tax

Stamp duty land tax. *From 26 September 2005*: Interest runs from the end of 30 days after the effective date of transaction (normally completion), or the date of a disqualifying event, until the tax is paid. In the case of a deferred payment, interest runs from the date the payment is due until the tax is paid. A penalty carries interest from the date determined until the date of payment.

Stamp duty. *For instruments executed from 1 October 1999*: Interest runs from the end of 30 days after the date the instrument is executed until the tax is paid. Amounts less than £25 are not charged.

Stamp duty reserve tax. Interest is charged from 14 days after the transaction date for exchange transactions and otherwise from seven days after the end of the month of the transaction. Amounts less than £25 are not charged.

Rates: see p 5.

Repayment supplement

Stamp duty land tax. *From 26 September 2005*: Interest is added to repayments of overpaid stamp duty land tax and runs from the date tax was paid or an amount was lodged with HMRC, or the date a penalty was made, to the date the order for repayment is issued.

Stamp duty. *For instruments executed from 1 October 1999*: Interest is added to repayments of overpaid stamp duty and runs from 30 days after the date the instrument is executed or the date of payment if later. Amounts less than £25 are not paid.

Stamp duty reserve tax. Interest is paid from the date the tax was paid to the date the order for repayment is issued.

Rates: see p 8.

Penalties

Offence	Penalty
Stamp duty land tax and stamp duty reserve tax	
Inaccuracy in return or other document (FA 2007 Sch 24).	See **Penalties — modernised penalty regime** on p 14
Inaccuracy in return or other document as a result of third party providing incorrect (or withholding) information (FA 2007 Sch 24).	See **Penalties — modernised penalty regime** on p 14
Failure to notify HMRC of an error in an assessment (within 30 days) (FA 2007 Sch 24).	See **Penalties — modernised penalty regime** on p 14
Failure to comply with HMRC investigatory powers with effect from 1 April 2010 (FA 2008 Sch 36).	(*a*) Initial penalty of £300; (*b*) if failure/obstruction continues, a further penalty of up to £60 per day; (*c*) if failure/obstruction continues after penalty under (*a*) imposed, a tax-related amount determined by the Upper Tribunal.
Provision of inaccurate information or document when complying with an information notice with effect from 1 April 2010 (FA 2008 Sch 36).	Up to £3,000 per inaccuracy.
Stamp duty – for instruments executed from 1 October 1999	
Failure to present instrument for stamping within 30 days after execution (or the day in which it is first received in the UK if executed outside the UK) (Stamp Act 1891 s 15B; SI 1999/2537). (Extended to instruments executed from 24 July 2002 for transfers of UK land and buildings, wherever executed (FA 2002 s 114).)	If presented within one year after the end of the 30-day period: the lower of £300 or the amount of the unpaid duty. If presented more than one year after the end of the 30-day period: the greater of £300 or the amount of unpaid duty.
Stamp duty land tax – contracts completed after 30 November 2003	
Failure to deliver a land transaction return by the filing date (FA 2003 Sch 10 paras 3, 4).	£100 if return delivered within three months of filing date, otherwise £200. If not delivered within 12 months, penalty up to amount of tax chargeable.
Failure to comply with notice to deliver return within specified period (FA 2003 Sch 10 para 5).	Up to £60 for each day on which the failure continues after notification.
Fraudulently or negligently delivering an incorrect return or failing to remedy an error without unreasonable delay (FA 2003 Sch 10 para 8).	*Up to the difference between the amount payable and the amount that would have been chargeable on the basis of the return delivered.* **Repealed and replaced by penalty under FA 2007 Sch 24 above after 31 March 2010.**
Fraudulently or negligently giving a self-certificate for a chargeable transaction or failing to remedy an error in respect of such certificate without unreasonable delay (FA 2003 Sch 11 para 3).	*Up to the amount of tax chargeable.* **Repealed for transactions after 11 March 2008.**
Failure to keep and preserve records under FA 2003 Sch 10 para 9 or Sch 11 para 4 (FA 2003 Sch 10 para 11, Sch 11 para 6).	Up to £3,000 unless the information is provided by other documentary evidence.
Failure to comply with notice to produce documents etc under FA 2003 Sch 10 para 14 (FA 2003 Sch 10 para 16).	(*a*) Initial penalty of £50; (*b*) further penalty for each day the failure continues up to £30 if penalty determined by HMRC, or £150 if determined by the court. **Repealed with effect from 1 April 2010. Penalties still apply after 31 March 2010 to notices issued before 1 April 2010.**
Failure (From 1 August 2005) to disclose certain SDLT proposals or arrangements (TMA 1970 s 98C; SI 2005/1868; SI 2005/1869; SI 2010/2743).	(*a*) Up to £600 per day during 'initial period' (but tribunal can determine a higher penalty up to £1 million); (*b*) further penalty up to £600 per day while failure continues. Both the initial penalty in (*a*) above and the secondary penalty in (*b*) above can be increased up to £5,000 per day that failure continues from 10 days after the order is made.
Failure (From 1 August 2005) to provide prescribed information relating to disclosure certain SDLT proposals or arrangements (TMA 1970 s 98C; SI 2005/1868; SI 2005/1869; SI 2010/2743).	(*a*) Initial penalty up to £5,000; (*b*) further penalty up to £600 per day while failure continues. This can be increased up to £5,000 per day after a tribunal has issued a disclosure order.

Offence	Penalty
Failure (From 1 August 2005) to provide scheme reference number relating to certain SDLT proposals or arrangements (TMA 1970 s 98C; SI 2005/1868; SI 2005/1869; SI 2010/2743);	(*a*) Penalty of £100 in respect of each scheme to which the failure relates;
for second failure, occurring within three years from the date on which the first failure began;	(*b*) penalty of £500 in respect of each scheme to which the failure relates;
for subsequent failures, occurring within three years from the date on which the previous failure began.	(*c*) penalty of £1,000 in respect of each scheme to which the failure relates.
Stamp duty reserve tax	
Failure to notify HMRC and pay tax (TMA 1970 s 93, SI 1986/1711 as applied in practice by HMRC; see under 'Penalties and appeals —stamp duty reserve tax' on HMRC website).	If notified within one year of the payment deadline: the lower of £100 or the amount of the unpaid duty. If notified more than one year after the payment deadline: £100 plus up to the amount of unpaid duty, subject to a reduction for mitigating factors.

Value added tax

Rates

(VATA 1994 s 2)

	From 4.1.11		1.1.10–3.1.11		1.12.08–31.12.09	
	Rate	VAT fraction	Rate	VAT Fraction	Rate	VAT Fraction
Standard rate	20%	$^1/_6$	17.5%	$^7/_{47}$	15.0%	$^3/_{23}$
Reduced rate (see p 138)	5.0%	$^1/_{21}$	5.0%	$^1/_{21}$	5.0%	$^1/_{21}$
Flat-rate scheme for farmers	4.0%*		4.0%[1]		4.0%*	

[1]   Flat rate addition to sale price

Registration limits

UK taxable supplies

(VATA 1994 Sch 1 para 1, Sch 1A para 1)

A person who is UK-established (from 1 December 2012[3], previously both UK and non-UK established persons) and makes taxable supplies is liable to be registered:
- (a)   at the end of any month, or
- (b)   at any time, if:

	(a) turnover in the past year[1] (b) turnover in the next 30 days[2] exceeds:	Unless, in the case of (a), turnover for next year not expected to exceed:
1.4.12 onwards	**£77,000**	**£75,000**
1.4.11–31.3.12	£73,000	£71,000
1.4.10–31.3.11	£70,000	£68,000
1.5.09–31.3.10	£68,000	£66,000
1.4.08–30.4.09	£67,000	£65,000
1.4.07–31.3.08	£64,000	£62,000
1.4.06–31.3.07	£61,000	£59,000
1.4.05–31.3.06	£60,000	£58,000
1.4.04–31.3.05	£58,000	£56,000

[1]   The value of taxable supplies in the year then ending.
[2]   If there are reasonable grounds for believing the value of taxable supplies will exceed limit.
[3]   For supplies made on or after 1 December 2012 non-UK established businesses are required to register for VAT regardless of the value of taxable supplies made in the UK.

Supplies from other EC countries ('distance selling')

(VATA 1994 Sch 2)

A business person in another EC country not registered or liable to be registered in the UK is liable to be registered on any day if, in the period beginning with 1 January in that year, the value of supplies by that person to non-taxable persons in the UK exceeds:

1.1.93 onwards	**£70,000**

Acquisitions from other EC countries

(VATA 1994 Sch 3)

A person not registered or liable to be registered under the above rules is liable to be registered:

(a)   at the end of any month if, in the period beginning with 1 January in that year, the value of taxable goods acquired by that person for business purposes (or for non-business purposes if a public body, charity, club, etc) from suppliers in other EC countries exceeds the following limits; or

(b)   at any time, if there are reasonable grounds for believing the value of such acquisitions in the next 30 days will exceed the following limits:

1.4.12 onwards	£77,000
1.4.11–31.3.12	£73,000
1.4.10–31.3.11	£70,000
1.5.09–31.3.10	£68,000
1.4.08–30.4.09	£67,000
1.4.07–31.3.08	£64,000
1.4.06–31.3.07	£61,000
1.4.05–31.3.06	£60,000
1.4.04–31.3.05	£58,000
10.4.03–31.3.04	£56,000

Deregistration limits

UK taxable supplies

(VATA 1994 Sch 1 para 4)

A registered taxable person who is UK-established (from 1 December 2012[1], previously both UK and non-UK established persons) ceases to be liable to be registered if, at any time, HMRC are satisfied that the value of taxable supplies in the year then beginning will not exceed:

1.4.12 onwards	£75,000
1.4.11–31.3.12	£71,000
1.4.10–31.3.11	£68,000
1.5.09–31.3.10	£66,000
1.4.08–30.4.09	£65,000
1.4.07–31.3.08	£62,000
1.4.06–31.3.07	£59,000
1.4.05–31.3.06	£58,000
1.4.04–31.3.05	£56,000
10.4.03–31.3.04	£54,000
25.4.02–9.4.03	£53,000

Unless the reason for not exceeding the limit during that year is that the person will cease making taxable supplies or suspend making taxable supplies for 30 days or more.

[1] For supplies made on or after 1 December 2012 non-UK established businesses are required to register for VAT regardless of the value of taxable supplies made in the UK.

Supplies from other EC countries ('distance selling')

(VATA 1994 Sch 2)

A person registered under these provisions ceases to be liable to be registered if, at any time:
(a) relevant supplies in year ended 31 December last before that time did not exceed following limit; and
(b) HMRC are satisfied that value of relevant supplies in year immediately following that year will not exceed following limit:

1.1.93 onwards	£70,000

Acquisitions from other EC countries

(VATA 1994 Sch 3)

A person registered under these provisions ceases to be liable to be registered if, at any time:
(a) relevant acquisitions in year ended 31 December last before that time did not exceed following limits; and
(b) HMRC are satisfied that value of relevant acquisitions in year immediately following that year will not exceed following limits:

1.4.12 onwards	£77,000
1.4.11–31.3.12	£73,000
1.4.10–31.3.11	£70,000
1.5.09–31.3.10	£68,000
1.4.08–30.4.08	£67,000
1.4.07–31.3.08	£64,000
1.4.06–31.3.07	£61,000
1.4.05–31.3.06	£60,000
1.4.04–31.3.05	£58,000
10.4.03–31.3.04	£56,000
25.4.02–9.4.03	£55,000
1.4.01–24.4.02	£54,000

Annual accounting scheme

(SI 1995/2518 regs 49–55)

A business may, subject to conditions, complete one VAT return a year. Before 1 April 2006, only businesses with taxable turnover up to £150,000 could join the scheme immediately; other businesses had to have been registered for 12 months.

	Can join if taxable supplies in next year not expected to exceed:	Must leave at end of accounting year if taxable supplies exceeded:
1.4.06 onwards	**£1,350,000**	**£1,600,000**
1.4.04–31.3.06	£660,000	£825,000
1.4.01–31.3.04	£600,000	£750,000

Cash accounting scheme

(SI 1995/2518 regs 56–65)

A business may, subject to conditions, account for and pay VAT on the basis of cash paid and received. It can join the scheme at any time as follows.

	Can join if taxable supplies in next year not expected to exceed:	Must leave at end of VAT period if taxable supplies in previous year exceed:	Unless turnover for next year not expected to exceed:
1.4.07 onwards	**£1,350,000**	**£1,600,000**	**£1,350,000**
1.4.04–31.3.07	£660,000	£825,000	£660,000
1.4.01–31.3.04	£600,000	£750,000	£600,000

Flat-rate scheme for small businesses

(SI 1995/2518 regs 55A–55V)

A business which expects its taxable supplies in the next year to be no more than £150,000 and (before 1 April 2009) its total business income to be no more than £187,500 (including VAT) can opt to join a flat-rate scheme. The appropriate percentage below is applied to total turnover generated, including exempt income, to calculate net VAT due.

Category of business	Appropriate %		
	From 4.1.11	1.1.10–3.1.11	1.12.08–31.12.09
Accountancy or book-keeping	14.5	13	11.5
Advertising	11	10	8.5
Agricultural services	11	10	7
Any other activity not listed elsewhere	12	10.5	9
Architect	14.5	13	11
Boarding or care of animals	12	10.5	9.5
Business services that are not listed elsewhere	12	10.5	9.5
Catering services, including restaurants and takeaways	12.5	11	10.5
Civil and structural engineer or surveyor	14.5	13	11
Computer and IT consultancy or data processing	14.5	13	11.5
Computer repair services	10.5	9.5	10
Dealing in waste or scrap	10.5	9.5	8.5
Entertainment or journalism	12.5	11	9.5
Estate agency and property management services	12	10.5	9.5
Farming or agriculture that is not listed elsewhere	6.5	6	5.5
Film, radio, television or video production	13	11.5	9.5
Financial services	13.5	12	10.5
Forestry or fishing	10.5	9.5	8
General building or construction services	9.5	8.5	7.5
Hairdressing or other beauty treatment services	13	11.5	10.5
Hiring or renting goods	9.5	8.5	7.5
Hotel or accommodation	10.5	9.5	8.5
Investigation or security	12	10.5	9
Labour-only building or construction services[1]	14.5	13	11.5
Laundry or dry-cleaning services	12	10.5	9.5

Category of business	Appropriate %		
	From 4.1.11	1.1.10–3.1.11	1.12.08–31.12.09
Lawyer or legal services	14.5	13	12
Library, archive, museum or other cultural activity	9.5	8.5	7.5
Management consultancy	14	12.5	11
Manufacturing fabricated metal products	10.5	9.5	8.5
Manufacturing food	9	8	7
Manufacturing that is not listed elsewhere	9.5	8.5	7.5
Manufacturing yarn, textiles or clothing	9	8	7.5
Membership organisation	8	7	5.5
Mining or quarrying	10	9	8
Packaging	9	8	7.5
Photography	11	10	8.5
Post Offices	5	4.5	2
Printing	8.5	7.5	6.5
Publishing	11	10	8.5
Pubs	6.5	6	5.5
Real estate activity not listed elsewhere	14	12.5	11
Repairing personal or household goods	10	9	7.5
Repairing vehicles	8.5	7.5	6.5
Retailing food, confectionery, tobacco, newspapers or children's clothing	4	3.5	2
Retailing pharmaceuticals, medical goods, cosmetics or toiletries	8	7	6
Retailing that is not listed elsewhere	7.5	6.5	5.5
Retailing vehicles or fuel	6.5	6	5.5
Secretarial services	13	11.5	9.5
Social work	11	10	8
Sport or recreation	8.5	7.5	6
Transport or storage, couriers, freight, removals and taxis	10	9	8
Travel agency	10.5	9.5	8
Veterinary medicine	11	10	8
Wholesaling agricultural products	8	7	5.5
Wholesaling food	7.5	6.5	5
Wholesaling that is not listed elsewhere	8.5	7.5	6

[1] That is, services where value of materials supplied is less than 10% of turnover of such services; any other services are 'general building or construction services'.

[2] Once in the scheme a business may continue to use it until its total business income exceeds £230,000, and if income does exceed this limit, the business can still remain in the scheme if the income in the following year is estimated not to exceed £191,500.

Partial exemption

(SI 1995/2518 regs 106–107)

A registered person who makes taxable and exempt supplies is partly exempt and may not be able to deduct (or reclaim) all his input tax. Where, however, input tax attributable to exempt supplies in a prescribed accounting period or tax year is within the de minimis limits below, all such input tax is attributable to taxable supplies and recoverable (subject to the normal rules).

De minimis limits	£625 per month on average and 50% of all input tax for the period concerned

Capital goods scheme

(SI 1995/2518 regs 112–116)

Input tax adjustment following change in taxable use of capital goods

Item	Value	Adjustment period
Computer equipment	£50,000 or more	Five years
Ships, boats or other vessels[1]	£50,000 or more	Five years
Aircraft[1]	£50,000 or more	Five years
Land and buildings	£250,000 or more	Ten years (for adjustment periods commenced before 1 January 2011, five years where interest had less than ten years to run on acquisition)

[1] Applies for goods acquired on or after 1 January 2011.

Adjustment formula where adjustment period begins before 1 January 2011

$$\frac{\text{Total input tax on item}}{\text{Length of adjustment period}} \times \text{adjustment percentage}$$

Adjustment formula where adjustment period begins on or after 1 January 2011

$$\frac{\text{Total VAT on item}}{\text{Length of adjustment period}} \times \text{adjustment percentage}$$

The adjustment percentage is the percentage change in the extent to which the item is used (or treated as used) in making taxable supplies between the first interval in the adjustment period and a subsequent interval. (The first interval generally ends on the last day of the tax year in which the input tax was incurred.) For goods acquired on or after 1 January 2011 total VAT includes any non-business VAT and the extent to which a capital item is used for business purposes must be determined when ascertaining taxable use for each subsequent interval.

Zero-rated supplies

A zero-rated supply is a taxable supply, but the rate of tax is nil (VATA 1994 Sch 8).

Group 1 – Food

Group 2 – Sewerage services and water

Group 3 – Books etc

Group 4 – Talking books for the blind and handicapped and wireless sets for the blind

Group 5 – Construction of buildings etc

Group 6 – Protected buildings

Group 7 – International services

Group 8 – Transport

Group 9 – Caravans and houseboats

Group 10 – Gold

Group 11 – Bank notes

Group 12 – Drugs, medicines, aids for the handicapped etc

Group 13 – Imports, exports etc

Group 15 – Charities etc

Group 16 – Clothing and footwear

Reduced rate supplies

(VATA 1994 Sch 7A)

Group 1 – Domestic fuel and power

Group 2 – Installation of energy-saving materials

Group 3 – Grant-funded installation of heating equipment or security goods or connection of a gas supply

Group 4 – Women's sanitary products

Group 5 – Children's car seats and bases

Group 6 – Residential conversions

Group 7 – Residential renovations and alterations

Group 8 – Contraceptive products (from 1 July 2006)

Group 9 – Welfare advice or information (from 1 July 2006)

Group 10 – Installation of mobility aids for the elderly (from 1 July 2007)

Group 11 – Smoking cessation products (from 1 July 2007)

Exempt supplies

(VATA 1994 Sch 9)

Group 1 – Land

Group 2 – Insurance

Group 3 – Postal services

Group 4 – Betting, gaming and lotteries

Group 5 – Finance

Group 6 – Education

Group 7 – Health and welfare

Group 8 – Burial and cremation

Group 9 – Subscriptions to trade unions, professional and other public interest bodies

Group 10 – Sport, sports competitions and physical education

Group 11 – Works of art etc

Group 12 – Fund-raising events by charities and other qualifying bodies

Group 13 – Cultural services etc

Group 14 – Supplies of goods where input tax cannot be recovered

Group 15 – Investment gold

EC Sales Lists

(SI 1995/2518 regs 2, 21–23)

All VAT-registered businesses in the UK must provide HMRC with details of goods and services supplied to a VAT-registered customer in another EU country.

The requirement for returns is as follows:

Supplies of		Frequency
Goods	Supplies of goods are in excess of £35,000 (£70,000 before 1 January 2012) in any of the current or last four quarters	Monthly
Goods	Supplies of goods are below £35,000 (£70,000 before 1 January 2012) per quarter in the current and previous four quarters	Quarterly on 31 March, 30 June, 30 September and 31 December
Services supplied to a business where the place of supply is where the customer belongs		Quarterly as above
Goods and services where a business is required to submit monthly lists for goods		Monthly for all supplies, or monthly for goods and quarterly for services
Goods or services supplied by a business completing annual VAT returns	Total annual taxable turnover does not exceed £145,000; annual value of supplies to other EU countries not more than £11,000 (and do not include New Means of Transport)	On application — annual on agreed due date
Goods only supplied	Total annual taxable turnover does not exceed the VAT registration threshold plus £25,500; annual value of supplies to other EU countries not more than £11,000 (and do not include New Means of Transport	On application — annual in simple format on agreed due date

The due date for returns is 21 days after the end of the period if submitted online and 14 days after the end of the period if submitted on paper.

Country	Code
Austria	AT
Belgium	BE
Bulgaria	BG
Cyprus[9]	CY
Czech Republic	CZ
Denmark[2]	DK
Estonia	EE
Finland[3]	FI
France[4]	FR
Germany[5]	DE
Greece	EL
Hungary	HU
Ireland	IE
Italy[6]	IT
Latvia	LV
Lithuania	LT
Luxembourg	LU
Malta	MT
Netherlands	NL
Poland	PL
Portugal[7]	PT
Romania	RO
Slovak Republic	SK
Slovenia	SI
Spain[8]	ES
Sweden	SE

[1] Countries not listed in the table above are not part of the EU VAT area and so sales to those countries should not be included on the EC sales list. The following are not part of the EU VAT area; Andorra, The

Channel Islands, Gibraltar, Mount Athos, San Marino, and Vatican City. The UK and the Isle of Man are part of the EU VAT area, but sales to these should not be included on the list.

2 Does not include the Faroe Islands and Greenland.
3 Does not include Aland Islands.
4 Includes Monaco, but excludes Martinique, Guadeloupe, Reunion, St Pierre and Miquelon, and French Guiana.
5 Does not include Busingen and Isle of Heligoland.
6 Does not include communes of Livigno and Campione d'Italia and the Italian waters of Lake Lugano.
7 Includes the Azores and Madeira.
8 Includes the Balearic Islands but excludes Ceuta, Melilla, and the Canary Islands.
9 Includes British sovereign base areas of Akrotiri and Dhekelia, but excludes those areas in United Nations buffer zone and to the north of that where the Republic of Cyprus does not have effective control.

Intrastat

(SI 1992/2790)

All VAT-registered businesses in the UK must complete boxes 8 and 9 on the VAT return showing the total value of goods supplied to and acquired from other EC member states respectively. Businesses with a total value of such supplies or acquisitions exceeding a threshold must make supplementary declarations containing further information each month. Thresholds are set for each calendar year and recent thresholds are shown below. If a person's supplies or acquisitions in the previous calendar year exceeded the current year's threshold, supplementary declarations must be made for the full current year. If the cumulative total of supplies or acquisitions in a year exceeds that calendar year's threshold, supplementary declarations must be made for the rest of the year, starting in the month in which the threshold is exceeded. From April 2012 declarations must be submitted electronically and will be due 21 days after the end of the month in which there is EU trade to declare.

Year	Supplies threshold	Acquisitions threshold
2012	£250,000	£600,000
2011	£250,000	£600,000
2010	£250,000	£600,000
2009	£270,000	£270,000
2008	£260,000	£260,000
2007	£260,000	£260,000

Some of the EU country codes and the areas included for intrastat purposes differ from those used for EC sales list purposes. The intrastat codes are as follows.

Country	Code
Austria	AT
Belgium	BE
Bulgaria	BG
Cyprus[9]	CY
Czech Republic	CZ
Denmark[2]	DK
Estonia	EE
Finland[3]	FI
France[4]	FR
Germany[5]	DE
Greece[10]	GR
Hungary	HU
Ireland	IE
Italy[6]	IT
Latvia	LV
Lithuania	LT
Luxembourg	LU
Malta	MT
Netherlands[11]	NL
Poland	PL
Portugal[7]	PT
Romania	RO
Slovak Republic	SK
Slovenia	SI
Spain[8]	ES
Sweden	SE
United Kingdom[12]	GB

[1]   Andorra and Liechtenstein are both outside the customs territory (and therefore the statistical territory) of the EU.

[2]   Does not include the Faroe Islands.

[3]   Includes Aland Islands.

[4]   Includes Monaco, but excludes Martinique, Guadeloupe, Reunion, St Pierre and Miquelon, and French Guiana.

[5]   Includes Isle of Heligoland but excludes Busingen.

[6]   Does not include communes of Livigno and Campione d'Italia, the Italian waters of Lake Lugano and the Vatican.

[7]   Includes the Azores and Madeira.

[8]   Includes the Balearic Islands but excludes Ceuta, Melilla, and the Canary Islands.

[9]   Includes UK sovereign base areas but excludes Northern Cyprus.

[10] Includes Mount Athos.

[11] Excludes all dependent and associated territories.

[12] Includes the Isle of Man and the Channel Islands but excludes Gibraltar.

Car fuel

(VATA 1994 ss 56, 57)

Where an employer pays mileage allowances, he may use the advisory fuel rates on p 81 to calculate the input VAT to reclaim on the fuel element. Receipts must still be retained.

VAT-inclusive scale figures are used to assess VAT due on petrol provided at below cost price for private journeys by registered traders or their employees, where the petrol has been provided from business resources. The figures represent the tax-inclusive value of the fuel supplied to each individual and relate to return periods beginning on the dates shown.

	12 months £	3 months £	1 month £
From 1 May 2012: CO_2 band			
120 or below	665	166	55
125	1,000	250	83
130	1,065	266	88
135	1,135	283	94
140	1,200	300	100
145	1,270	316	105
150	1,335	333	111
155	1,400	350	116
160	1,470	366	122
165	1,535	383	127
170	1,600	400	133
175	1,670	416	138
180	1,735	433	144
185	1,800	450	150
190	1,870	467	155
195	1,935	483	161
200	2,000	500	166
205	2,070	517	172
210	2,135	533	177
215	2,200	550	183
220	2,270	567	189
225 or above	2,335	583	194

	12 months £	3 months £	1 month £
From 1 May 2011–30 April 2012: CO_2 band			
120 or below	630	157	52
125	945	236	78
130	1,010	252	84
135	1,070	268	89
140	1,135	283	94
145	1,200	299	99
150	1,260	315	105
155	1,325	331	110
160	1,385	346	115
165	1,450	362	120
170	1,515	378	126
175	1,575	394	131
180	1,640	409	136
185	1,705	425	141
190	1,765	441	147
195	1,830	457	152
200	1,890	472	157
205	1,955	488	162
210	2,020	504	168
215	2,080	520	173
220	2,145	536	178
225 or above	2,205	551	183

	12 months £	3 months £	1 month £
From 1 May 2010–30 April 2011: CO_2 band			
120 or below	570	141	47
125	850	212	70
130	850	212	70
135	910	227	75
140	965	241	80
145	1,020	255	85
150	1,080	269	89
155	1,135	283	94
160	1,190	297	99
165	1,250	312	104
170	1,305	326	108
175	1,360	340	113
180	1,420	354	118
185	1,475	368	122
190	1,530	383	127
195	1,590	397	132
200	1,645	411	137
205	1,705	425	141
210	1,760	439	146
215	1,815	454	151
220	1,875	468	156
225	1,930	482	160
230 or above	1,985	496	165

	12 months £	3 months £	1 month £
1 May 2009–30 April 2010: CO_2 band			
120 or below	505	126	42
125	755	189	63
130	755	189	63
135	755	189	63
140	805	201	67
145	855	214	71
150	905	226	75
155	960	239	79
160	1,010	251	83
165	1,060	264	88
170	1,110	276	92
175	1,160	289	96
180	1,210	302	100
185	1,260	314	104
190	1,310	327	109
195	1,360	339	113
200	1,410	352	117
205	1,465	365	121
210	1,515	378	126
215	1,565	390	130
220	1,615	403	134
225	1,665	416	138
230	1,715	428	142
235 or above	1,765	441	147

	12 months £	3 months £	1 month £
1 May 2008–30 April 2009: CO_2 band			
120 or below	555	138	46
125	830	207	69
130	830	207	69
135	830	207	69
140	885	221	73
145	940	234	78
150	995	248	82
155	1,050	262	87
160	1,105	276	92
165	1,160	290	96
170	1,215	303	101
175	1,270	317	105
180	1,325	331	110
185	1,380	345	115
190	1,435	359	119
195	1,490	373	124
200	1,545	386	128
205	1,605	400	133
210	1,660	414	138
215	1,715	428	142
220	1,770	442	147
225	1,825	455	151
230	1,880	469	156
235 or above	1,935	483	161

	12 months £	3 months £	1 month £
1 May 2007–30 April 2008: CO_2 band			
140 or below	730	182	60
145	780	195	65
150	830	207	69
155	880	219	73
160	925	231	77
165	975	243	81
170	1,025	256	85
175	1,075	268	89
180	1,120	280	93
185	1,170	292	97
190	1,220	304	101
195	1,270	317	105
200	1,315	329	109
205	1,365	341	113
210	1,415	353	117
215	1,465	365	121
220	1,510	378	126
225	1,560	390	130
230	1,610	402	134
235	1,660	414	138
240 or above	1,705	426	142

Interest and penalties

Default interest

(VATA 1994 s 74)

Interest runs on the amount of any VAT assessed (or paid late by voluntary disclosure):

- from the reckonable date (normally the latest date on which a return is required for the period in question);
- until the date of payment (although in practice it runs to the date shown on the notice of assessment or notice of voluntary disclosure if paid within 30 days of that date).

The period of interest cannot commence more than three years before the date of assessment or payment.

The rates of interest are as follows:

Period	Rate
From 29 September 2009	**3%**
24 March 2009–28 September 2009	2.5%
27 January 2009–23 March 2009	3.5%
6 January 2009–26 January 2009	4.5%
6 December 2008–5 January 2009	5.5%
6 November 2008–5 December 2008	6.5%
6 January 2008–5 November 2008	7.5%
6 August 2007–5 January 2008	8.5%
6 September 2006–5 August 2007	7.5%
6 September 2005–5 September 2006	6.5%
6 September 2004–5 September 2005	7.5%
6 December 2003–5 September 2004	6.5%
6 August 2003–5 December 2003	5.5%*

Interest on VAT overpaid in cases of official error

(VATA 1994 s 78)

Where VAT has been overpaid or underclaimed due to an error by HMRC, then on a claim HMRC must pay interest:

- from the date they receive payment (or authorise a repayment) for the return period in question;
- until the date on which they authorise payment of the amount on which interest is due.

This provision does not require HMRC to pay interest on an amount on which repayment supplement is due.

The rates of interest are as follows:

Period	Rate
from 29 September 2009	**0.5%**
27 January 2009–28 September 2009	0%
6 January 2009–26 January 2009	1%
6 December 2008–5 January 2009	2%
6 November 2008–5 December 2008	3%
6 January 2008–5 November 2008	4%
6 August 2007–5 January 2008	5%
6 September 2006–5 August 2007	4%
6 September 2005–5 September 2006	3%
6 September 2004–5 September 2005	4%
6 December 2003–5 September 2004	3%
6 August 2003–5 December 2003	2%*
6 November 2001–5 August 2003	3%

* Due to an administrative error the rate of default and statutory interest was too high by one percentage point between 6 August 2003 and 5 September 2003. HMRC will not seek to recover amounts overpaid by HMRC and will seek to identify businesses overcharged (see Business Brief 17/05 as of 9 September 2005).

Repayment supplement – VAT

(VATA 1994 s 79)

Where a person is entitled to a repayment the payment due is increased by a supplement of the greater of:

- (i)   5% of that amount; or
- (ii)   £50.

The supplement will only be paid if:

(a)   the return or claim is received by HMRC not later than the last day on which it is required to be made;

(b)   HMRC do not issue a written instruction making the refund within the relevant period; and

(c)   the amount shown on the return or claim does not exceed the amount due by more than 5% of that amount or £250, whichever is the greater.

The 'relevant period' is 30 days beginning with the receipt of the return or claim or, if later, the day after the last day of the VAT period to which the return or claim relates.

Penalties and surcharges

Offence	Penalty
Inaccuracy in return or other document (FA 2007 Sch 24).	See **Penalties — modernised penalty regime** on p 14.
Failure to notify obligation to register for VAT, change in supplies made by person exempted from registration, acquisition affecting exemption, acquisition of goods from another member state and un-authorised issue of an invoice (FA 2008 Sch 41).	See **Penalties — modernised penalty regime** on p 14.
Inaccuracy in return or other document as a result of third party providing incorrect (or withholding) information (FA 2007 Sch 24).	See **Penalties — modernised penalty regime** on p 14.
Failure to inform HMRC of an error in an assessment within 30 days of the date of the assessment (FA 2007 Sch 24).	See **Penalties — modernised penalty regime** on p 14.
Failure to comply with HMRC investigatory powers with effect from 1 April 2009 (FA 2008 Sch 36).	(*a*) Initial penalty of £300; (*b*) if failure/obstruction continues, a further penalty of up to £60 per day; (*c*) if failure/obstruction continues after penalty under (*a*) imposed, a tax-related amount determined by the Upper Tribunal.
Provision of inaccurate information or document when complying with an information notice (FA 2008 Sch 36).	Up to £3,000 per inaccuracy.
Failure to submit a return electronically if required to do so by SI 1995/2518 reg 25 for prescribed accounting periods starting on or after 1 April 2012. Before 1 April 2012, failure of a *specified person* to make a *specified return* using an electronic return system for prescribed accounting periods ending on or after 31 March 2011 (SI 1995/2518 reg 25A). 'Specified person' was broadly a person registered for VAT on or after 1 April 2010, or one registered before that date who at 31 December 2009 or any later date has an annual VAT exclusive turnover of £100,000 or more. Penalty will only apply to prescribed accounting periods ending on or after 31 March 2013 where the person is required to make an electronic return only as a result of the removal of the turnover test from 1 April 2012.	Annual VAT exclusive turnover of: £22,800,001 or more — £400 £5,600,001 to £22,800,000 — £300 £100,001 to £5,600,000 — £200 £100,000 or under — £100
Failure to submit return or pay VAT due within time limit (where a return is late but the VAT is paid on time or no VAT is due, a default is recorded but no surcharge arises) (VATA 1994 s 59). Failure to pay tax due under the payment on account scheme on time (VATA 1994 s 59A).	The greater of £30 and a specified percentage of outstanding VAT for period, depending on number of defaults in surcharge period: first default in period 2%, second default 5%, third default 10%, fourth and further defaults 15%. (Surcharge assessments are not issued for sums of less than £200 unless the rate of the surcharge is 10% or more.) **Due to be replaced by penalties under FA 2009 Schs 55 and 56 from a date to be appointed.**
Evasion of VAT: conduct involving dishonesty (VATA 1994 s 60*).	*Amount of tax evaded or sought to be evaded (subject to mitigation).* **Repealed and replaced for periods beginning on or after 1 April 2008 and ending on or after 1 April 2009 subject to the exceptions shown below***.
Issuing incorrect certificate stating that certain supplies fall to be zero-rated or taxed at the reduced rate (VATA 1994 s 62).	Difference between tax actually charged and tax which should have been charged.
Misdeclaration or neglect (VATA 1994 s 63).	*15% of VAT which would have been lost if inaccuracy had not been discovered.* **Repealed and replaced for periods beginning on or after 1 April 2008 and ending on or after 1 April 2009.**

Offence	Penalty
Repeated misdeclarations (VATA 1994 s 64).	*15% of VAT which would have been lost if second and subsequent inaccuracies within penalty period had not been discovered.* **Repealed and replaced for periods ending on or after 1 April 2008 and ending on or after 1 April 2009**.
Material inaccuracy in EC sales statement (VATA 1994 s 65).	£100 for each material inaccuracy in two-year penalty period (which commences following notice of second material inaccuracy).
Failure to submit an EC sales statement (VATA 1994 s 66).	Greater of £50 or a daily penalty (maximum 100 days) £5 for the first, £10 for the second, £15 for the third or subsequent failure in the default period.
Failure to notify liability for registration or a change in nature of supplies by person exempted from registration (VATA 1994 s 67).	*Greater of £50 and a specified percentage of the tax for which the person would have been liable, depending on the period of failure: nine months or less 5%; over nine and up to 18 months 10%; over 18 months 15%.* **Repealed after 31 March 2010**.
Failure to notify acquisition of excise duty goods or new means of transport (VATA 1994 s 67).	*Greater of £50 and: 5% of the tax for which the person would have been liable if period of failure is three months or less, 10% if over three and up to six months and 15% if over six months.* **Repealed after 31 March 2010**.
Unauthorised issue of invoices (VATA 1994 s 67).	*Greater of £50 and 15% of amount shown as or representing VAT.* **Repealed after 31 March 2010**.
Breach of walking possession agreement (VATA 1994 s 68).	50% of VAT due or amount recoverable.
Failure to preserve records for prescribed period (VATA 1994 ss 69, 69B).	£500.
Failure to preserve records specified in HMRC direction (VATA 1994 ss 69, 69B).	£200 for each day of failure (maximum 30 days).
Breaches of regulatory provisions, including failure to notify cessation of liability or entitlement to be registered, failure to keep records and non-compliance with any regulations made under VATA 1994 (VATA 1994 s 69).	Greater of £50 and a daily penalty (maximum 100 days) of a specified amount depending on number of failures in preceding two years: £5* per day if no previous failures; £10* per day if one previous failure; £15* per day if two or more previous failures.
Where failure consists of not paying VAT or not making a return in the required time.	*$1/6$, $1/3$ and $1/2$ of 1% of the VAT due respectively, if greater.
Breaches of regulatory provisions involving failure to pay VAT or submit return by due date (VATA 1994 s 69).	Greater of £50 and a daily penalty (for no more than 100 days) of a specified amount depending on number of failures in preceding two years: greater of £5 and $1/6$% of VAT due if no previous failures; greater of £10 and $1/3$% of VAT due if one previous failure; greater of £15 and $1/2$% of VAT due if two or more previous failures.
Failure to comply with the requirements of the investment gold scheme (VATA 1994 s 69A).	17.5% of the value of transactions concerned.
Import VAT (FA 2003 ss 24–41):	From 27 November 2003:
– failures relating to non-compliance	maximum penalty of £2,500
– evasion.	maximum penalty equal to VAT sought to be evaded.
Failure to notify the use of a designated avoidance scheme (VATA 1994 Sch 11A paras 10, 11).	15% of the tax avoided (applies to businesses with supplies of £600,000 or more from 1 August 2004).
Failure to disclose certain schemes within 30 days of the due date or the first return affected (VATA 1994 Sch 11A paras 10, 11).	£5,000 (applies to businesses with supplies exceeding £10 million from 1 August 2004).

*Penalties under VATA 1994 s 60 will continue to be charged for acts or omissions not relating to an inaccuracy in a document or failure to notify HMRC of an under-assessment (SI 2008/568 and SI 2009/571).

Index